behold, the man

Titles in the Seedbed Daily Text series:

The Advent Mission: Advent by Omar Rikabi
Behold, the Man: John by J. D. Walt
Between You and Me: 2 John, 3 John, Philemon, Titus, and Jude by Omar Rikabi
The Christian New Year: Advent by J. D. Walt
The Domino Effect: Colossians by J. D. Walt
First Love: Philippians by J. D. Walt
The First Real Christian: James by J. D. Walt
First Word. Last Word. God's Word: The Bible by J. D. Walt
God Is Here: Advent by Casey Page Culbreth
The Gospel of the Holy Spirit: Mark by J. D. Walt
Listen to Him: Lent by J. D. Walt
People Who Say Such Things: Faith by J. D. Walt
Protagonist: Advent by Matt LeRoy and Josh LeRoy
Reset: Advent by J. D. Walt
Right Here, Right Now, Jesus: Prayer by J. D. Walt
Soundtrack: Lent by J. D. Walt
This Is How We Know: 1 John by J. D. Walt
(un)Puzzled: Ephesians by J. D. Walt
What Happens in Corinth: 1 Corinthians by J. D. Walt
Wilderness: Exodus by J. D. Walt

The Seedbed Daily Text

behold, the man

ohn

J. D. WALT

Copyright 2021 by J. D. Walt

All rights reserved. No part of this publication may be reproduced, stored in a retrieval system, or transmitted, in any form or by any means—electronic, mechanical, photocopying, recording, or otherwise—without prior written permission, except for brief quotations in critical reviews or articles.

Unless otherwise noted, Scripture quotations are taken from the Holy Bible, New International Version®, NIV® Copyright © 1973, 1978, 1984, 2011 by Biblica, Inc.™ Used by permission of Zondervan. All rights reserved worldwide. www.zondervan.com. The "NIV" and "New International Version" are trademarks registered in the United States Patent and Trademark Office by Biblica, Inc.™ All rights reserved worldwide.

Scripture quotations marked ESV are from the ESV® Bible (The Holy Bible, English Standard Version®), copyright © 2001 by Crossway, a publishing ministry of Good News Publishers. Used by permission. All rights reserved.

Printed in the United States of America

Cover and page design by Strange Last Name
Typesetting by PerfecType, Nashville, Tennessee

Walt, J. D. (John David)
Behold the man / J.D. Walt. – Franklin, Tennessee : Seedbed Publishing, ©2021.

pages ; cm. – (The Seedbed daily text)

ISBN 9781628248494 (paperback)
ISBN 9781628248500 (Mobi)
ISBN 9781628248517 (ePub)
ISBN 9781628248524 (uPDF)
OCLC 1246362331

1. Jesus Christ -- Meditations. 2. Spiritual exercises. I. Title. II. Series.

BT306.43.W34 2021 232.9/01 2021937469

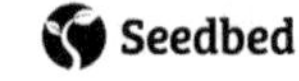

SEEDBED PUBLISHING
Franklin, Tennessee
seedbed.com

Contents

An Invitation to Awakening

This resource comes with an invitation.

The invitation is as simple as it is comprehensive. It is not an invitation to commit your life to this or that cause or to join an organization or to purchase another book. The invitation is this: to wake up to the life you always hoped was possible and the reason you were put on planet Earth. It begins with following Jesus Christ.

In case you are unaware, Jesus was born in the first century BCE into a poor family from Nazareth, a small village located in what is modern-day Israel. While his birth was associated with extraordinary phenomena, we know little about his childhood. At approximately thirty years of age, Jesus began a public mission of preaching, teaching, and healing throughout the region known as Galilee. His mission was characterized by miraculous signs and wonders; extravagant care of the poor and marginalized; and multiple unconventional claims about his own identity and purpose. In short, he claimed to be the incarnate Son of God with the mission and power to save people from sin, deliver them from death, and bring them into the now-and-eternal kingdom of God—"on earth as it is in heaven" (Matt. 6:10).

In the spring of his thirty-third year, during the Jewish Passover celebration, Jesus was arrested by the religious authorities, put on trial in the middle of the night, and at their urging, sentenced to death by a Roman governor. On the day known to history as Good Friday, Jesus was crucified on a Roman cross and then was buried in a borrowed tomb. On the following Sunday, according to multiple eyewitness accounts, he was physically raised from the dead. He appeared to hundreds of people, taught his disciples, and prepared for what was to come.

Forty days after the resurrection, Jesus ascended bodily into the heavens where, according to the Bible, he sits at the right hand of God as the Lord of heaven and earth. Ten days after his ascension, in a gathering of 120 people on the day of Pentecost, a Jewish day of celebration, something truly extraordinary happened. A loud and powerful wind swept over the people gathered. Pillars of what appeared to be fire descended upon the followers of Jesus. The Holy Spirit, the presence and power of God, filled the people, and the church was born. After this, the followers of Jesus went forth and began to do the very things Jesus did—preaching, teaching, and healing—and planting churches and making disciples all over the world. Today, more than two thousand years later, the movement has reached us. This is the Great Awakening, and it has never stopped.

Yes, two thousand years hence and more than two billion followers of Jesus later, this awakening movement of Jesus Christ and his church stands stronger than ever. Billions of ordinary people the world over have discovered in Jesus Christ an awakened life they never imagined possible. They have overcome challenges, defeated addictions, endured untenable hardships and suffering with unexplainable joy, and stared death in the face with the joyful confidence of eternal life. They have healed the sick, gathered the outcasts, embraced the oppressed, loved the poor, contended for justice, labored for peace, cared for the dying, and, yes, even raised the dead.

We all face many challenges and problems. They are deeply personal, yet when joined together, they create enormous and complex chaos in the world, from our hearts to our homes to our churches and our cities. All of this chaos traces to two originating problems: sin and death. Sin, far beyond mere moral failure, describes the fundamental broken condition of every human being. Sin separates us from God and others, distorts and destroys our deepest identity as the image-bearers of God, and poses a fatal problem from which we cannot save ourselves. It results in an ever-diminishing quality of life and ultimately ends in eternal death. Because Jesus lived a life of sinless perfection, he is able to save us from sin and restore us to a right relationship with God, others, and ourselves. He did this through his sacrificial death on the cross on our behalf. Because Jesus rose from the dead, he is able to deliver us from death and bring us into a quality of life both eternal and unending.

This is the gospel of Jesus Christ: pardon from the penalty of sin, freedom from the power of sin, deliverance from the grip of death, and awakening to the supernatural empowerment of the Holy Spirit to live powerfully for the good of others and the glory of God. Jesus asks only that we acknowledge our broken selves as failed sinners, trust him as our Savior, and follow him as our Lord. Following Jesus does not mean an easy life; however, it does lead to a life of power and purpose, joy in the face of suffering, and profound, even world-changing, love for God and people.

All of this is admittedly a lot to take in. Remember, this is an invitation. Will you follow Jesus? Don't let the failings of his followers deter you. Come and see for yourself.

Here's a prayer to get you started:

> Our Father in heaven, it's me (say your name). I want to know you. I want to live an awakened life. I confess I am a sinner. I have failed myself, others, and you in many ways. I know you made me for a purpose, and I want to fulfill that purpose with my one life. I want to follow Jesus Christ. Jesus, thank you for the gift of your life, death, resurrection, and ascension on my behalf. I want to walk in relationship with you as Savior and Lord. Would you lead me into the fullness and newness of life I was made for? I am ready to follow you. Come, Holy Spirit, and fill me with the love, power, and purposes of God. I pray these things by faith in the name of Jesus, amen.

It would be our privilege to help you get started and grow deeper in this awakened life of following Jesus. For some next steps and encouragements visit seedbed.com/awaken.

How the Daily Text Works

It seems obvious to say, but the Daily Text is written every day. Mostly, it is written the day before it is scheduled to release online.

Before you read further, you are cordially invited to subscribe to and receive the daily e-mail. Visit seedbed.com/dailytext to get started. Also, check out the popular Facebook group, Seedbed Daily Text.

Eventually, the daily postings become part of a Daily Text discipleship resource. That's what you hold in your hands now.

It's not exactly a Bible study, though the Bible is both the source and subject. You will learn something about the Bible along the way: its history, context, original languages, and authors. The goal is not educational in nature, but transformational. Seedbed is more interested in folks knowing Jesus than knowing *about* Jesus.

To that end, each reading begins with the definitive inspiration of the Holy Spirit, the ongoing, unfolding text of Scripture. Following that is a short and, hopefully, substantive insight from the text and some aspect of its meaning. For insight to lead to deeper influence, we turn the text into prayer. Finally, influence must run its course toward impact. This is why we ask each other questions. These questions are not designed to elicit information but to crystallize intention.

Discipleship always leads from inspiration to intention and from attention to action.

Using the Daily Text as a Discipleship Curricular Resource for Groups

While Scripture always addresses us personally, it is not written to us individually. The content of Scripture cries out for a community to address. The Daily Text is made for discipleship in community. This resource can work in several different ways. It could be read like a traditional book, a few pages or chapters at a time. Though unadvisable, the readings could be crammed in on the night before the meeting. Keep in mind, the Daily Text is not called the Daily Text for kicks. We believe Scripture is worthy of our most focused and consistent attention. Every day. We all have misses, but let's make every day more than a noble aspiration. Let's make it our covenant with one another.

For Use with Bands

In our judgment, the best and highest use of the Daily Text is made through what we call banded discipleship. A band is a same-gender group of three to five people who read together, pray together, and meet together to become the love of God for one another and the world. With banded discipleship, the daily readings serve more as a common text for the band and grist for the interpersonal conversation mill between meetings. The band meeting is reserved for the specialized activities of high-bar discipleship.

To learn more about bands and banded discipleship, visit discipleshipbands.com. Be sure to download the free *Discipleship Bands: A Practical Field Guide* or order a supply of the printed booklets online. Also be sure to explore Discipleship Bands, our native app designed specifically for the practice of banded discipleship, in the App Store or Google Play.

For Use with Classes and Small Groups

The Daily Text has also proven to be a helpful discipleship resource for a variety of small groups, from community groups to Sunday school classes. Here are some suggested guidelines for deploying the Daily Text as a resource for a small group or class setting:

1. Hearing the Text

Invite the group to settle into silence for a period of no less than one and no more than five minutes. Ask an appointed person to keep time and to read the biblical text covering the period of days since the last group meeting. Allow at least one minute of silence following the reading of the text.

2. Responding to the Text

Invite anyone from the group to respond to the reading by answering these prompts: What did you hear? What did you see? What did you otherwise sense from the Lord?

3. Sharing Insights and Implications for Discipleship

Moving in an orderly rotation (or free-for-all), invite people to share insights and implications from the week's readings.

What did you find challenging, encouraging, provocative, comforting, invasive, inspiring, corrective, affirming, guiding, or warning? Allow group conversation to proceed at will. Limit to one sharing item per turn, with multiple rounds of discussion.

4. Shaping Intentions for Prayer

Invite each person in the group to share a single discipleship intention for the week ahead. It is helpful if the intention can also be framed as a question the group can use to check in from the prior week. At each person's turn, he or she is invited to share how their intention went during the previous week. The class or group can open and close their meeting according to their established patterns.

Introduction

"It is shallow enough for a child not to drown, yet deep enough for an elephant to swim in it." That is how Augustine reflected on the magisterial gospel of John.

Stretching out before us are twenty-one chapters, 879 verses, 15,635 words (Greek words, that is), all revealed by the Spirit of God and all pointing to a singular subject. In John 19:5 (ESV), the most unlikely proclaimer of the gospel, the Roman governor of a backwater province, Pontius Pilate, points to our subject most poignantly:

"Behold, the man!"

In addition to this, in your hands are just shy of eighty-six thousand words, spanning 118 chapters. If read daily, it will take just under seventeen weeks (just over four months). These words are mere reflection and yet their sole agenda is to help us together do the one thing necessary.

"Behold, the man!"

From the prologue through the post-resurrection, through the seven sayings and seven signs, from the woman at the well to the woman caught in adultery, and from Nathanael to Nicodemus, the apostle John leads us on a journey from heaven to earth and back again.

"Behold, the man!"

To behold means more than to look. It carries a far deeper sense of perception. Beholding captures the essence of what Jesus means when he speaks of having eyes to see and ears to hear (see Matthew 13). Beholding brings hearing and seeing into a unified and seamless way of perceiving the revelation of God as a singular reality. As the ancient Gloria Patri has it, "As it was in the beginning, is now and ever shall be, world without end, amen, amen!"

Whether this is your first time through John's gospel or your hundredth time, there is more of Jesus to behold. Even more challenging, there is more of Jesus to become like. This is perhaps the deepest truth of the gospel—as we truly behold Jesus, we become like him. Paul made it crystal clear in his second letter to the Corinthian Christians when he said:

> And we all, with unveiled face, beholding the glory of the Lord, are being transformed into the same image from one degree of glory to another. For this comes from the Lord who is the Spirit. (2 Cor. 3:18 ESV)

"Behold, the man!"

Prepare now for the journey of beholding—as Athanasius put it in the early days—the one who became like us so we could become like him. Prepare to enter the healing waters of the gospel of John.

behold, the man

God Is Jesus

1

JOHN 1:1–2 | **In the beginning was the Word, and the Word was with God, and the Word was God. He was with God in the beginning.**

Consider This

Welcome to the gospel of our Lord Jesus Christ according to Saint John. While the scope of the gospel is as vast as eternity, the agenda of the gospel, from the first word to the last, is singular. It is to reveal this all-consuming reality: God is Jesus.

Do we realize just how astonishing this is? Can we fathom what we are actually saying?

God is Jesus.

We are saying that a human being—a real, living, breathing human being is the Creator of all that is, the very God of heaven and earth. Pick someone out of a crowd today. Take a good look at them, and try to grasp the reality that a person, just like the person you are looking at, could possibly be almighty God.

God is Jesus.

It seems reasonable to posit an invisible, omnipotent, omniscient, and omnipresent deity and call this being God. It seems reasonable to posit an invisible Spirit who is distinct from and yet indivisibly one with God.

It seems patently unreasonable, even absurd, to posit that a visible, approachable, flesh-and-blood human being could possibly be the omnipotent, omniscient, and omnipresent God of the cosmos. And yet the Bible couldn't be more emphatically clear on this point.

In the beginning was the Word, and the Word was with God, and the Word was God. He was with God in the beginning.

God is Jesus.

As the Nicene Creed, the consensus faith of the church at all times and in all places, has it:

> God from God, Light from Light,
> true God from true God,
> begotten, not made,
> of one Being with the Father.
> Through him all things were made.

God is Jesus.

It's one thing to make the claim that Jesus is God. It strikes me as of another order to say God is Jesus. The gospel of John, as well as the other three eyewitness accounts, does not set out to convince or prove that Jesus is God as though we were the jury who would render a verdict. No, we are the ones on trial. The gospel of John purposes to reveal the single most important truth in the history of history—the only truth with the power to save us: God is Jesus.

The Prayer

Abba Father, thank you for Jesus. Thank you for the mercy of sending your Son. Forgive us for sitting in judgment on him. As we open the pages on this gospel, open the eyes of our hearts to perceive this revelation of all revelation: God is Jesus. It is in his name that we pray, amen.

The Questions

- Do you sense the change in order of magnitude between saying Jesus is God and saying God is Jesus. Why is that? Of course, we believe God is Father and God is Holy Spirit. So why is it so critical to grapple with the implications that God is Jesus? What would it mean to approach the gospel of John, not as those seeking proofs, but as those who are hungering for divine revelation?

2 Jesus Created the World He Saved

JOHN 1:3–5 | Through him all things were made; without him nothing was made that has been made. In him was life, and that life was the light of all mankind. The light shines in the darkness, and the darkness has not overcome it.

Consider This

More than anything in life, we desperately need a proper view and conception of Jesus Christ, the Lord of heaven and earth—the one who was and is and is to come. He is the Alpha and the Omega, the one about whom it is written "is the same yesterday and today and forever" (Heb. 13:8).

In order to come anywhere near grasping the unimaginable depths to which the Son of God went to rescue and save us, we must stretch to fathom the inconceivable heights from whence he came.

Through him all things were made; without him nothing was made that has been made.

Jesus created the world. It was Jesus, the Word of God, whose words fashioned the universe. The one who is light said, "Let there be light" (Gen. 1:3). The one who is life, spoke life into being.

Here's how the apostle Paul puts it:

> The Son is the image of the invisible God, the firstborn over all creation. For in him all things were created: things in heaven and on earth, visible and invisible, whether thrones or powers or rulers or authorities; all things have been created through him and for him. He is before all things, and in him all things hold together. (Col. 1:15–17)

On the one hand, Jesus is the God who sits on the throne of heaven. On the other, he is the man who carries his own cross for the whole world. He is the God of glory to whom all worship is due. He is the man of sorrows, born to suffering, who takes away the sins of the world.

The light shines in the darkness, and the darkness has not overcome it.

The Prayer

Abba Father, we thank you for your Son, our Savior and Lord, Jesus Christ. Open the eyes of our hearts that we might ever increasingly see him for who he most truly is. It is in his name we pray, amen.

The Questions

- Would you say you possess a significantly expansive and expanding conception of Jesus? Is it more difficult for you to fathom the God-ness of Jesus or the human-ness of Jesus? Will you ask the Holy Spirit to magnify the Son of God in your own heart and mind?

3 The Power of Preemptive Grace

JOHN 1:6–13 | There was a man sent from God whose name was John. He came as a witness to testify concerning that light, so that through him all might believe. He himself was not the light; he came only as a witness to the light.

The true light that gives light to everyone was coming into the world. He was in the world, and though the world was made through him, the world did not recognize him. He came to that which was his own, but his own did not receive him. Yet to all who did receive him, to those who believed in his name, he gave the right to become children of God—children born not of natural descent, nor of human decision or a husband's will, but born of God.

Consider This

Surely these must be the saddest words in all of Scripture.

He was in the world, and though the world was made through him, the world did not recognize him. He came to that which was his own, but his own did not receive him.

To be at home and unrecognized is worse than being ignored.

To be at home and not be received is worse than rejection.

These are the wounds that never heal, for they are the deepest and most vexing wounds of the cross. The pain of crucifixion lasts a day, but the suffering born of rejection lives eternally. The injuries from nails and spears become scars. The wounds of rejection are forever open.

Herein lies the greatest mystery of the cross. These never-healing wounds of Jesus are ever healing the wounds of we who inflicted them upon him. Charles Wesley captured it with this turn of phrase: "Died He for me, who caused his pain? For me, who Him to death pursued?"*

---

* Charles Wesley, "And Can It Be That I Should Gain?" 1738. Public domain.

The cross is not something that happens at the end of the gospel. The cross is the whole of the gospel from first to last. At the heart of all that ever has been and ever will be is a God who embraces those who reject him.

Yet to all who did receive him, to those who believed in his name, he gave the right to become children of God—

In fact, Jesus preemptively embraced us knowing that we would reject him. The power of the gospel is not that Jesus forgives our sin. It is that he decided to forgive our sin even before we sinned. If only we will receive it. He is "the Lamb who was slain from the creation of the world" (Rev. 13:8). And for all eternity, he is the slain one at the center of the throne of whom it will be sung for endless ages, "Worthy is the Lamb, who was slain, to receive power and wealth and wisdom and strength and honor and glory and praise!" (Rev. 5:12).

The Prayer

Abba Father, forgive us for rejecting your Son and, so, rejecting you. We marvel at this unfathomable grace that, in the face of our rejection, you have embraced us anyway. Grant us the grace to receive your mercy and make us to be ambassadors of the same. We pray in Jesus' name, amen.

The Questions

- Can you remember a time when you experienced the wounds of rejection? Have you responded to Jesus' invitation to receive his grace and embrace his forgiveness?

If not, why not? What do you think about responding to rejection by preemptively embracing the person from whom you sense rejection?

4 The Mind-Blowing Implications of the Word Becoming Flesh

JOHN 1:14–18 ESV | And the Word became flesh and dwelt among us, and we have seen his glory, glory as of the only Son from the Father, full of grace and truth. (John bore witness about him, and cried out, "This was he of whom I said, 'He who comes after me ranks before me, because he was before me.'") For from his fullness we have all received, grace upon grace. For the law was given through Moses; grace and truth came through Jesus Christ. No one has ever seen God; the only God, who is at the Father's side, he has made him known.

Consider This

The message of the gospel of John is as simple as it is incomprehensible. If you want to see the one and only true God of all that is and was and is to come, look at Jesus. Jesus has not come to show us that he is God. God has come to show us that he is Jesus. Jesus has come to show us what God is like, but in an even greater sense, I think God has come to show us what human beings are like.

So, what if humanity has always been in the heart of God? What if being created in the image of God actually means to be truly human? Otherwise, does being created in the image of God mean everything but being human? Otherwise, what does "the Word became flesh" actually mean?

What if human beings were always meant to be the bearers and sharers of divine power? And what if Jesus has come to show us what it looks like for a human person to live and move and have their being in the realm and reality of divine power—which is holy love? Wouldn't this make better sense of what it means to be created in the image of God, indeed, to be image-bearers?

Note, I am not making bold assertions here but asking probing—and admittedly unsettling and mind-blowing—questions. And, please understand, I am not asking them of you. I am asking us to ask them of the text. Flesh and blood cannot reveal such things; only Word and Spirit can. When "the Word became flesh and dwelt among us," this is what began to happen, and it never stopped.

The Prayer

Abba Father, Lord Jesus Christ, Holy Spirit, we know that to speak your name is to stand on holy ground. Open the fullness of who we are that we might begin even to grasp the fullness of who you are. Even more, awaken our faith to the reality that we might be filled with that very same fullness. We pray in the name of Jesus, who with you and the Holy Spirit reign together as one God forever, amen.

The Questions

- Do you tend to have a transactional view of salvation or is it a more comprehensive vision? What do you make of this notion of humanity always being at the core of the image of God?

5 A God Who Wears Sandals

JOHN 1:19–27 ESV | And this is the testimony of John, when the Jews sent priests and Levites from Jerusalem to ask him, "Who are you?" He confessed, and did not deny, but confessed, "I am not the Christ." And they asked him, "What then? Are you Elijah?" He said, "I am not." "Are you the Prophet?" And he answered, "No." So they said to him, "Who are you? We need to give an answer to those who sent us. What do you say about yourself?" He said, "I am the voice of one crying out in the wilderness, 'Make straight the way of the Lord,' as the prophet Isaiah said."

(Now they had been sent from the Pharisees.) They asked him, "Then why are you baptizing, if you are neither the Christ, nor Elijah, nor the Prophet?" John answered them, "I baptize with water, but among you stands one you do not know, even he who comes after me, the strap of whose sandal I am not worthy to untie."

Consider This

A phenomenon was unfolding out in the countryside on the banks of the Jordan River. Word spread like wildfire. Droves of people gathered. God was up to something, and it was not happening in the temple.

The religious leaders, the ones we would expect to be the lead God-seekers, did not come. They sent their cronies. They wanted to find out not so much what was going on but who was behind it all. They wanted to know who John was. Where were his credentials? What were his qualifications? From where did he get his so-called authority? He gave them this:

"I am the voice of one crying out in the wilderness, 'Make straight the way of the Lord.'"

God stands among you and you do not recognize him because you do not know him. He stands among you in the midst of the crowd, unrecognized, hidden in the ordinary, in the frail frame of a human person. God is not in the temple. God is not some presence in the air creating a spiritual atmosphere in which people can experience him. No. God is somewhere in the crowd. He has a face. And he is wearing sandals.

Remember, God is a human being.

The Prayer

Almighty God, thank you for revealing yourself to us as Jesus of Nazareth. We think we grasp this until we really contemplate it. We can be so spiritually minded that we forget to be human. Help us with this. We pray in Jesus' name, amen.

The Questions

- Why are institutions, particularly religious institutions, skeptical and even hostile to things happening outside of their purview and control? How are baptism controversies these days just another verse of the same song the religious authorities have always been singing? How could anyone have possibly comprehended that God could be a human being back then? Even now?

6 Some Revelation Required

JOHN 1:28–34 | This all happened at Bethany on the other side of the Jordan, where John was baptizing.

The next day John saw Jesus coming toward him and said, "Look, the Lamb of God, who takes away the sin of the world! This is the one I meant when I said, 'A man who comes after me has surpassed me because he was before me.' I myself did not know him, but the reason I came baptizing with water was that he might be revealed to Israel."

Then John gave this testimony: "I saw the Spirit come down from heaven as a dove and remain on him. And I myself did not know him, but the one who sent me to baptize with water told me, 'The man on whom you see the Spirit come down and

remain is the one who will baptize with the Holy Spirit.' I have seen and I testify that this is God's Chosen One."

Consider This

Unless Jesus is revealed to us, we stand no chance of recognizing him. Sure, we can read about him from the pages of Scripture. Others can preach, teach, and otherwise tell us about him until they are blue in the face, and we can be confident we have understood them perfectly. In fact, we can give our mental, intellectual, and even willful assent to all of the truth and truths concerning him. Still, unless Jesus is revealed to us, we stand no chance of recognizing him. Only the Holy Spirit can reveal Jesus to us.

Now, to be sure, the Holy Spirit can reveal Jesus to us through reading Scripture or through the witness of others or by teaching and preaching and so forth. It is important that we realize that just because these things are happening and just because their essential content is accurate does not mean Jesus is being revealed by the Holy Spirit.

"And I myself did not know him, but the one who sent me to baptize with water told me, 'The man on whom you see the Spirit come down and remain is the one who will baptize with the Holy Spirit.'"

The Holy Spirit revealed the truth about Jesus to John—and to everyone who has ever truly known him since. Note how it worked. The Spirit revealed and John recognized. We will see this pattern unfold many times with particular people before this gospel is done.

Since the day of Pentecost, the Holy Spirit has been laboring to reveal Jesus to the whole world. The big questions are: Who will recognize him? And among those who recognize him, who will receive him? Yes, these are the questions.

The Prayer

Abba Father, thank you for your Son, Jesus, the one who is both the revealer and the revelation. Fill me with your Holy Spirit that I might more deeply perceive the depths of who he is. It is in his name I pray, amen.

The Questions

- What keeps people from recognizing Jesus? Is your faith in Jesus grounded more in an intellectual assent to the truths about Jesus or has Jesus been revealed to you as the Truth? See the difference? If it is the Spirit who reveals Jesus and people who recognize him, what is our part in the process, if any?

7 How to See beyond Sight

JOHN 1:35–39 ESV | The next day again John was standing with two of his disciples, and he looked at Jesus as he walked by and said, "Behold, the Lamb of God!" The two disciples

heard him say this, and they followed Jesus. Jesus turned and saw them following and said to them, "What are you seeking?" And they said to him, "Rabbi" (which means Teacher), "where are you staying?" He said to them, "Come and you will see." So they came and saw where he was staying, and they stayed with him that day, for it was about the tenth hour.

Consider This

Don't you love how John lets us know the hour of the day? Why is that important? Think about it. This is not a "once upon a time" story we are reading here. This is a historical account. It has particularity.

The big story in today's text is John's clarion call to action: *"Behold, the Lamb of God!"*

To behold means to offer the totality of one's attention to something or someone. To say, "Behold the Lamb of God!" carries a completely different sense than, "Look at that guy over there." To behold requires far more than one's eyes. It requires a complete yielding of one's deepest self.

We can see something once or twice and consider that we have seen it. With beholding, the more we look, the more we see. To behold Jesus means moving in the ever-deepening kind of humility that requires us to confess that, though we love him, we scarcely know him.

The truth is, we can't behold without the Holy Spirit's help. Beholding moves us into the realm of revelation where perception transcends observation, where believing gives way to true seeing.

The Prayer

Abba Father, teach my heart to behold. I know it's not a matter of how hard I try but how attuned I am to your Spirit. Come, Holy Spirit, and open the eyes of my heart that I might behold Jesus. I pray in his name, amen.

The Questions

- What does this call to "behold" bring to mind for you? What will be required of you to become one who "beholds" or who grows in beholding? What keeps people from "beholding"? What keeps you from it?

8 Remembering the Days of Small Beginnings

JOHN 1:40–46 ESV | One of the two who heard John speak and followed Jesus was Andrew, Simon Peter's brother. He first found his own brother Simon and said to him, "We have found the Messiah" (which means Christ). He brought him to Jesus. Jesus looked at him and said, "You are Simon the son of John. You shall be called Cephas" (which means Peter).

The next day Jesus decided to go to Galilee. He found Philip and said to him, "Follow me." Now Philip was from Bethsaida, the city of Andrew and Peter. Philip found Nathanael and said to him, "We have found him of whom Moses in the Law and also the prophets wrote, Jesus of Nazareth, the son of Joseph."

Nathanael said to him, "Can anything good come out of Nazareth?" Philip said to him, "Come and see."

Consider This

We tend to think of well-established successful movements and organizations as beginning in that same fashion. That is rarely the case. Because of the explosive growth of the Christian movement in the first century and to the present day, we naturally read the stories of its origins in the light of its later success. We celebrate those early disciples and outright champion the Twelve. It is so easy to retrospectively romanticize the early days as a smashing success.

Did you catch this phrase from today's text?

One of the two who heard John speak and followed Jesus was Andrew, Simon Peter's brother.

Andrew was "one of the two" who heard and responded to John.

Wait! One of the two? The great John the Baptist, the phenom forerunner of the Son of God, the one who first identified him to the world, only managed to come up with two followers for Jesus?

Think about it. By any standard, we would file an outcome of two responses on day one (or day two) in the Epic Fail folder. We might console ourselves to remember that one of those two brought his brother and the other one produced a sarcastic, cynical colleague (a.k.a. Nathanael).

Why are we so seduced by the shallow metrics of numbers when it comes to our churches and kingdom efforts? Three joiners and a tepid fourth doesn't seem like anything we would even have the guts to report. Even twelve would be considered an embarrassment we would desperately want to somehow explain away.

As ego-inflating (or deflating) as the case may be, when it comes to the kingdom of God, numbers are, at best, an unreliable source and, at worst, a deceptive measure of success.

Of all those droves of people listening to John, only two raised their hands. It just so happens that one of them turned out to be the apostle to Europe and the other the apostle to Africa—both were founding fathers of what is today a two-thousand-year-and-counting global movement of more than two billion people.

This is how God starts a movement. This is how Jesus saves the world. It should cause all of us to pause and reconsider what success might look like in the eyes of God—to remember the mustard seed and the loaves and fish and a band of twelve that started with two. And yes, to never, ever despise the days of small beginnings.

The Prayer

Abba Father, thank you for teaching us the secret of the seed. Cultivate in us the audacity of faith to trust the small starts and humble origins. Come, Holy Spirit, and retrain our vision, remake our mind, and retool our expectations that we might be freed from the ways of the world and fit with the wisdom of the kingdom. We pray in Jesus' name, amen.

The Questions

- Have you ever thought of Jesus' beginnings as being weak and unimpressive? What is it about numbers that so seduces us? What will it take to shift our mindset on what constitutes true success? How do we live in the midst of a world (even the church) that remains in the old and broken way of seeing and thinking?

Why We Never Have to Climb the Stairway to Heaven

9

JOHN 1:47–51 | When Jesus saw Nathanael approaching, he said of him, "Here truly is an Israelite in whom there is no deceit."

"How do you know me?" Nathanael asked.

Jesus answered, "I saw you while you were still under the fig tree before Philip called you."

Then Nathanael declared, "Rabbi, you are the Son of God; you are the king of Israel."

Jesus said, "You believe because I told you I saw you under the fig tree. You will see greater things than that." He then added, "Very truly I tell you, you will see 'heaven open, and the angels of God ascending and descending on' the Son of Man."

Consider This

Jesus saw Nathanael before he (Jesus) could actually see him. He saw him standing under a fig tree. Not only did Jesus demonstrate a kind of miraculous foresight of Nathanael, he also revealed his insight into him. It's interesting, though, how he led with the insight:

When Jesus saw Nathanael approaching, he said of him, "Here truly is an Israelite in whom there is no deceit."

Jesus perceived and named a distinctive quality of heart he saw in Nathanael: guilelessness or, stated positively, pureheartedness. You will remember in his Sermon on the Mount, Jesus said, "Blessed are the pure in heart, for they will see God" (Matt. 5:8). Is this not what Jesus is saying about Nathanael?

Note Nathanael's response:

"Rabbi, you are the Son of God; you are the king of Israel."

Nathanael saw based on the outward revelation that Jesus saw him before he could have possibly seen him (under the fig tree). Jesus then gave Nathanael a word that will come to capture the very essence of the kingdom of God on earth—all that has come before and all that will come after:

"Very truly I tell you, you will see 'heaven open, and the angels of God ascending and descending on' the Son of Man."

Nathanael, this true Israelite, would have immediately recalled Jacob's dream:

> He had a dream in which he saw a stairway resting on the earth, with its top reaching to heaven, and the angels of God were ascending and descending on it. . . .

> When Jacob awoke from his sleep, he thought, "Surely the Lord is in this place, and I was not aware of it." He was afraid and said, "How awesome is this place! This is none other than the house of God; this is the gate of heaven." (Gen. 28:12, 16–17)

Nathanael must have felt the ground quake beneath his feet. He must have trembled in awe. He must have stood there in stunned silence, for we never hear another word from him. He was standing in the presence of the Word of God, which is the house of God—the house of God before there ever was a physical house for God—the Word of God before there ever was a physical scroll on which such revelation would be written. Nathanael was standing at the gate of heaven which had come down to earth. He knew he had not climbed up the ladder. He knew God had climbed down. Something tells me he knew that he knew he was tabernacling with the Word made flesh and yet something else tells me he had no idea of it: "Surely the Lord is in this place, and I was not aware of it" (Gen. 28:16).

We passed over this word of Jesus to Nathanael.

"You will see greater things than that."

I think it is a word to us as we prepare to proceed into the gospel. We have been standing at the gate, if you will, of heaven. We are now passing through it and into the realm.

The Prayer

Abba Father, we can hardly fathom what we are considering. Jesus is the gateway to heaven, not when we die, but then and now and always—and this gate is open to us. Come, Holy Spirit, and grant us purity of heart. Grace us with repentance from our deceit. Open the eyes of our hearts that we might behold Jesus as never before. It is in his name we pray, amen.

The Questions

- So often we ask God to reveal himself to us in fresh and new ways, and yet so often we fail to approach Scripture with this same kind of asking. Are you guilty of this? The gospel of John is perhaps the most sensationally dynamic book in the Bible. How can we get past our assumption that we have already read it and seen what there is to see? How can we approach with fresh eyes? Do you have an expectation of seeing greater things than you have ever seen before as we proceed into this sacred text?

10 From Reality-Show Reading to Reading Revelatory Signs

JOHN 2:1–8 ESV | On the third day there was a wedding at Cana in Galilee, and the mother of Jesus was there. Jesus also was invited to the wedding with his disciples. When the wine ran out, the mother of Jesus said to him, "They have no wine." And Jesus said to her, "Woman, what does this have to

do with me? My hour has not yet come." His mother said to the servants, "Do whatever he tells you."

Now there were six stone water jars there for the Jewish rites of purification, each holding twenty or thirty gallons. Jesus said to the servants, "Fill the jars with water." And they filled them up to the brim. And he said to them, "Now draw some out and take it to the master of the feast." So they took it.

Consider This

This is such an interesting story to include in the Bible. Can you think of anywhere else we see such a gratuitous miracle as this? Aren't miracles, or "signs" as John calls them, reserved for emergency situations like impending disaster, sure death, or intractable illness? This is a wedding feast, for crying out loud! It wasn't like they ran out of food. It feels more like an episode from the Kardashians. It seems crass to say, but they simply wanted to keep the open bar open—not exactly a 9-1-1. And Jesus didn't want to get involved.

That's my reality-show read of the text. Remember, though, there is a much bigger reality afoot and unfolding here, the real one. This is not a reality show. It is a revelatory sign. Will you chance a few theological double takes with me?

1. John began with the creation of the world. Is he moving to the re-creation of his image-bearers—a man and a woman—at the place where they are most fully on display, a wedding? I've never participated in a wedding where Jesus' presence at this wedding in Cana of Galilee was not noted. Might gender

identity and marriage matter more to God than the present times might lead one to think?

2. Might Jesus be stirring us to remember that the world began with a wedding and that it will end with a wedding, one whose feast will never end and whose wine will never run out? Indeed, might this new creation be one whose wine will ever reveal a vintage, all at once ancient and brand-new?

3. About this wine—it's new wine, like five minutes old. Who drinks this stuff? It turns out to be the best wine of all. And those stone jars? Verses ago John reminded us the law came through Moses. That's what these jars pointed to: the purity signified by ritual cleansing. Could this miraculous transformation of water into wine signify the quantum leap about to be made from the tutelage of the law to the transforming power of the grace and truth of the gospel?

There are two ditches we want to stay between when it comes to reading Scripture: the ditch of an oversimplified reading and the ditch of an oversophisticated reading. We neither want to read something into the text that shouldn't be there (i.e., cheap analogies), nor do we want to read something out of the text that is not there (i.e., complex allegories). It's why we humbly ask questions of the text, make tentative observations, and allow them to be tried and tested by the Holy Spirit and one another as we read further.

For now, note how all of this is drawing us out of self-centered reading (I call it reality-show reading), which forces the text to be first and last about ourselves. The Bible is first, middle, and last about revealing the name and nature of God to the world. The design of divine revelation is not to give us tips on how to live a better life or be a better Christian. No, divine revelation designs to draw our knees to the earth, our faces to the ground, and our hearts into the heavens where we cry out, "Holy! Holy! Holy!"

The Prayer

Abba Father, thank you for the awe-inspiring word and work of your Son, Jesus. Thank you for the Holy Spirit, who opens the text to our lives and opens our lives to the text. We humbly bow before you at the scene of this mysterious wedding in Cana of Galilee. Reveal yourself to us in fullness. We pray in Jesus' name, amen.

The Questions

- Why do you think we begin at a wedding in this gospel? What do you observe about the nature of God being revealed in this text? How are you challenged in your approach to reading Scripture?

Where the Wine Never Runs Out

11

JOHN 2:9–11 | **[A]nd the master of the banquet tasted the water that had been turned into wine. He did not realize where it had come from, though the servants who had drawn the water knew. Then he called the bridegroom aside and said, "Everyone brings out the choice wine first and then the**

cheaper wine after the guests have had too much to drink; but you have saved the best till now."

What Jesus did here in Cana of Galilee was the first of the signs through which he revealed his glory; and his disciples believed in him.

Consider This

No one had any idea the Bridegroom had come to this wedding. In fact, it has me wondering: *What if he comes in secret to every wedding? Would we recognize him? Is it even in our minds to look for him?* I once saw a giant billboard that was solid black with white letters that said, "Loved the wedding. Invite me to the marriage. God." Seems apropos to mention.

Permit me a few more theological speculations on this mysterious story.

1. Do you remember how this story began? "On the third day a wedding took place in Cana of Galilee" (v. 1a). Might this be a foreshadowing of the last and greatest sign of the gospel? Fill in the blank, "On the third day, ______________________."

2. The next thing we were told is this: "Jesus' mother was there" (v. 1b). There is only one other place in John's gospel where we see Mary—at the cross. Could this entire opening story be mysteriously foreshadowing the closing story?

3. Now to this curious word from Jesus back to his mother: "'Woman, why do you involve me?' Jesus replied. 'My hour has not yet come'" (v. 4). What is Jesus' hour? As Jesus was riding into Jerusalem for the last time (okay, the next to the

last time), he said this, "The hour has come for the Son of Man to be glorified" (John 12:23). More pointers from the first sign to the last?

4. Then there's the matter of the water and the wine. Go with me again to the cross: "[O]ne of the soldiers pierced Jesus' side with a spear, bringing a sudden flow of blood and water" (John 19:34).

5. Now to this word from the maître d': "Everyone brings out the choice wine first and then the cheaper wine after the guests have had too much to drink; but you have saved the best till now" (John 2:10). Could this word at the first sign be telling us the story of the last sign—the death and resurrection of Jesus—the best saved for last?

6. Finally, to the wine. Did you pick up just how much wine Jesus miraculously made? The text told us yesterday: six stone jars, each containing between twenty and thirty gallons (see John 2:6). Let's average that at twenty-five gallons a piece and do the math. I get 150 gallons of wine. To give us an idea of how much that is, the standard bottle of wine contains twenty-five ounces. That means it takes five bottles of wine to make one gallon. It comes to 750 bottles of the choicest wine for these already inebriated guests at this small-town wedding. Take a look at the wine section the next time you are in the grocery store. That's how much wine we are talking about. Why so much? Could it be a sign pointing to the endless abundance of everlasting life given freely to us in the Holy Spirit?

That's where we are headed: abundant life, living water, bread with no expiration date, fruitful branches, and more.

Between this first sign and the last sign we are going to behold Jesus like never before. Prepare yourselves. This is not abundance as a magnification of whatever we tend to think of as a lot—this is abundance of another magnitude, of another order.

The Prayer

Abba Father, thank you for your Son, Jesus, who is abundant life and who gives us abundant life by giving us himself. Thank you that, by your Spirit, Jesus will make us this kind of gift of abundance to others. We want that. In Jesus' name, amen.

The Questions

- What about your own notion of abundance must diminish in order for you to begin to grasp the abundance Jesus offers? What do you make of all these allusions from the first sign to the last in this gospel? How does that impact you?

12 There's a New Temple in Town

JOHN 2:12–17 ESV | **After this he went down to Capernaum, with his mother and his brothers and his disciples, and they stayed there for a few days.**

The Passover of the Jews was at hand, and Jesus went up to Jerusalem. In the temple he found those who were selling oxen and sheep and pigeons, and the money-changers sitting there. And making a whip of cords, he drove them all out of the temple, with the sheep and oxen. And he poured out the coins of the money-changers and overturned their tables. And he told those who sold the pigeons, "Take these things away; do not make my Father's house a house of trade." His disciples remembered that it was written, "Zeal for your house will consume me."

Consider This

This feels like a ripe moment for a well-placed flashback. Let's go back and visit this site about a thousand years earlier. Let's remember the dedication of Solomon's temple, predecessor to the one at issue today:

> When Solomon finished praying, fire came down from heaven and consumed the burnt offering and the sacrifices, and the glory of the Lord filled the temple. The priests could not enter the temple of the Lord because the glory of the Lord filled it. When all the Israelites saw the fire coming down and the glory of the Lord above the temple, they knelt on the pavement with their faces to the ground, and they worshiped and gave thanks to the Lord, saying,
>
> "He is good;
> his love endures forever." (2 Chron. 7:1–3)

Yes, on this day a thousand years later, the glory of God was filling the temple again. The Word made flesh, the literal Temple of the living God, had come to dwell in his own temple. Try this: the Temple paid a visit to the temple, where he discovered that the temple had become something less than the Temple.

The NIV says it like this: "Stop turning my Father's house into a market!" (v. 16).

The temple is the dwelling place of God, and in the absence of God dwelling there, we will fill it with everything under the sun.

Richard Halverson, former chaplain to the United States Senate, famously said:

> In the beginning the church was a fellowship of men and women centering on the living Christ. Then the church moved to Greece, where it became a philosophy. Then it moved to Rome, where it became an institution. Next it moved to Europe where it became a culture, and finally it moved to America, where it became an enterprise.

According to today's text, before the church was even the church it was already quite an enterprise. In the absence of the manifest presence of God, the best we can seem to come up with is some kind of enterprise. I think that's what happens when God leaves the building. What was formerly filled with his presence becomes filled with our buzzing, enterprising activity.

Could it be that before the temple can be filled again, it must first be emptied? It was as though on that day in Jerusalem, Jesus was putting everyone on notice: there was a new Temple in town, not a fixed building for religious observance, but a moving Tabernacle of demonstrative power.

Let's flash-forward to another temple-filling day, the day of Pentecost:

> Suddenly a sound like the blowing of a violent wind came from heaven and filled the whole house where they were sitting. They saw what seemed to be tongues of fire that separated and came to rest on each of them. All of them were filled with the Holy Spirit and began to speak in other tongues as the Spirit enabled them. (Acts 2:2–4)

Notice how the glory of the Lord did not come to fill the building but to fill the disciples of Jesus.

The same is true now.

The Prayer

Abba Father, thank you for your Son, Jesus, the Temple of the living God. We can hardly grasp the fullness of your presence dwelling in Jesus, and now you ask us to imagine this same glory dwelling in us who follow him. Stretch our feeble minds and shallow hearts to begin to grasp this mystery: we are the temple of God. In Jesus' name, amen.

The Questions

- What would it mean for Jesus to come cleanse or empty his temple today? Is your life being filled with other things that might be usurping or even displacing the presence of God? Do you think we can be the temple of God by ourselves?

13 Has Jesus Entrusted Himself to You?

JOHN 2:18–25 | The Jews then responded to him, "What sign can you show us to prove your authority to do all this?"

Jesus answered them, "Destroy this temple, and I will raise it again in three days."

They replied, "It has taken forty-six years to build this temple, and you are going to raise it in three days?" But the temple he had spoken of was his body. After he was raised from the dead, his disciples recalled what he had said. Then they believed the scripture and the words that Jesus had spoken.

Now while he was in Jerusalem at the Passover Festival, many people saw the signs he was performing and believed in his name. But Jesus would not entrust himself to them, for he knew all people. He did not need any testimony about mankind, for he knew what was in each person.

Consider This

Has Jesus entrusted himself to you?

We are beginning to see a recurring word early on in this gospel. We've already seen the word or some form of it seven times. In the original Greek it is *pisteuo* (pronounced pist-yoo-o). The word is most commonly translated into English as "believe." In my judgment, the word holds a much richer meaning than that conveyed by the term *believe*. It means to place faith in or to have confidence in or to trust.

We live in the age of easy believism. It's easy to believe something because belief has largely come to be associated with some kind of mental or intellectual assent. The word is most commonly used to signify our agreement with some concept or proposition. As a consequence, a person can believe in something without actually demonstrating any confidence or trust in that which is believed.

Many claim to believe in God, and yet so few seem to actually trust God. Trust or faith means belief in action. Faith does not mean mental assent to a propositional truth. Faith means demonstrated trust.

Here's what I find so interesting about this text:

But Jesus would not entrust himself to them, for he knew all people.

It's the same basic word translated as "believe" in the earlier instances.

We think of discipleship as the process by which we grow in our faith and trust in Jesus. What if discipleship is actually the process by which we grow to become the kind of people Jesus can trust?

The Prayer

Abba Father, thank you for your Son, Jesus. Thank you for this gracious and patient invitation to entrust ourselves to him. Thank you for his infinite trustworthiness. Fill us with the Holy Spirit in ways that grow us up to become the kind of people Jesus can entrust himself to. It is in his name we pray, amen.

The Questions

- How does this understanding of discipleship as becoming people Jesus can trust challenge you? What impact has this notion of easy believism had on the church and its witness in the world? What if Jesus will only entrust himself to us to the extent we actually entrust ourselves to him? What keeps us from trusting him more?

14 The Prison of a Good Reputation

JOHN 3:1–4 ESV | Now there was a man of the Pharisees named Nicodemus, a ruler of the Jews. This man came to Jesus by night and said to him, "Rabbi, we know that you are a teacher come from God, for no one can do these signs that you do unless God is with him." Jesus answered him, "Truly,

truly, I say to you, unless one is born again he cannot see the kingdom of God." Nicodemus said to him, "How can a man be born when he is old? Can he enter a second time into his mother's womb and be born?"

Consider This

We are about to witness our first defection. We would call Nicodemus a pillar of the synagogue. He was the guy who never missed. Everyone knew exactly where he sat, and should the rare occurrence happen and he not be there, the seat remained empty. He was among the top givers. He was a member of the Sanhedrin, which for us would be a mix between a federal judge and a United States senator. He was a man of great esteem and honor. We cannot speak ill of Nicodemus. He had been a paragon of faithfulness to all he had been taught.

People like Nicodemus don't tend to risk their status and standing in the community. So why did he do it? Henry David Thoreau once wrote: "The mass of men lead lives of quiet desperation."* I think Nicodemus had gotten in touch with the quiet desperation just under the polished surface of his life. Though he had everything, he knew deep down he was missing the most important thing.

It may not be as hard for a non-churched pillar of the community to awaken to faith as it is for a leader or a respected pillar of the church to be awakened. Why is it so hard for leaders in the church to admit that they aren't quite

---

* Henry David Thoreau, *Walden* (Boston: Houghton, Mifflin & Co., 1906), 8.

the people everyone thinks they are? What keeps us from mustering the humility it takes to confess that, though we may be seminary-level Bible readers, we remain stuck in junior-high faith? Why do we choose to be admired at the expense of being known?

Though he came under cover of darkness, it seems Nicodemus was done with such charades. He knew there must be more than what he knew, and he was ready to sacrifice his pride to know it. This was the day Nicodemus broke free from the prison of his good reputation.

Why is it so easy for a sinner to come to the Lord and so hard for a saint?

The Prayer

Abba Father, thank you for your Son, Jesus, who invites us to come out from under the covering of our reputation and get honest about our own souls. Come, Holy Spirit, and fill us with the courage to be real, that we might grow in the Lord beyond our imagining. We pray in Jesus' name, amen.

The Questions

- How do you see yourself in Nicodemus? Can you identify the quiet desperation in your own life? Why is it hard for those of us who have been in the church so long to find our way to the altar of humility and honesty about our real condition? Are we worried about what others might think?

Saving Nicodemus

15

JOHN 3:5–15 | Jesus answered, "Very truly I tell you, no one can enter the kingdom of God unless they are born of water and the Spirit. Flesh gives birth to flesh, but the Spirit gives birth to spirit. You should not be surprised at my saying, 'You must be born again.' The wind blows wherever it pleases. You hear its sound, but you cannot tell where it comes from or where it is going. So it is with everyone born of the Spirit."

"How can this be?" Nicodemus asked.

"You are Israel's teacher," said Jesus, "and do you not understand these things? Very truly I tell you, we speak of what we know, and we testify to what we have seen, but still you people do not accept our testimony. I have spoken to you of earthly things and you do not believe; how then will you believe if I speak of heavenly things? No one has ever gone into heaven except the one who came from heaven—the Son of Man. Just as Moses lifted up the snake in the wilderness, so the Son of Man must be lifted up, that everyone who believes may have eternal life in him."

Consider This

Nicodemus was stuck in the box of conventional religion. Jesus worked to bring him into the wide-open, mysterious place of Holy Spirit–filled faith. Remember from yesterday:

> Jesus replied, "Very truly I tell you, no one can see the kingdom of God unless they are born again."

> "How can someone be born when they are old?" Nicodemus asked. "Surely they cannot enter a second time into their mother's womb to be born!" (vv. 3–4)

See how Nicodemus is bumping up against the cardboard walls of his religious box?

Today, Jesus might put it like this: "Just because you are in the church doesn't mean you see the kingdom." I'll risk offense and take it a step further: Just because you've been baptized doesn't mean you are a real Christian.

Jesus took something we understand to teach us about something we can't yet comprehend. In this instance, birth. We are kept from seeing the light of revelation because we are blinded by the light we already see.

Flesh gives birth to flesh, but the Spirit gives birth to spirit.

What are we to do? I must humble myself and confess that my own knowledge is incomplete, that my own experience is inadequate, that my religious reputation must be put in the ground so true faith might arise in its place.

Nicodemus blindly trusted in his heritage—his first birth. All the while, Jesus offered him an inheritance—the second birth. He will quietly wrestle with this in the hidden shadows as the gospel publicly unfolds.

The Prayer

Abba Father, thank you for your Son, Jesus, who patiently works with us, persuading without pushing, that we might let go of the old so something genuinely new might happen. Come, Holy Spirit, and fill us with courage to let go of that which will not matter in the end so we might take up what endlessly matters to you. We pray in Jesus' name, amen.

The Questions

- Can you remember/recount an experience of waking up from boxed-in religion and breaking into living faith? What keeps us in our boxes? Why will we not humble ourselves? Think about the pain and struggle of the labor that precedes birth. Play that analogy out with the notion of the second birth. Reflect on the difference between a heritage and an inheritance. (Note: heritage can also be a source of immense brokenness.) What is it time for you to let go of? What do you hope might be born in its wake?

The Problem with John 3:16

16

JOHN 3:16–21 | **For God so loved the world that he gave his one and only Son, that whoever believes in him shall not perish but have eternal life. For God did not send his Son into the world to condemn the world, but to save the world through him. Whoever believes in him is not condemned, but whoever does not believe stands condemned already because they have not believed in the name of God's one and only Son. This is the verdict: Light has come into the world, but people**

loved darkness instead of light because their deeds were evil. Everyone who does evil hates the light, and will not come into the light for fear that their deeds will be exposed. But whoever lives by the truth comes into the light, so that it may be seen plainly that what they have done has been done in the sight of God.

Consider This

So, what's the problem with John 3:16? It's only the most succinct, power-packed verse in all of the Bible. The problem is not with the verse. The problem is how the verse has been presented over the past hundred years or so.

The church has tended to present John 3:16 as the finish line instead of the starting line. Believe the truth about Jesus and go to heaven when you die. The gospel has been flattened into a series of propositional statements we are asked to agree with like a software agreement. All is bad. I'm a sinner. Jesus is the Savior. Believe in him. All is good.

The gospel is not first a truth to be accepted. The gospel is an invitation to meet the one true and living God in the person of Jesus Christ. He is the Way who shows us the way. He is the Truth who reveals the truth to us. He is the Life who gives us life.

For God so loved the world that he gave his one and only Son, that whoever believes in him shall not perish but have eternal life.

If this is the starting line, how might we speak of the finish line? Thanks for asking. Serendipitously, it can be found in

1 John 3:16: "This is how we know what love is: Jesus Christ laid down his life for us. And we ought to lay down our lives for our brothers and sisters."

The primary and most compelling way the world can know the love of God is to experience it through those who claim to love him.

If John 3:16 captures the first half of the gospel, 1 John 3:16 shows us the agenda of the second half of the gospel. Being loved and becoming love—this is the gospel.

But to be clear: love is not soft, squishy sentimentality; love is hard. But love is the only true power, and love can do impossible things.

The Prayer

Abba Father, thank you for your Son, Jesus, through whom you revealed your love for us and in whom you show us what love is. Come, Holy Spirit, and empower this kind of love in us who follow him, for the sake of the world you love. In Jesus' name, amen.

The Questions

- We readily receive the first half of the gospel. What keeps us from going to the second half? What do you think about this tendency to reduce the gospel to a series of propositional truths? What are the strengths and weaknesses of this approach?

17 Why Friends Don't Let Friends Carry the Policy Manual to the Big Game

JOHN 3:22–30 | After this, Jesus and his disciples went out into the Judean countryside, where he spent some time with them, and baptized. Now John also was baptizing at Aenon near Salim, because there was plenty of water, and people were coming and being baptized. (This was before John was put in prison.) An argument developed between some of John's disciples and a certain Jew over the matter of ceremonial washing. They came to John and said to him, "Rabbi, that man who was with you on the other side of the Jordan—the one you testified about—look, he is baptizing, and everyone is going to him."

To this John replied, "A person can receive only what is given them from heaven. You yourselves can testify that I said, 'I am not the Messiah but am sent ahead of him.' The bride belongs to the bridegroom. The friend who attends the bridegroom waits and listens for him, and is full of joy when he hears the bridegroom's voice. That joy is mine, and it is now complete. He must become greater; I must become less."

Consider This

John was doing the most significant work in the world. He was the forerunner of the Son of God, for crying out loud. The gospel of the kingdom of God was unfolding before his very eyes. He was, in essence, the first proclaimer of it all. And we get this:

An argument developed between some of John's disciples and a certain Jew over the matter of ceremonial washing.

What?! Arguments over ceremonial washing?! I'm not sure who I would rather not be, John's disciples or that "certain Jew." We all know it's true though. Anyone who breaks free from the status quo of nominal faith will sooner or later find themselves surrounded by the likes of John's disciples and certain other characters who have become masters of majoring on the minors. They love to play gotcha with the ceremonial-washing policy manual.

They came to John and said to him, "Rabbi, that man who was with you on the other side of the Jordan—the one you testified about—look, he is baptizing, and everyone is going to him."

To them, Jesus was only known as "that man who was with you on the other side of the Jordan." They were John's disciples and they had completely missed the point of his life's work.

Don't get me wrong, these weren't the bad guys. While they understood themselves to be all about God, somewhere along the way they took a wrong turn and detoured into an adventure in missing the point. They saw Jesus as the competition. Their T-shirts said, "We must become more. He must become less."

Sometimes we can be so committed to the mission of God that we miss the actual message of the gospel. Not John—

"The bride belongs to the bridegroom."

The bride never did and never will belong to this organization or that ministry or the church down the street. The bride belongs to the bridegroom. It seems obvious to say, until I am confronted by my own misguided competitive spirit. Jesus is baptizing all kinds of people, in all kinds of places, and in all kinds of ways. Why do I find it so easy to take issue with those places and people where Jesus is clearly baptizing more with them than with me? What if I really believed John on this point?

To this John replied, "A person can receive only what is given them from heaven."

Do I really believe that? Or do I think I can take the hill for Jesus without Jesus—because that's what it really comes down to, doesn't it? When it comes down to my follower counts against theirs (a.k.a. vanity metrics), I must come to grips that I have lost the scent of the real Jesus.

Jesus is not looking for employees. He's not after servants. He's enlisting friends. John got it.

"The friend who attends the bridegroom waits and listens for him, and is full of joy when he hears the bridegroom's voice. That joy is mine, and it is now complete."

It's all about the bridegroom, isn't it—being his friend, listening to his voice?

The Prayer

Abba Father, thank you for your Son, Jesus, the Bridegroom, who counts all who follow him as friends. Deliver us from the pettiness of so many small distractions, and so many big ones. Free us for the joy of following Jesus as we are filled with the Holy Spirit. In Jesus' name we pray, amen.

The Questions

- How do you see the difference between working for Jesus and belonging to him? What might it look like today to be a friend of the Bridegroom who waits and listens for him? How can we humbly, graciously, and yet firmly deal with the heel-biting, policy-manual people who are completely missing the point?

18 Is God Mad?

JOHN 3:31–36 ESV | He who comes from above is above all. He who is of the earth belongs to the earth and speaks in an earthly way. He who comes from heaven is above all. He bears witness to what he has seen and heard, yet no one receives his testimony. Whoever receives his testimony sets his seal to this, that God is true. For he whom God has sent utters the words of God, for he gives the Spirit without measure. The Father loves the Son and has given all things into his hand. Whoever believes in the Son has eternal life; whoever does not obey the Son shall not see life, but the wrath of God remains on him.

Consider This

Wrath. It's a hard, unpleasant word. It feels like the unmitigated emotion of rage. It doesn't sound like the God and

Father of our Lord Jesus Christ to me. I just don't get the impression that God is angry from my reading of Scripture.

So, what is the wrath of God? What if the wrath of God is simply the presence of God as experienced by anyone unprepared for it? By way of analogy, consider the sun. The wrath of the sun is not found in its emotional state but as a natural consequence of its presence. Without the protection of the atmosphere, we could not live in the presence of the sun. By the mercy of God, we have been covered by a protective atmosphere in which we can not only look upon the sun but also enjoy and flourish in its warmth.

What if God's wrath is akin to the experience of the presence of the sun without any atmospheric protection? What if we thought of God's holiness as the luminously fierce brightness of ten thousand suns? It would be a wrathful experience for anyone unprepared for such a holy presence. They simply could not exist there. It's why we understand hell as eternal separation from God. As I understand it, the biblical notion of wrath refers to a fixed state of being rather than a volatile state of emotion.

Whoever believes in the Son has eternal life; whoever does not obey the Son shall not see life, but the wrath of God remains on him.

To say that God's wrath remains on a person is to say that it had already been on them. In fact, because sin entered the world, we are born into the unfortunate state of the wrath of God. Sin cannot tolerate the presence of the holiness of God. My friend Timothy Tennent has described sin as the willful choosing of the absence of God. When our ancestors sinned in the garden of Eden, they effectively chose life in the absence of God's presence. God did not leave them. In fact, it was the mercy of God to move them out of the garden where they could remain alive.

We are born into the condition of sin and into the unfortunate reality of the wrath of God. In his mercy, God has made provision for the short span of our lives. But this is the miracle: "For God so loved the world that he gave his one and only Son, that whoever believes in him shall not perish but have eternal life" (John 3:16). In his mercy, by the death of Jesus Christ, God protects all who will receive this offering on their behalf from eternal death. In his grace, by the resurrection of Jesus Christ from the dead, God offers us life on life on life, which is his presence, which is perfect, holy love. We are invited to choose life.

Whoever believes in the Son has eternal life; whoever does not obey the Son shall not see life, but the wrath of God remains on him.

It is an absurdity to suggest that it is somehow unfair that Jesus Christ is the only way to be reconciled with God. It is an unimaginable mercy—the free gift of eternal life for undeserving sinners. I like the way C. S. Lewis talked about this. Let's give him the last word today.

> When the author walks on to the stage the play is over. God is going to invade, all right: but what is the good of saying you are on His side then, when you see the

> whole natural universe melting away like a dream and something else—something it never entered your head to conceive—comes crashing in; something so beautiful to some of us and so terrible to others that none of us will have any choice left? For this time it will be God without disguise; something so overwhelming that it will strike either irresistible love or irresistible horror into every creature. It will be too late then to choose your side. There is no use saying you choose to lie down when it has become impossible to stand up. That will not be the time for choosing: it will be the time when we discover which side we really have chosen, whether we realised it before or not. Now, today, this moment, is our chance to choose the right side. God is holding back to give us that chance. It will not last for ever. We must take it or leave it.*

The Prayer

Abba Father, thank you for your Son, Jesus. Just thank you.

The Questions

- If someone were to come up with a singular cure to all cancer and it was the only known cure, would we be upset with them or think it unfair that there were not other cures available? Why do people reject the exclusivity of the offer of salvation of Jesus Christ offered universally to anyone who will believe? Do you understand/believe God's wrath

* C. S. Lewis, *Mere Christianity* (New York: HarperCollins, 2011), 65.

to mean God is angry at you? What do you make of the sun analogy? Does this help give you a better understanding of the urgent necessity of our being faithful witnesses of Jesus Christ to others?

Jesus and the Basket of Deplorables

19

JOHN 4:1–9 ESV | Now when Jesus learned that the Pharisees had heard that Jesus was making and baptizing more disciples than John (although Jesus himself did not baptize, but only his disciples), he left Judea and departed again for Galilee. And he had to pass through Samaria. So he came to a town of Samaria called Sychar, near the field that Jacob had given to his son Joseph. Jacob's well was there; so Jesus, wearied as he was from his journey, was sitting beside the well. It was about the sixth hour.

A woman from Samaria came to draw water. Jesus said to her, "Give me a drink." (For his disciples had gone away into the city to buy food.) The Samaritan woman said to him, "How is it that you, a Jew, ask for a drink from me, a woman of Samaria?" (For Jews have no dealings with Samaritans.)

Consider This

And he had to pass through Samaria.

Did he have to go through Samaria? Of course not. What Jew had to go through Samaria? Samaria was a defiled land.

When Israel fell to the Assyrians, all of the inhabitants of the land were taken into exile. Years later, the Assyrians exported their own people back to Samaria. For Jews, Samaritans were the ultimate basket of deplorables. They worshipped all sorts of gods and did their best to make life miserable for the Jews. Suffice it to say, the term "good Samaritan" was the ultimate oxymoron.

So why did Jesus have to go through Samaria? Because that is what God does. In the eyes of God there are no deplorables, only wayward sons and daughters. I think Jesus had to go to Samaria because of a divine appointment with an outcast woman in an exiled land. The disciples peeled off for lunch, leaving Jesus alone, when along came his lunch appointment.

A woman from Samaria came to draw water. Jesus said to her, "Give me a drink."

The stage was set—Jacob's well, high noon, a Samaritan woman, and the Son of God—and they were about to engage in a conversation we are still talking about. Here was Jesus in a place where no one could have predicted, with a person no one would have expected, entering into a conversation no one could have ever imagined.

That's what God is like. And I'm pretty sure it's what he wants us to be like.

The Prayer

Abba Father, thank you for your Son, Jesus, who crushes our categories of who is in and who is out and where we should and should not be. Come, Holy Spirit, and so fill us with the love of God that such prejudgments can no longer remain in us. We pray in Jesus' name, amen.

The Questions

- Where do you think the Samaritans are in today's world? Do we think that by connecting with and conversing with certain kinds of people that it will be read as our affirmation of them and their activities? So, what if that happened? Why do we disassociate with people we consider to be deplorable? What does this say about our understanding of God?

20 The Gospel of John as Holy Spirit Field Guide

JOHN 4:10–15 | Jesus answered her, "If you knew the gift of God and who it is that asks you for a drink, you would have asked him and he would have given you living water."

"Sir," the woman said, "you have nothing to draw with and the well is deep. Where can you get this living water? Are you greater than our father Jacob, who gave us the well and drank from it himself, as did also his sons and his livestock?"

Jesus answered, "Everyone who drinks this water will be thirsty again, but whoever drinks the water I give them will never thirst. Indeed, the water I give them will become in them a spring of water welling up to eternal life."

The woman said to him, "Sir, give me this water so that I won't get thirsty and have to keep coming here to draw water."

Consider This

I think of John's gospel as Jesus' Holy Spirit field guide. Scan back through the text so far and you will see it clearly, and there is oh so much more to come. The Lord revealed to John concerning Jesus: "The man on whom you see the Spirit come down and remain is the one who will baptize with the Holy Spirit" (1:33). Jesus taught Nicodemus that he must be born by water and the Spirit, noting, "Flesh gives birth to flesh, but the Spirit gives birth to spirit" (3:6). Jesus is the one, as we learned last week, in whom the Spirit dwells "without limit" (3:34).

Today, in this arid scene at high noon, Jesus does it again. He comes to a water well to teach us about the well of the Holy Spirit. Note the curious opener:

"If you knew the gift of God and who it is that asks you for a drink, you would have asked him and he would have given you living water."

What is this "gift of God"? You already know what I think. The gift of God is the life in the living water. The gift of God is the life in eternal life. The gift of God is *The Life of God in the Soul of Man*, to borrow the title phrase from Henry Scougal's classic work. The gift of God is nothing less and nothing more than the Holy Spirit.

Jesus wants to introduce us to the unseen reality of the person of the Holy Spirit.

"Indeed, the water I give them will become in them a spring of water welling up to eternal life."

Remember proud Nicodemus, hiding in the cover of night, sneaking through the shadows of his discontented soul, knowing there must be more to this life than the respectability of his religious reputation. "How can this be?" he quizzically asked Jesus (see John 3:1–9).

And now this nameless woman of ill repute, slinking in shame to the ancient well, hiding at high noon, her wounded soul parched by a scorn she knew all too well. She knew there had to be more to this life than what she had known. She pleads, *"Where can you get this living water?"*

All of us are somewhere on the spectrum between these two extremes. We mostly live in the mediocre middle attuned to neither our pride nor shame, settling for the status quo of whatever we think life and faith should be. Might we get in touch with our discontent, name it, and settle for it no longer? Must we reach the point of desperation to make a move? He will wait, but aren't we more than tired of wasting his time? Aren't we weary of wasting any more of our numbered days?

If I know you, I suspect you are with me. And if that's the case, then we are with her:

"Sir, give me this water . . ."

The Prayer

Abba Father, thank you for your Son, Jesus, who reveals your heart for us and who gives us the Holy Spirit. Teach us the ways of your Spirit, that we might walk in the power of love. We pray in Jesus' name, amen.

The Questions

- Here's the question to which we must become piercingly honest: Do I know the gift of God? If I know the gift of God, have I become convinced there is more of this gift that I don't know than I do know? If I have become convinced there is more of the gift of God that I don't know than I do know, what will this mean for me going forward?

21 Why You Can't Hide from God

JOHN 4:16–26 ESV | Jesus said to her, "Go, call your husband, and come here." The woman answered him, "I have no husband." Jesus said to her, "You are right in saying, 'I have no husband'; for you have had five husbands, and the one you now have is not your husband. What you have said is true." The woman said to him, "Sir, I perceive that you are a prophet. Our fathers worshiped on this mountain, but you say that in Jerusalem is the place where people ought to worship." Jesus said to her, "Woman, believe me, the hour is coming when neither on this mountain nor in Jerusalem will you worship the Father. You worship what you do not know; we worship

what we know, for salvation is from the Jews. But the hour is coming, and is now here, when the true worshipers will worship the Father in spirit and truth, for the Father is seeking such people to worship him. God is spirit, and those who worship him must worship in spirit and truth." The woman said to him, "I know that Messiah is coming (he who is called Christ). When he comes, he will tell us all things." Jesus said to her, "I who speak to you am he."

Consider This

There is one core universal truth, which if we could truly believe it, would save us from a world of heartache and pain. That truth? It is impossible to hide from God.

Let's go back to the garden.

> Then the man and his wife heard the sound of the LORD God as he was walking in the garden in the cool of the day, and they hid from the LORD God among the trees of the garden. But the LORD God called to the man, "Where are you?"
>
> He answered, "I heard you in the garden, and I was afraid because I was naked; so I hid." (Gen. 3:8–10)

This woman, interestingly enough, was hiding at high noon. No one visited the well in the heat of the day. Her pride sent her into hiding. Nicodemus hid under the cover of night. His pride sent him into hiding. Jesus knew them both, inside and out, before he ever laid eyes on them.

We tend to think of pride and shame as though they are two opposite poles of the same spectrum. They aren't. Pride and shame are two expressions of the same thing: brokenness. Pride is the external way we protect our internal brokenness brought on by shame. We cover our shame with our pride. That is why we blame others instead of owning our own faults. For a person shackled by shame, to admit doing wrong is tantamount to saying they are bad. Because of our shame, we cannot own our guilt. Shame is a mortal wound to our deepest identity. Pride is a fig leaf Band-Aid.

Herein lies the ancient psychology of sacrificial love. I cannot cover my own guilt and shame. No amount of external covering can heal my internal wounding. Only Jesus can do this.

Jesus said to her, "I who speak to you am he."

The Prayer

Abba Father, thank you for your Son, Jesus, the one who knows us better than we know ourselves. Thank you for calling us out of hiding. Give us courage to lay down our pride and come out of the shadows of our shame and insecurity. In Jesus' name, amen.

The Questions

- Why do we think we can hide from God? What do you think about this idea of pride being our primary way of covering over our shame and insecurity? Do you see yourself more in Nicodemus or in the woman at the well? Why?

The Critical Difference between Fasting and Dieting

22

JOHN 4:27–38 | Just then his disciples returned and were surprised to find him talking with a woman. But no one asked, "What do you want?" or "Why are you talking with her?"

Then, leaving her water jar, the woman went back to the town and said to the people, "Come, see a man who told me everything I ever did. Could this be the Messiah?" They came out of the town and made their way toward him.

Meanwhile his disciples urged him, "Rabbi, eat something."

But he said to them, "I have food to eat that you know nothing about."

Then his disciples said to each other, "Could someone have brought him food?"

"My food," said Jesus, "is to do the will of him who sent me and to finish his work. Don't you have a saying, 'It's still four months until harvest'? I tell you, open your eyes and look at the fields! They are ripe for harvest. Even now the one who reaps draws a wage and harvests a crop for eternal life, so that the sower and the reaper may be glad together. Thus the saying 'One sows and another reaps' is true. I sent you to reap what you have not worked for. Others have done the hard work, and you have reaped the benefits of their labor."

Consider This

"I have food to eat that you know nothing about."

I'm neither a scholar nor the son of a scholar, but I think Jesus must have been fasting.

Whether he was or not, for my money, this verse captures the ethos and essence of fasting in the way of Jesus. Fasting is not so much about abstaining from eating food as it is about finding an entirely new source of food.

"My food," said Jesus, "is to do the will of him who sent me and to finish his work."

This is an intense idea. Food is a good thing, until it has become the main thing, and for so many of us (present company included) food has become the main thing. Can we just call it? My food is not to do the will of God but, rather, pizza and steak and barbecue and lots of chips and salsa and Panda Express and . . . I'll stop there. My life, all too often, revolves around food. I think about it way too much. No sooner have I finished lunch than I start thinking about dinner.

"My food," said Jesus, "is to do the will of him who sent me and to finish his work."

Don't you think Jesus would like to take us to this place with him—where we are fed at the deepest level from doing the will of God? Wouldn't that be awesome? Again, food is a good thing, until it has become the main thing. I think if my food were doing the will of God that normal food might taste even better.

So how might we get to such a place in our experience of eternal life? It brings me back to the practice of fasting. I've been learning a lot about fasting over the past couple of years. I've mostly thought about fasting in the same way I think about dieting—as a temporary alteration of my normal pattern in order to gain some kind of positive benefit. In my experience, dieting does not produce lasting change. I am coming to think that dieting is all wrong, because it just means swapping out one kind of food for another (until you can't stand it anymore or the Swiss roll cake comes calling). What needs to change is not so much the food I eat but my overall relationship with food. With this kind of change, my diet will cease to be an aberration from the norm and begin to be a new normal.

The same might be said of fasting. What needs to change is not my technical practice of fasting but my overall relationship with God. With this kind of change, my fasting will cease to be an aberration from the norm and begin to be a new normal.

Now, the fascinating thing about fasting in the way of Jesus is it will not only change your relationship with God, it will change your relationship with food. I'll push it a step further and speculate that my disordered relationship with food may actually be a symptom that I have a disordered relationship with God.

"My food," said Jesus, "is to do the will of him who sent me and to finish his work."

Come, Holy Spirit!

The Prayer

Abba Father, thank you for your Son, Jesus, who teaches us how to pray and to fast and to truly live. Open my mind to the mystery of this way of the cross, which I believe is the way of the Spirit. Fill me with the Holy Spirit, that I might be liberated from my slavery to everything else but Jesus. It is in his name I pray, amen.

The Questions

- How do you see that our relationship with food could be trying to tell us something about our relationship with God? Or does that seem off track to you? Would you like to grow toward the reality of gaining sustenance and nourishment from doing the will of God?

23 Do You Have a Testimony?

JOHN 4:39–45 | Many of the Samaritans from that town believed in him because of the woman's testimony, "He told me everything I ever did." So when the Samaritans came to him, they urged him to stay with them, and he stayed two days. And because of his words many more became believers.

They said to the woman, "We no longer believe just because of what you said; now we have heard for ourselves, and we know that this man really is the Savior of the world."

After the two days he left for Galilee. (Now Jesus himself had pointed out that a prophet has no honor in his own country.) When he arrived in Galilee, the Galileans welcomed him. They had seen all that he had done in Jerusalem at the Passover Festival, for they also had been there.

Consider This

Did you catch what was happening in the first few verses of today's text? Samaria woke up. According to John's gospel, this looks like the first great awakening of Jesus' ministry—and in Samaria, of all places!

Many of the Samaritans from that town believed in him because of the woman's testimony . . . And because of his words many more became believers.

"Because of the woman's testimony . . ." It has me asking: What is my testimony? Would people believe in Jesus as a result of hearing my testimony? How about you? Do you have a testimony? It does not have to be a dramatic before-and-after story. A testimony is your own authenticating word about the working of the Holy Spirit in your life.

A testimony is a witness to the working of God. The Greek word is *martureo*. It's where the word *martyr* comes from. It means witness. It's a form of the word we see in Acts 1:8, which says, "But you will receive power when the Holy Spirit comes on you; and you will be my witnesses in Jerusalem, and in all Judea and Samaria, and to the ends of the earth."

We are witnesses because of the Holy Spirit. My witness is not so much about my story, but about the activity of the Holy Spirit in me. We need more witnesses. We need to hear more testimony about how the Holy Spirit has revealed Jesus in us and to us and for us and through us. Why? Because the Holy Spirit loves to awaken people through the power of our testimony.

What is your testimony?

The Prayer

Abba Father, thank you for your Son, Jesus, whose words convict and convince us, and thank you for the Holy Spirit who makes us his witnesses. Increase the power of our testimony to your reality. We pray in Jesus' name, amen.

The Questions

- So, how about it? What is your testimony? Would you be willing to ask the Holy Spirit to increase and deepen your testimony? Can you think of an instance where the Holy Spirit convinced you through the testimony of another person?

24 Interpreting Signs from God

JOHN 4:46–54 ESV | So he came again to Cana in Galilee, where he had made the water wine. And at Capernaum there

was an official whose son was ill. When this man heard that Jesus had come from Judea to Galilee, he went to him and asked him to come down and heal his son, for he was at the point of death. So Jesus said to him, "Unless you see signs and wonders you will not believe." The official said to him, "Sir, come down before my child dies." Jesus said to him, "Go; your son will live." The man believed the word that Jesus spoke to him and went on his way. As he was going down, his servants met him and told him that his son was recovering. So he asked them the hour when he began to get better, and they said to him, "Yesterday at the seventh hour the fever left him." The father knew that was the hour when Jesus had said to him, "Your son will live." And he himself believed, and all his household. This was now the second sign that Jesus did when he had come from Judea to Galilee.

Consider This

I've seen something in today's text all at once ordinary and exceptional, and it's something I've never noticed before. It is verse 50:

The man believed the word that Jesus spoke to him and went on his way.

The man took Jesus at his word. Now the piercing question: Do we take Jesus at his word, or do we need to see a sign or wonder in order to truly believe?

"Unless you see signs and wonders you will not believe."

This father wanted Jesus to go with him to heal his son who was on the precipice of death. Instead, Jesus did the greater miracle of a distance healing while requiring greater faith of the boy's father.

This is more than an isolated miracle. This healing of the Roman official's son, like the water into wine, rises to the level of a sign. I think of a sign as a miracle on steroids. There's more here than meets the eye. A sign opens up an endless well of revelation. On the one hand, it cannot be pinned down to one meaning; on the other, it can't mean whatever we want it to mean. A sign is a demonstration that never stops demonstrating. A sign beckons us to take off our shoes and recognize we are standing on holy ground. In the presence of a sign we bow and behold and ask Jesus, through the Holy Spirit, to reveal and even particularize his meaning to us. The operative word is not *dissect,* but *discover*. This is not science. It's mystery.

Rather than me speculating about the meaning of this sign, how about we get on our knees before Jesus, the God of this mysterious sign, and ask him to reveal himself and his meaning to us?

The Prayer

Abba Father, thank you for your Son, Jesus, who not only performs signs but charges them with inexhaustible mystery and meaning. Come, Holy Spirit, and interpret to us this sign of the healing of the Roman official's son. We confess our tendency and posture is too often that of trying to master meaning. Teach us to bow before the mystery and behold your majesty in a way we've not seen before. We pray in Jesus' name, amen.

The Questions

- Find a posture of humility and ask Jesus to reveal and interpret this sign to you. If the Holy Spirit shows you something and you believe it is for more than just yourself, would you consider sharing it?

25 Why the Why of Jesus Matters More Than the What, Who, When, Where, and How

JOHN 5:1–9 ESV | After this there was a feast of the Jews, and Jesus went up to Jerusalem.

Now there is in Jerusalem by the Sheep Gate a pool, in Aramaic called Bethesda, which has five roofed colonnades. In these lay a multitude of invalids—blind, lame, and paralyzed. One man was there who had been an invalid for thirty-eight years. When Jesus saw him lying there and knew that he had already been there a long time, he said to him, "Do you want to be healed?" The sick man answered him, "Sir, I have no one to put me into the pool when the water is stirred up, and while I am going another steps down before me." Jesus said to him, "Get up, take up your bed, and walk." And at once the man was healed, and he took up his bed and walked.

Now that day was the Sabbath.

Consider This

Jesus was not doing things right. Nor was he doing the right things. In fact, he was doing the wrong things in the wrong ways.

Messiah wouldn't begin on the banks of the Jordan with a rogue prophet's announcement. Messiah wouldn't go to the temple and turn it upside down. Messiah wouldn't lead a first mission trip to Samaria. Messiah wouldn't heal the sick son of the avowed enemy. Messiah wouldn't set up headquarters in Galilee. Messiah wouldn't hang out at the magic fountain of healing with the most marginal people in the world.

Let's be clear. Despite the fanfare centered around these events so many years later, they were not particularly noteworthy events in the news of their day. They were small, unexpected, unconventional, extraordinary signs—noticed only by those with eyes to see and ears to hear.

The same is true still. Just because we read the stories, know about them, and even preach and teach around them does not mean we grasp their significance as signs bearing revelatory significance. I'm not talking about some kind of secret knowledge reserved only for a select few. In fact, these events are on eternal display now for anyone and everyone to observe. It requires a quality of heart, mind, soul, and strength to begin to perceive the meaning of these messianic signs. The simple quality is humility.

It's why the importance of what Jesus did is only exceeded by the significance of with whom, when, where, and in what manner he did it. We must humble and submit ourselves to the entirety of the whole scene and context. One need not be a scholar to understand such things, though our understanding would be greatly impoverished without the work of godly scholars. Important as they are, these are all penultimate issues. The ultimate concern pointed to by all these matters is ultimately unknowable, save by the revelation of almighty God: the why.

Why does Messiah do what he does, when he does, where he does, with whom he does, and in what manner he does? Only God knows; therefore, only God can say. This is why we love the Word of God. This why we must be filled with the Holy Spirit. And all of this is to the end that the why of God the Father, revealed by his Son, Jesus Messiah, the Word of God, would become our own all-consuming why and empowered way through the person of the Holy Spirit.

If we would know and do the will of God, as revealed to us by the Son of God, we must release our assumptions, let go of our preferences, renounce all rights to ourselves, become humble, like powerless children, and follow Jesus to kingdom come—and all of this under the eternal banner of divine love.

I will say it emphatically, at the risk of offending readers and to the point of indicting myself: anything less than this is less than the will of God and only a passing shadow of the faith once handed down to the saints. It is to this faith we must be ever awakening.

The Prayer

Abba Father, thank you for your Son, Jesus, who upends all our worldly assumptions and reverses all of our native ways. We thank you for the foolishness of the cross, manifest in far more than his death but through his entire eternal life to the present day. Open our ears and eyes to perceive the gospel, grasp the love of God, and give ourselves unreservedly to Jesus. Come, Holy Spirit, and empower our participation in the very nature of God for the glory of kingdom come, on earth as it is in heaven (see Matthew 6:9–13). In Jesus' name we pray, amen.

The Question

- What do you think about this notion of humility being the prerequisite to perceiving and processing the revelation of God in Scripture?

26 Why God Leaves the Building

JOHN 5:10–15 ESV | So the Jews said to the man who had been healed, "It is the Sabbath, and it is not lawful for you to take up your bed." But he answered them, "The man who healed me, that man said to me, 'Take up your bed, and walk.'" They asked him, "Who is the man who said to you, 'Take up

your bed and walk'?" Now the man who had been healed did not know who it was, for Jesus had withdrawn, as there was a crowd in the place. Afterward Jesus found him in the temple and said to him, "See, you are well! Sin no more, that nothing worse may happen to you." The man went away and told the Jews that it was Jesus who had healed him.

Consider This

What a remarkable contrast we see in this story. I find it noteworthy that we can get two completely disparate headlines. The *Galilean Gazette* might write: "Miracle Worker Heals Paraplegic Beggar." The *Jerusalem Journal*, on the other hand, might frame it something like: "Sabbath Breaker Identified as Notorious Bethesda Beggar." Same event—two completely different stories. And here's the kicker: both of them are true.

Then there's the story of the gang down at the pool: "Lame Bro Hits the Lottery after Thirty-Eight Years of Playing!" How about the story told by the man healed? "He touched me. Okay, he didn't touch me, but I'm healed and I'm not sure who he even is."

What do our ears hear and what do our eyes see? It depends on who we are following. If we are following the crowd, we see the sensation. If we are following the religious leadership, we see the scandal. The trouble is both of these outcomes obscure the sign.

The sensational story is not that the man was miraculously healed. People apparently received some form of healing from that pool every day. The sensation is that God, in the person of Jesus Messiah, healed him. The scandal was not Sabbath-breaking. The scandal was Sabbath breaking out. Why weren't these broken men at the temple? The establishment had no use for them. The scandal? The Temple, in the person of Jesus Christ, visited them. This is the sign.

The sensational, scandalous sign? God goes to the temple only to ransack it. God goes to the most impossible and unconventional places to set up the temple, or better said, to tabernacle. The sign is reversal: the bringing down of the so-called righteous and the raising up of the so-called rejects. Down with the proud and up with the humble. Jesus reverses the status quo with kingdom come.

Here's something to think about: Have we re-created the temple complex in our churches? Or is the tabernacle moving us out into places where the kingdom of Jesus longs to come?

How about our own lives? Temple complex or tabernacle movement?

The Prayer

Abba Father, thank you for your Son, Jesus, the Word made flesh who tabernacled and tabernacles among us. Come, Holy Spirit, and make us as persons and as a people to become the tabernacling of Jesus in the world. Help us to fathom what that could be like. We pray in Jesus' name, amen.

The Questions

- What headline would you write over the story? Why do religious authorities and their brood so resist and even attack the unlikely, unexpected, and unconventional work of Jesus still today? What about this temple versus tabernacle contrast? See it in your church? In your life? Can you recall a church who truly tabernacled out in the world? How about a person or family?

Why Our Relationship with God May Not Be What We Thought It Was

27

JOHN 5:16–23 | So, because Jesus was doing these things on the Sabbath, the Jewish leaders began to persecute him. In his defense Jesus said to them, "My Father is always at his work to this very day, and I too am working." For this reason they tried all the more to kill him; not only was he breaking the Sabbath, but he was even calling God his own Father, making himself equal with God.

Jesus gave them this answer: "Very truly I tell you, the Son can do nothing by himself; he can do only what he sees his Father doing, because whatever the Father does the Son also does. For the Father loves the Son and shows him all he does. Yes, and he will show him even greater works than these, so that you

will be amazed. For just as the Father raises the dead and gives them life, even so the Son gives life to whom he is pleased to give it. Moreover, the Father judges no one, but has entrusted all judgment to the Son, that all may honor the Son just as they honor the Father. Whoever does not honor the Son does not honor the Father, who sent him."

Consider This

Throughout this gospel, John will bring us on the inside of sidebars like we see in today's text. In response to the persecution of the religious leaders about Sabbath-breaking, Jesus revealed a much bigger picture of reality. This vision will continue to unfold as the gospel progresses.

Jesus gave them this answer: "Very truly I tell you, the Son can do nothing by himself; he can do only what he sees his Father doing, because whatever the Father does the Son also does."

Jesus revealed here something profoundly new about the nature of God to these paragons of monotheism (one God). Within the oneness of God are three persons: the Father, the Son (both explicitly noted here), and the Holy Spirit (referenced throughout). To behold one is to witness all. "See what I do," says Jesus, "and you see what my Father is doing."

We can't come down too hard on these Pharisees. After all, the bedrock foundation of their understanding of God was revealed to them in the opening words of the Shema, which says, "Hear, O Israel: The Lord our God, the Lord is one" (Deut. 6:4). A God who is one and yet two, much less three persons, would have been incomprehensible. It would likely have the same effect if someone came to us claiming to be the fourth person of the quadrinity today.

"For the Father loves the Son and shows him all he does. Yes, and he will show him even greater works than these, so that you will be amazed."

This is why John's gospel, with its seven "I Am" statements and seven signs, is such a magisterial proclamation and demonstration of the identity of Jesus as the complete revelation of the nature of God. The bottom-line, breaking news here: God is relationship. God is one God in three persons—Father, Son, and Holy Spirit—and is made manifest and known in all of their glorious interrelationships.

To say we have a relationship with God is not to say we have a relationship with the Father and a relationship with the Son and a relationship with the Holy Spirit as though there were three relationships. Neither is it to say we have a relationship with this conglomerate of divine persons. To be in relationship with God means we are brought on the inside of the very relationship of the Father and the Son and the Holy Spirit. "My prayer is . . . that all of them would be one, Father, just as you are in me and I am in you. May they also be in us so the world will believe you have sent me" (John 17:20–21).

It's one thing to become friends with another person. It's quite another to be brought into the inside of their friendships with others—into their community. This is the essence of the gift of our relationship with God. We are born again (i.e., baptized) by the power of the Holy Spirit into the family of God. From there we grow up into the grace of God, discipled by Jesus to abide in the very life of God (the bond of Father, Son, and Holy Spirit), whose name and nature is love.

Our calling is to do nothing by ourselves but only what we see Jesus doing, which is in point of fact, what the Father is doing.

The gospel of John is like the ocean. We are edging into the deep end.

The Prayer

Abba Father, thank you for your Son, Jesus, who is the image of God in human flesh. We thank you for the way he brings us into his relationship with you. Come, Holy Spirit, and open our eyes to the wonders of the Godhead and bring us deeper into this fellowship. We pray in Jesus' name, amen.

The Questions

- What difference does it make to understand our relationship with God as being brought into the relationships of Father, Son, and Holy Spirit, rather than simply having a relationship? What might it look like for us to behold the things Jesus is doing in this gospel and then to do such things ourselves? Could it even be possible?

The Gospel Is Not Good to Great—It's Death to Life

28

JOHN 5:24–30 | "Very truly I tell you, whoever hears my word and believes him who sent me has eternal life and will not be judged but has crossed over from death to life. Very truly I tell you, a time is coming and has now come when the dead will hear the voice of the Son of God and those who hear will live. For as the Father has life in himself, so he has granted the Son also to have life in himself. And he has given him authority to judge because he is the Son of Man.

"Do not be amazed at this, for a time is coming when all who are in their graves will hear his voice and come out—those who have done what is good will rise to live, and those who have done what is evil will rise to be condemned. By myself I can do nothing; I judge only as I hear, and my judgment is just, for I seek not to please myself but him who sent me."

Consider This

"Whoever hears my Word and believes him who sent me has eternal life and will not be judged but has crossed over from death to life."

This is the gospel of Jesus Christ.

Hear the Word of Jesus. Believe. Claim eternal life. Rise from the dead and walk into life.

It is not a future hope but a present reality. The gospel does not take effect when we die. The crossover is now. The gospel does not make good people better. Jesus raises dead people to life.

Have you crossed over?

"Whoever hears my Word . . ."

Note, Jesus doesn't say, "whoever *reads* my Word." Faith comes by hearing. The two most fundamental faculties of perception are seeing and hearing. We tend to make much more of reading and thinking than we do about hearing and seeing. We are born seeing and hearing, not reading and thinking.

Going forward I want to encourage us to speak the words of Jesus aloud so our ears can hear them. There's something to that. I think it will lead to a new way of seeing.

The Prayer

Abba Father, thank you for your Son, Jesus, whose words are life. Indeed, heaven and earth will pass away, but your words will never pass away. Train our ears to hear and our eyes to see so the words of Jesus break forth into the vision of Jesus. We want to see Jesus. It is in his name we pray, amen.

The Questions

- Do you tend to put more stock into seeing and hearing or reading and thinking? Do you see the difference? Is the gospel more of a self-improvement reality for you or is it becoming a crossing over from death to life? Has your concept of eternal life been more framed around something that happens after you die or is it a right-now reality?

Reading the Bible and Missing God

29

JOHN 5:31–40 ESV | **"If I alone bear witness about myself, my testimony is not true. There is another who bears witness about me, and I know that the testimony that he bears about me is true. You sent to John, and he has borne witness to the truth. Not that the testimony that I receive is from man, but I say these things so that you may be saved. He was a burning and shining lamp, and you were willing to rejoice for a while in his light. But the testimony that I have is greater than that of John. For the works that the Father has given me to accomplish, the very works that I am doing, bear witness about me that the Father has sent me. And the Father who sent me has himself borne witness about me. His voice you have never heard, his form you have never seen, and you do not have his word abiding in you, for you do not believe the one whom he has sent. You search the Scriptures because you think that in them you have eternal life; and it is they that bear witness about me, yet you refuse to come to me that you may have life."**

Consider This

As much as we love the Bible, we have to agree—it's not about the Bible. At the end of the day, the question we must answer does not concern the Bible, but Jesus. We can read, ruminate, memorize, research, and get every question right, but if we miss Jesus in all that, we've missed the whole thing.

"You search the Scriptures because you think that in them you have eternal life; and it is they that bear witness about me, yet you refuse to come to me that you may have life."

However, if we miss the whole Bible and we get Jesus, we've got all we need. The whole purpose and point of the Bible is to introduce us to Jesus Christ and lead us in the way of following him into the kingdom of God—"on earth as it is in heaven" (Matt. 6:10).

So, am I saying we don't really need the Old Testament? Nothing could be further from the truth. What do you think Jesus is talking about here? When he said, "These are the very Scriptures that testify about me" (v. 39 NIV), he didn't mean the Gospels or the Epistles. They didn't exist when he said this. Jesus was talking about the Old Testament. In fact, anytime anyone in the New Testament references "the Scriptures," they mean the Old Testament.

Though he isn't named, you will find Jesus in every book of the Old Testament. In fact, that's why we study the Old Testament—to find Jesus, to more deeply understand him, to better follow him, that we might love God with all that we are.

We should heed Jesus' warning. As it was possible for the most devoted God-seekers in the first century, it is the same for the most faithful Jesus-followers in the twenty-first century: we can read the Bible with great frequency and intensity and be a million miles from Jesus.

The Bible can give us truth, wisdom, counsel, guidance, hope, encouragement, inspiration, caution, warning, rebuke, correction, and so on, but it can't give us life. Only Jesus gives life.

Let's keep that in focus going forward.

Only Jesus gives life.

The Prayer

Abba Father, thank you for your Son, Jesus, who is the Word of God made flesh. Thank you for the Scriptures and the mysterious and masterful ways they always point us to Jesus. Teach us to read them by the inspiration of your Holy Spirit, that we might come to know him better. It is in his name we pray, amen.

The Questions

- How would you describe your relationship and understanding of the Old Testament? Would you agree that the Old Testament has worlds to teach us about Jesus? What keeps us from really diving into the Old Testament? Have you ever been around Christians who are all about the Bible but seem to bear little resemblance to Jesus? How does that happen?

30 How Jesus Makes the Old Testament New

JOHN 5:41–47 ESV | "I do not receive glory from people. But I know that you do not have the love of God within you. I have come in my Father's name, and you do not receive me. If another comes in his own name, you will receive him. How can you believe, when you receive glory from one another and do not seek the glory that comes from the only God? Do not think I will accuse you to the Father. There is one who accuses you: Moses, on whom you have set your hope. For if you believed Moses, you would believe me; for he wrote of me. But if you do not believe his writings, how will you believe my words?"

Consider This

You know the trial is going bad when opposing counsel calls your star witness and turns him into your accuser. That's the nutshell of today's text.

"There is one who accuses you: Moses, on whom you have set your hope. For if you believed Moses, you would believe me; for he wrote of me. But if you do not believe his writings, how will you believe my words?"

Did Jesus actually tell these Moses fanboys they didn't believe what Moses wrote? Yep. He did. Translation: "If you don't believe what I say then you have no idea what Moses was saying." It's another way of saying you can know the Bible upside down and inside out and completely miss the point. File it in the folder that says, "It should give us great caution."

Something about the use of the term *BC* and the way we commonly understand it (i.e., before Christ) bleeds over into our understanding of the Old Testament as being before Christ. Now, if Jesus is the Lamb slain from before the foundation of the world (see Revelation 13:8), can there even be such a thing as "before Christ"? And if Jesus can be found throughout the Old Testament, how is anything before Christ?

Remember that time after Jesus rose from the dead and he came alongside those two guys walking down the road to Emmaus? They reported to Jesus all of the cataclysmic events of Jesus' crucifixion. Then this:

> He said to them, "How foolish you are, and how slow to believe all that the prophets have spoken! Did not the Messiah have to suffer these things and then enter his glory?" And beginning with Moses and all the Prophets, he explained to them what was said in all the Scriptures concerning himself. (Luke 24:25–27)

So here are the questions we need to consider: When we read Moses and the Prophets (i.e., the Old Testament), do we see Jesus? If not, then why not?

One sign that we are reading the Old Testament with Jesus is when what happened to those two disciples on the road to Emmaus begins to happen for us: "They asked each other, 'Were not our hearts burning within us while he talked with us on the road and opened the Scriptures to us?'" (Luke 24:32).

The Prayer

Abba Father, thank you for Jesus, who is the Word made flesh. He is the one who came to fulfill the law of Moses, and who makes his fulfillment of the law effective in and for us by the Holy Spirit who writes the law on our hearts. We pray in Jesus' name, amen.

The Questions

- Why do people perceive such a disconnect between the Old Testament and the New Testament? Have you ever experienced such a revelation of Jesus in the Old Testament that it caused a burning in your heart? Are you ready to dive deeper into the Old Testament with Jesus? If not, what is holding you back?

31 Have You Been Tested by Jesus?

JOHN 6:1–6 ESV | After this Jesus went away to the other side of the Sea of Galilee, which is the Sea of Tiberias. And a large crowd was following him, because they saw the signs that he was doing on the sick. Jesus went up on the mountain, and there he sat down with his disciples. Now the Passover, the feast of the Jews, was at hand. Lifting up his eyes, then, and seeing that a large crowd was coming toward him, Jesus said to Philip, "Where are we to buy bread, so that these people

may eat?" He said this to test him, for he himself knew what he would do.

Consider This

We are headed into sign number four, which might be called the pivot sign of the seven. At least it's the middle one. For memory's sake let's rehearse. Sign One: water into wine. Sign Two: long-distance healing. Sign Three: healing by pool. Sign Four will be John's account of the feeding of the multitudes.

Crowds were following him because they had seen the signs. Jesus wanted them to see through the signs into the depths of who he is. It's like he wanted to draw the crowd out of the hustle of village life and into a more reflective place. We might think of it like a place with no Wi-Fi or cell signal.

Jesus had set the scene for a sign. He was going to set a feast on the hillside overlooking the Sea of Galilee that would feed his followers until the end of time. He was going to feed his sheep with a kind of food that will all at once satisfy their stomachs yet stir an insatiable appetite in their souls.

I wonder what those multitudes, moving together like so many sheep, talked about on their way to be with Jesus. I wonder if their souls (or even their subconscious awareness) were stoked by the memory of these words: "The Lord is my shepherd; I shall not want. He makes me lie down in green pastures. He leads me beside still waters. He restores my soul" (Ps. 23:1–3a ESV).

There was another conversation always stirring between Jesus and his disciples. Remember, through everything he does, Jesus is discipling his followers. He's training them (and us) for the mission of the church he founded. It's interesting to me, though, that he's not focusing on strengths or looking for the can-do performer types. He is looking for people who know their human limitations. He's not looking for people who know what they can do but for those who know what they can't do. It seems counterintuitive and goes against all that seems right to us. Here's what I mean:

Lifting up his eyes, then, and seeing that a large crowd was coming toward him, Jesus said to Philip, "Where are we to buy bread, so that these people may eat?" He said this to test him, for he himself knew what he would do.

He wanted Philip and the other disciples to grasp the absurdity of a can-do attitude in the face of sheer impossibility. The test of Jesus is always to bring us to the end of ourselves, to the places of impossibility, where we finally come to grips with our limitations. He always has in mind what he is going to do. To pass the test of Jesus is to fail the test of self-reliance.

How are you doing with that? I have found that preparing for this test requires a lot of unlearning.

The Prayer

Abba Father, thank you for your Son, Jesus, who always has in mind what he is going to do. Thank you for the ways he tests and trains us to unlearn our own ways so that we might learn his ways. Come, Holy Spirit, and replace our can-do mentality with the plans you already have in mind. We pray in Jesus' name, amen.

The Questions

- How do you deal with this counterintuitive way of Jesus—that it's not about our strengths but his? What have you had to unlearn in your discipleship to Jesus so far? Are you facing an impossible situation that requires complete reliance on Jesus?

When You Know You Are Not Enough

32

JOHN 6:7–15 ESV | Philip answered him, "Two hundred denarii worth of bread would not be enough for each of them to get a little." One of his disciples, Andrew, Simon Peter's brother, said to him, "There is a boy here who has five barley loaves and two fish, but what are they for so many?" Jesus said, "Have the people sit down." Now there was much grass in the place. So the men sat down, about five thousand in number. Jesus then took the loaves, and when he had given thanks, he distributed them to those who were seated. So also the fish, as much as they wanted. And when they had eaten their fill, he told his disciples, "Gather up the leftover fragments, that nothing may be lost." So they gathered them up and filled twelve baskets with fragments from the five barley loaves left by those who had eaten. When the people saw the sign that he had done, they said, "This is indeed the Prophet who is to come into the world!"

Perceiving then that they were about to come and take him by force to make him king, Jesus withdrew again to the mountain by himself.

Consider This

Now to the sign. Philip told Jesus it would cost half a year's wages to even serve these people communion (i.e., for each one to have a bite!), much less serve them a meal.

While Philip was whining, Andrew went into action and came up with a whopping five loaves and two fish—hardly a bag of groceries.

Now it was Jesus' turn. He received the meager rations, blessed them, and multiplied them until, we are told, all had eaten "as much as they wanted." In case it wasn't clear to us that this wasn't a mere appetizer, we are told again, "they had eaten their fill."

What a sign! It's a picture of how Jesus can take something limited and make it unlimited. He can take scarcity and turn it into abundance. He can take not nearly enough and make it more than enough. Five barley loaves and two fish fed somewhere around ten thousand people (including women and children). The only thing more absurd than Jesus asking Philip how to feed all these people was Jesus actually feeding all these people.

I wonder what Philip thought about this. I'll chance a guess. I bet he was pondering, *If Jesus can do this with loaves and fish, imagine what he could do with my life.*

That's the secret of the kingdom of King Jesus. We don't have to be enough. We only have to be his. In the hands of Jesus, our lives can all at once be profoundly limited and more than enough. We boast only in the cross! Paul's word to the Ephesians comes to mind:

> Now to him who is able to do immeasurably more than all we ask or imagine, according to his power that is at work within us, to him be glory in the church and in Christ Jesus throughout all generations, for ever and ever! Amen. (3:20–21)

The Prayer

Abba Father, thank you for your Son, Jesus, who is immeasurably more than all we could ever ask or imagine. He is the loaves and fish by which you have loved the whole world and in whom all who will believe can be saved. Come, Holy Spirit, and stretch our belief beyond our paltry limitations and into the shape of God's possibilities for our lives to bless others. We pray in Jesus' name, amen.

The Questions

- What are you seeing in today's sign? Do you tend to be more of a scarcity person or an abundance person? Why is that? How, practically speaking, can you grow more and more into an abundance person?

33 Getting Away When Things Are Going Well

JOHN 6:16–21 ESV | **When evening came, his disciples went down to the sea, got into a boat, and started across the sea to Capernaum. It was now dark, and Jesus had not yet come to them. The sea became rough because a strong wind was blowing. When they had rowed about three or four miles, they saw Jesus walking on the sea and coming near the boat, and they were frightened. But he said to them, "It is I; do not be afraid." Then they were glad to take him into the boat, and immediately the boat was at the land to which they were going.**

Consider This

Let's begin today by remembering the last words from yesterday's text: "Perceiving then that they were about to come and take him by force to make him king, Jesus withdrew again to the mountain by himself" (6:15 ESV).

Many agendas compete for the attention of Jesus. Only one must prevail: the agenda of Jesus. Jesus could not be made king because he was already King. Rather than take on their agenda by confrontation, he did so by subversion. Jesus "withdrew again to the mountain by himself." There's a word hiding in that phrase I never noticed until now. The word is *again*. This was no isolated run-for-the-hills reaction. Withdrawing was not the exception for Jesus but the rule.

Many years ago, a teacher pointed me to a passage in Luke's gospel that continues to both challenge and encourage me: "Yet the news about him spread all the more, so that crowds of people came to hear him and to be healed of their sicknesses. But Jesus often withdrew to lonely places and prayed" (5:15–16).

If I'm honest, and you know I try to be, this practice of withdrawing into the fellowship of Father, Son, and Holy Spirit is not the rule for me but the exception. It might read: "But John David every now and then, when he was particularly stressed out, withdrew to lonely places and prayed." It is usually some kind of chaos or storm I'm trying to escape that drives me to withdraw into the refuge of God's presence. That's not bad. It's just not Jesus. It was Jesus' extraordinary success, and the ever-present agenda of the world in light of this success, that moved him to flee into the haven of his Father's fellowship.

Here's the payoff: the next time Jesus appeared in the Scriptures, he was walking straight into the heart of a storm and all of its unpredictable chaos. The thing we tend to run from, Jesus runs to. Before, I tended to put all the emphasis on the miraculous meal for the multitudes and the sensational headline of Jesus walking on water. That's beginning to change for me. I'm starting to read the signs posted amid the signs and wonders. It's like he's posting those quiet and slightly hidden signs in the midst of so many other things.

They say, "Follow Me."

The Prayer

Abba Father, we thank you for your Son, Jesus, who always leads us to you. Whether it be miraculous signs, mountaintop solitude, or the chaotic storms of our lives, we want to follow him. Come, Holy Spirit, and groove deeper patterns of the ways of Jesus into our lives. We pray in Jesus' name, amen.

The Questions

- Would you say withdrawing into the fellowship of God is the rule or the exception for you? What do you think of this notion of being driven into the fellowship of God by successes and not just by difficulties? What signs between the signs are you beginning to take note of in the gospel? In your everyday life?

34 Why Jesus Is Not Looking for Employees

JOHN 6:22–29 | **The next day the crowd that had stayed on the opposite shore of the lake realized that only one boat had been there, and that Jesus had not entered it with his disciples, but that they had gone away alone. Then some boats from Tiberias landed near the place where the people had eaten the bread after the Lord had given thanks. Once the crowd realized that neither Jesus nor his disciples were there, they got into the boats and went to Capernaum in search of Jesus.**

When they found him on the other side of the lake, they asked him, "Rabbi, when did you get here?"

Jesus answered, "Very truly I tell you, you are looking for me, not because you saw the signs I performed but because you ate the loaves and had your fill. Do not work for food that spoils, but for food that endures to eternal life, which the Son of Man will give you. For on him God the Father has placed his seal of approval."

Then they asked him, "What must we do to do the works God requires?"

Jesus answered, "The work of God is this: to believe in the one he has sent."

Consider This

Two kinds of food: food that spoils and food that endures to eternal life.

"Do not work for food that spoils, but for food that endures to eternal life."

So how does one work for food that endures to eternal life? At this point it would be very easy to read into the text many things that might be true but aren't actually there. For instance, we might misread it to mean we must work for eternal life, as though it could be earned. We might interpret it to have something to do with the building up of one's soul or character. After all, didn't Paul say to the Philippians, "He who began a good work in you will carry it on to completion until the day of Christ Jesus" (1:6)?

I may be wrong, but I doubt that John had read Paul's letter at the time of his writing. We need to look for clues in the larger context of the gospel to try to understand what he meant here. Remember when Jesus was at the well with the woman and they were talking about water. Remember Jesus' reply when his disciples asked him if he wanted something to eat:

> But he said to them, "I have food to eat that you know nothing about."
>
> Then his disciples said to each other, "Could someone have brought him food?"
>
> "My food," said Jesus, "is to do the will of him who sent me and to finish his work." (John 4:32–34)

Wouldn't it stand to reason for us too? The food that endures to eternal life "is to do the will of him who sent me and to finish his work."

So if this is our work, what did Jesus mean when he added, "which the Son of Man will give you" (John 6:27b)? He will give us the food that endures to eternal life which we must work for. How does that work? Herein lies the mystery. The people are tracking with us:

Then they asked him, "What must we do to do the works God requires?"

And here comes the money pitch:

Jesus answered, "The work of God is this: to believe in the one he has sent."

This is not a to-do list or a set of tasks or a magic formula. Neither is it a doctrine, creed, or proposition to assent to or agree with. This is a relationship. Just as Jesus abides in relationship with his Father, so he invites us to abide in relationship with him.

We don't do the will of God apart from God as though we were working for God. No, the work of God, which is the will of God, is the fruit of Jesus' love for us and our love for Jesus. This fruit is born in and manifest through our love for one another.

The working will of God, the deepest and most satisfying nourishment of life, happens as we live in such close relationship with Jesus that his love for the world can be directly made known to others through us.

The Prayer

Abba Father, we thank you for your Son, Jesus, whom to know is eternal life. Fill us with the courage to entrust our whole lives to him. Yes, Lord, this is our work: to trust Jesus. Come, Holy Spirit, and bring it all to life for us. We pray in Jesus' name, amen.

The Questions

- What do you think it means to work for food that does not spoil but that endures to eternal life? How do you see the difference in working for God versus Jesus working through us by the power of the Holy Spirit? If working means believing in this instance, what kind of perishable food are we devoting our lives to working for?

35 Why Jesus Must Be More Than the Solution to Our Problems

JOHN 6:30–37 ESV | So they said to him, "Then what sign do you do, that we may see and believe you? What work do you perform? Our fathers ate the manna in the wilderness; as it is written, 'He gave them bread from heaven to eat.'" Jesus then said to them, "Truly, truly, I say to you, it was not Moses who gave you the bread from heaven, but my Father gives you the true bread from heaven. For the bread of God is he who comes down from heaven and gives life to the world." They said to him, "Sir, give us this bread always."

Jesus said to them, "I am the bread of life; whoever comes to me shall not hunger, and whoever believes in me shall never thirst. But I said to you that you have seen me and yet do not believe. All that the Father gives me will come to me, and whoever comes to me I will never cast out."

Consider This

We want the bread to be the bread and not some kind of metaphor for God. When I am in debt, I want money. If I'm facing a hard circumstance, I want a solution. If I'm in a hard battle, I want victory. If I'm hungry, I want bread. I want God to provide all these things. All the while, God simply wills to provide himself. Jesus is the answer. And the answer might not involve a windfall of money to get out of debt or a solution to the problem or a victory in the battle. That's a problem. I really don't so much want Jesus as I want help.

Jesus can spot that from a mile away. Remember from yesterday's text: "Jesus answered, 'Very truly I tell you, you are looking for me, not because you saw the signs I performed but because you ate the loaves and had your fill'" (v. 26).

We want Jesus to help us more than we want Jesus to have us. In our shortsighted desperation, what we don't realize is help in this situation or that one is only a Band-Aid, a temporary fix. Jesus is himself the eternal solution. Watch this:

Jesus said to them, "I am the bread of life; whoever comes to me shall not hunger, and whoever believes in me shall never thirst."

We look for solutions when we need a Savior. Jesus is not God's solutions to all of our problems. Jesus is God's gift of himself to us. It sounds cliché to say, but the old adage comes to mind: "Give a man a fish and you feed him for a day. Teach a man to fish and you have fed him for a lifetime."

Give a person the answer to their prayer, and you help them for a time. Teach a person to abide in Jesus, and you have changed his life forever.

Jesus can solve our problems and, at times, he will. This is not his primary concern. Jesus most cares about becoming our life, our hope, our love, our joy, our all-in-all.

It sounds simple, but it will be the hardest thing we ever do—to entrust ourselves completely, unreservedly, and continuously to Jesus. This is the path of discipleship. True maturity does not come from pleading for answers to our prayers but from desperately seeking the one who answers.

The Prayer

Abba Father, we thank you for your Son, Jesus, who is himself the answer to our prayers. Grow us up to want Jesus more than we want our solutions, to love him for who he is beyond what he can do for us. Come, Holy Spirit, and give us this bread. We pray in Jesus' name, amen.

The Questions

- How do you relate to this point of desiring Jesus more than you want him to solve your problems? What will it take to grow in this kind of maturity? How might we get to the place where we can say, "Jesus, I will love you and cling to you even if you don't solve my problems"? What, if anything, holds you back from this kind of faith?

36 Would the Real Followers of Jesus Please Stand Up?

JOHN 6:36–46 ESV | "But I said to you that you have seen me and yet do not believe. All that the Father gives me will come to me, and whoever comes to me I will never cast out. For I have come down from heaven, not to do my own will but the will of him who sent me. And this is the will of him who sent me, that I should lose nothing of all that he has given me,

but raise it up on the last day. For this is the will of my Father, that everyone who looks on the Son and believes in him should have eternal life, and I will raise him up on the last day."

So the Jews grumbled about him, because he said, "I am the bread that came down from heaven." They said, "Is not this Jesus, the son of Joseph, whose father and mother we know? How does he now say, 'I have come down from heaven'?" Jesus answered them, "Do not grumble among yourselves. No one can come to me unless the Father who sent me draws him. And I will raise him up on the last day. It is written in the Prophets, 'And they will all be taught by God.' Everyone who has heard and learned from the Father comes to me—not that anyone has seen the Father except he who is from God; he has seen the Father."

Consider This

It all seems to be coming undone. Jesus found himself in a circle of doubters, scoffers, and accusers. We have gone from multiple awe-inspiring miraculous signs to this:

They said, "Is not this Jesus, the son of Joseph, whose father and mother we know? How does he now say, 'I came down from heaven'?"

If we are honest, and sympathetic at all to those eyewitnesses of all these happenings, it all does seem a bit incredulous. It is one thing to be impressed by the magnitude of the signs Jesus performed. It's a big leap from there to buying into the claim that he "came down from heaven." Right? Maybe if he were from out of town, but not this Nazarene we all know.

Let's get something straight. These skeptics are part of the ruling class. They are the respected establishment leaders—the people we look up to and admire. They are the beneficiaries of the status quo. They buy vintage wine. On the other hand, the people following Jesus are the common folk—in many cases, the poor. They are the left-behind ones and the forgotten—the people who need a break from the status quo if they ever hope to break free from it. They buy lottery tickets.

It's a long leap from then and there to here and now (and a stretched analogy), yet I want to pose the question to us who find ourselves somewhere in between the power players and the peasants: Who are we following?

We can claim to follow Jesus, but chances are if we are not following alongside the kind of people now who followed Jesus then, we are probably not following Jesus but, rather, some variety of establishment religion.

I think Jesus is ever clarifying who his followers are and aren't. He is as confrontational as he is comforting. The only way in is by opting in.

The Prayer

Abba Father, we thank you for your Son, Jesus, who mercifully exposes us and graciously welcomes us to come closer. We confess, all too often we want to follow him while keeping our distance from so many of his followers. Come, Holy Spirit, and convince us that we are them in the eyes of God. We pray in Jesus' name, amen.

The Questions

- Am I being unfair to suggest that if we aren't alongside the poor in following Jesus, we might not actually be following Jesus? What questions does that raise for you?

Holy Cannibalism, Batman! What in the World Is Jesus Talking About?

37

JOHN 6:47–57 | "Very truly I tell you, the one who believes has eternal life. I am the bread of life. Your ancestors ate the manna in the wilderness, yet they died. But here is the bread that comes down from heaven, which anyone may eat and not die. I am the living bread that came down from heaven. Whoever eats this bread will live forever. This bread is my flesh, which I will give for the life of the world."

Then the Jews began to argue sharply among themselves, "How can this man give us his flesh to eat?"

Jesus said to them, "Very truly I tell you, unless you eat the flesh of the Son of Man and drink his blood, you have no life in you. Whoever eats my flesh and drinks my blood has eternal life, and I will raise them up at the last day. For my flesh is real food and my blood is real drink. Whoever eats my flesh

and drinks my blood remains in me, and I in them. Just as the living Father sent me and I live because of the Father, so the one who feeds on me will live because of me."

Consider This

Years ago I had a mentor and friend who mentored by walking. We regularly took long walks together and talked about life and the things of God. Almost invariably at some point in the walk he would stop and, in a piercing fashion, ask me this question: "What do you think Jesus meant when he said, 'Unless you eat the flesh of the Son of Man and drink his blood, you have no life in you'?" It always took me by surprise. This question served as kind of a gear shift in our conversation, changing the pace, depth, and character of our walks. Over the years this question commanded hours of our dialogue.

Clearly, Jesus shifted into a new gear in this text. It's like he was grabbing the people by the lapels and trying to shock and shake them awake. Jesus was revealing a completely different kind of life—eternal life. It is different in quality, quantity, depth, love, power, and every other similar category we could name. Understandably, the people weren't grasping it. They said things like, "How can a person go back into their mother's womb?" (see John 3:4) and "How are you going to get any water from that well without a bucket?" (see John 4:11) and "It would take a fortune to feed all these people even a snack" (see John 6:7). Today's text is no different.

Then the Jews began to argue sharply among themselves, "How can this man give us his flesh to eat?"

Jesus was trying to tell them the how of eternal life while they were not yet grasping the what. I think this frustrated Jesus so much so that he literalized his own metaphor:

"Very truly I tell you, unless you eat the flesh of the Son of Man and drink his blood, you have no life in you."

Clearly, he was not advocating cannibalism, which, interestingly enough, the early Christians were accused of doing. Nor is it fair to argue the Catholic doctrine of transubstantiation (that the bread and wine actually become the physical flesh and blood of Jesus) from this text.

So let me ask you: What do you think Jesus meant when he said, "Unless you eat the flesh of the Son of Man and drink his blood, you have no life in you"?

The Prayer

Abba Father, we thank you for your Son, Jesus, who is the bread of life. Show us what it means to eat the flesh and drink the blood of the Son of Man. Come, Holy Spirit, and reveal this mystical reality to us in concrete fashion. We pray in Jesus' name, amen.

The Questions

- What do you think John 6:53 means? How would you describe eternal life? What is your present experience of eternal life? Are you satisfied with that, or are you wanting more?

38 The Most Mysterious Reality in the Most Concrete Terms

JOHN 6:58–71 ESV | "This is the bread that came down from heaven, not like the bread the fathers ate, and died. Whoever feeds on this bread will live forever." Jesus said these things in the synagogue, as he taught at Capernaum.

When many of his disciples heard it, they said, "This is a hard saying; who can listen to it?" But Jesus, knowing in himself that his disciples were grumbling about this, said to them, "Do you take offense at this? Then what if you were to see the Son of Man ascending to where he was before? It is the Spirit who gives life; the flesh is no help at all. The words that I have spoken to you are spirit and life. But there are some of you who do not believe." (For Jesus knew from the beginning who those were who did not believe, and who it was who would betray him.) And he said, "This is why I told you that no one can come to me unless it is granted him by the Father."

After this many of his disciples turned back and no longer walked with him. So Jesus said to the twelve, "Do you want to go away as well?" Simon Peter answered him, "Lord, to whom shall we go? You have the words of eternal life, and we have believed, and have come to know, that you are the Holy One of God." Jesus answered them, "Did I not choose you, the twelve? And yet one

of you is a devil." He spoke of Judas the son of Simon Iscariot, for he, one of the twelve, was going to betray him.

Consider This

So, what did Jesus mean when he said, "Unless you eat the flesh of the Son of Man and drink his blood, you have no life in you" (v. 53)?

Jesus most needs us to grasp what it means to believe. Believing means active, tangible, demonstrative trust. Way beyond the comforting, "I'll be here when you need my help" kind of faith, Jesus wants for us to know him beyond what knowledge can convey. He wants us to "taste and see that the LORD is good" (Ps. 34:8a). He wants our insatiable appetites and disordered desires to be integrated and satisfied by his life. As food is to the body, so is his life to our soul.

Let's be careful at this point. It's easy to make a wrong turn at this juncture and separate the visible from the unseen, the body from the soul, and the natural from the supernatural. God became a human person not to create dichotomies and dualities but to bring it all together.

When Jesus said, "It is the Spirit who gives life; the flesh is no help at all" (v. 63a), he was not discounting the human body or our physicality as human beings. He was rejoining that which had been separated from the fall of humanity. Jesus both exemplifies and executes the reuniting of the dust of the earth and the breath of God, the human body with the Holy Spirit, the source of life everlasting with the substance of frail humanity, indeed—"on earth as it is in heaven" (Matt. 6:10).

As Athanasius put it in the fourth century, "He became what we are that we may become what he is." He became like us so that we could become like him.

One word captures what Jesus is looking for from his followers: *union*. John 17:3 says: "Now this is eternal life: that they know you, the only true God, and Jesus Christ, whom you have sent." We might also look ahead to John 17:21 where Jesus prays, "that all of them may be one, Father, just as you are in me and I am in you. May they also be in us so that the world may believe that you have sent me."

Union—that's what he's after. This is what it means to "eat the flesh of the Son of Man and drink his blood" (John 6:53). Jesus reaches for the most concrete analogy possible to express the most mystical reality ever. He wants us to hunger and thirst for this most supernaturally natural possibility like we hunger and thirst for food and drink. This is eternal life. Let's give Jesus the last word: "Whoever eats my flesh and drinks my blood has eternal life, and I will raise them up at the last day. For my flesh is real food and my blood is real drink" (vv. 54–55).

The Prayer

Abba Father, we thank you for your Son, Jesus, whose life is the real life. We are weary of so many things that promise life and yet do not satisfy. We want the real food and real drink of eternal life. Come, Holy Spirit, and give us this life. In Jesus' name, amen.

The Questions

- Do you desire and are you ready for this kind of relationship with Jesus? Why do we settle for the things that promise life yet do not satisfy? What happens when we separate the body from the soul, the visible from the unseen, and the natural from the supernatural?

The Absurdity of Making Jesus Famous

39

JOHN 7:1–9 | After this, Jesus went around in Galilee. He did not want to go about in Judea because the Jewish leaders there were looking for a way to kill him. But when the Jewish Festival of Tabernacles was near, Jesus' brothers said to him, "Leave Galilee and go to Judea, so that your disciples there may see the works you do. No one who wants to become a public figure acts in secret. Since you are doing these things, show yourself to the world." For even his own brothers did not believe in him.

Therefore Jesus told them, "My time is not yet here; for you any time will do. The world cannot hate you, but it hates me because I testify that its works are evil. You go to the festival. I am not going up to this festival, because my time has not yet fully come." After he had said this, he stayed in Galilee.

Consider This

Something deep within all of us wants to be famous. No, we don't all want to be rock stars or celebrities, but deep down we desire to be acclaimed by others, which is the essence of fame. Even deeper, at the heart of our fame complex, lives our unspeakable desire to be godlike. Was not this the original temptation? "For God knows that when you eat from it your eyes will be opened, and you will be like God" (Gen. 3:5).

Another of the infinitely amazing things about Jesus is that he, "being in very nature God, did not consider equality with God something to be used to his own advantage; rather, he made himself nothing by taking the very nature of a servant, being made in human likeness" (Phil. 2:6–7).

In light of this contrast, note the words from Jesus' brothers: *"Leave Galilee and go to Judea, so that your disciples there may see the works you do. No one who wants to become a public figure acts in secret. Since you are doing these things, show yourself to the world."*

They thought Jesus wanted to be famous. Why would they think such a thing? It's because, deep down, they wanted to be famous. I hear a lot of Christian leaders these days call for their churches to "make Jesus famous." I think it's the most presumptuous and even ridiculous thing we could possibly say. Jesus unequivocally rejects the whole category of fame. The one who lives to love will not be made famous. The world looks for the famous ones; heaven searches for the holy ones. The world makes celebrities; the kingdom of God makes saints.

Jesus refuses the public captivity of celebrity. He hides himself in the nature of a servant. He will have no entourage of sycophants drafting on his fame. He drafts disciples—men and women who have walked the ways of the world and found them wanting, who are ready to abandon their lives to the only one who gives life—"no turning back, no turning back."*

The Prayer

Abba Father, we thank you for your Son, Jesus, who is the way and the truth and the life. There is no other way, no other truth, and no other life outside of him. Come, Holy Spirit, and help us give our whole lives to him, holding back nothing that we might receive everything. We pray in Jesus' name, amen.

The Questions

- Why do human beings crave fame or exalt celebrities and famous people? What may be holding you back from renouncing the ways of the world and abandoning your life to Jesus, who alone can give you life?

* "I Have Decided to Follow Jesus," lyrics attributed to Simon K. Marak, circa 1940. Public domain.

40 Undercover Boss: When Jesus Shows Up at Your Church

JOHN 7:10–15 ESV | **But after his brothers had gone up to the feast, then he also went up, not publicly but in private. The Jews were looking for him at the feast, and saying, "Where is he?" And there was much muttering about him among the people. While some said, "He is a good man," others said, "No, he is leading the people astray." Yet for fear of the Jews no one spoke openly of him.**

About the middle of the feast Jesus went up into the temple and began teaching. The Jews therefore marveled, saying, "How is it that this man has learning, when he has never studied?"

Consider This

There's been a television show for the past several years called *Undercover Boss*. In each episode the CEO of a large company shows up on the job disguised as a rank-and-file employee. For better or worse, the CEO gets to observe the company through the eyes of its workers. It usually results in several key changes in the company that make life better for those who work there.

Today's text gives us something of this scenario when Jesus made a secret visit to one of the key festivals of worship in Jerusalem. What might this have been like for him? Was he inspecting the liturgy and rituals, making sure they had crossed all the t's and dotted all the i's? Did he score the number of hymns versus praise choruses? Was he looking into the hearts of the people, seeing past the form of the festival and searching for the fire he wished were already built? Was he paying particular attention to who was not present at the feast, namely, the least, the last, and the lost?

And there was much muttering about him among the people.

Everyone was looking for him. No one realized he was already there. People were talking about him everywhere. No one realized he was listening in.

I sometimes wonder if it has become this way in my life. I'm searching for Jesus—meanwhile, he's sitting down the pew from me. I'm looking to experience him in the sacrament—meanwhile, he's the one right behind me in the line. I want to feel his presence in a song—while his voice sings out in the cries of the people far from me who have no sanctuary of protection from the sufferings of their lives.

What would be different if we knew Jesus were there, like the undercover CEO? In our churches? In our homes? In places of great need? Didn't he say something to that effect, like, "As you have done it to the least of these my brothers and sisters, you have done it unto me" (Matt. 25:40)?

I know. I know. That's not what this text is about. Or is it?

The Prayer

Abba Father, we thank you for your Son, Jesus, who hides himself in plain view. He is the King of the universe, yet he came in the disguise of a servant. Come, Holy Spirit, and awaken us to see him and, in seeing him, to know him and, in knowing him, to love him. We pray in Jesus' name, amen.

The Questions

- Do you live your day-to-day life with the awareness that Jesus is present? What would it mean to look for him? What would change about church if we knew that we knew he was there?

41 The Truth of Jesus vs. the Truths about Jesus

JOHN 7:16–24 ESV | So Jesus answered them, "My teaching is not mine, but his who sent me. If anyone's will is to do God's will, he will know whether the teaching is from God or whether I am speaking on my own authority. The one who speaks on his own authority seeks his own glory; but the one who seeks the glory of him who sent him is true, and in him there is no falsehood. Has not Moses given you the law? Yet none of you keeps the law. Why do you seek to kill me?" The crowd answered, "You have a demon! Who is seeking to kill you?" Jesus answered them, "I did one work, and you all marvel at it. Moses gave you circumcision (not that it is from Moses, but from the fathers), and you circumcise a man on the Sabbath. If on the Sabbath a man receives circumcision, so that the law of

Moses may not be broken, are you angry with me because on the Sabbath I made a man's whole body well? Do not judge by appearances, but judge with right judgment."

Consider This

Jesus was getting a track record. He was performing signs. He was preaching and teaching with an unusual authority. People were asking questions: Is he legit? Does he have a pedigree? Does he have credentials? Who has given him authorization to do and say such things? In the face of his claims to represent the God of Israel, the establishment made plans to kill him while the crowd called him demon-possessed.

How did he respond to these questions?

"If anyone's will is to do God's will, he will know whether the teaching is from God or whether I am speaking on my own authority."

Translation: Trust in me, and you will discover the truth of my words. It's not trust me because you already fully grasp the truth. No, it's trust me and you will discover the truth and the truth will set you free. Jesus offers the test of active trust. He is looking for people who will choose to belong to him even before they fully believe in him. How does one belong to Jesus? Start following him.

It strikes me that Jesus' invitation is a lot clearer and simpler than the church's invitation. Jesus never gives a four-step plan of salvation. He invites us to belong to him and to trust in him, which is signified very practically by following him in ways that lead to doing what he does and saying what he says. In doing so, we will discover that the truth becomes far more dynamic and alive than a fixed code of conduct.

I wonder if we have done the very thing with Jesus the first-century Jews did with Moses. They all revered the law, but none of them kept it. Is it because their loyalty had slowly drifted from the God of the law to the laws of God? Wouldn't it be possible for us to do the same thing with Jesus—to slowly drift from the truth who is Jesus to a collection of truth claims about Jesus?

Do we really think it is our job to reveal Jesus to people? Only the Holy Spirit can do that. Neither is it our job to try and convince people of a collection of truth claims, as though they had to get all that down pat before they could follow him.

I'm beginning to think evangelism looks a lot more like inviting people into simple and ordinary relationships where we read the Gospels together and explore this person of Jesus together and experiment with practicing his ways together. Our work is believing in Jesus, which means to actively trust him—in the midst of our relationships—unreservedly, unswervingly, and wholeheartedly. Jesus' work is revealing and winning people to himself. He will do it with signs and wonders where he wants to. He does it primarily in and through our relationships.

The Prayer

Abba Father, we thank you for your Son, Jesus, who not only is the truth but who will lead us into all truth. Grant us the grace to cast our lot with him, to belong to him, and to follow him with others as real disciples. We pray in Jesus' name, amen.

The Questions

- What do you think about this shift from the God of the law to the laws of God and, correspondingly, the truth who is Jesus to the truths about Jesus? Isn't the church supposed to be a group of people related together around Jesus such that Jesus is revealed to people through our relationships? Do we win people to Jesus or does Jesus win people to Jesus? What difference does it make?

The Difference between Certainty and Faith

42

JOHN 7:25–32 ESV | Some of the people of Jerusalem therefore said, "Is not this the man whom they seek to kill? And here he is, speaking openly, and they say nothing to him! Can it be that the authorities really know that this is the Christ? But we know where this man comes from, and when the Christ appears, no one will know where he comes from." So Jesus proclaimed, as he taught in the temple, "You know me, and you know where I come from. But I have not come of my own accord. He who sent me is true, and him you do not know. I know him, for I come from him, and he sent me." So they were seeking to arrest him, but no one laid a hand on him, because

his hour had not yet come. Yet many of the people believed in him. They said, "When the Christ appears, will he do more signs than this man has done?"

The Pharisees heard the crowd muttering these things about him, and the chief priests and Pharisees sent officers to arrest him.

Consider This

Let's not forget what we are dealing with here. Jesus is from Nazareth. Everybody knows it, including Jesus. Jesus is from heaven. Nobody knows it, except Jesus.

How would anyone know this? What would cause someone to believe this? For the Jews, this would have constituted pure heresy. God could never have been more than one according to the revealed faith of monotheism. And God could never have been an actual human being.

This is a real problem for the leaders of Israel and the temple. Add to this the growing uprising of faith among the people, and we have a problem of Houstonian proportion. Of course, they needed to do something about Jesus. Put yourself in their shoes. How would they understand anything other than that Jesus was a rogue prophet?

And that's the big problem with religion. It's not faith but certainty. Certainty destroys faith by crushing anything that challenges it. In our fallen state, we crave certainty because, with it, we can grasp control. Truth will not be controlled. It can only be embraced. Faith embraces truth, while certainty tries to pin it down. Is not this the great irony—these bastions of religious certainty, the ones with a lock on the truth, would ultimately pin Jesus, the Truth, down . . . to a cross?

The Pharisees heard the crowd muttering these things about him, and the chief priests and Pharisees sent officers to arrest him.

And lest we blame them, we must realize they are only earlier versions of us.

In defense of the truth, they arrested the Truth. In exalting the truth, they executed the Truth. Miracle of miracles, because of his arrest, we were set free. Because of his execution, we were exonerated. In the imprisonment of the grave, he rose from the dead. End of story.

The Prayer

Abba Father, we thank you for your Son, Jesus, who, in being taken captive, set us free from our captivity. Grant us the gift of faith and the courage to let go of the lie of certainty. Though truth be fixed, it will not be held captive by the control we wield with our certainty. Let faith arise. Come, Holy Spirit, and let faith arise. We pray in Jesus' name, amen.

The Questions

- What do you think of this distinction between certainty and faith? Why do we crave certainty? Why do we struggle with faith? Why do we think we would not be standing with the religious leaders had we been there at the time?

43 When Eternity Breaks into a Moment in Time

JOHN 7:33–39 | Jesus said, "I am with you for only a short time, and then I am going to the one who sent me. You will look for me, but you will not find me; and where I am, you cannot come."

The Jews said to one another, "Where does this man intend to go that we cannot find him? Will he go where our people live scattered among the Greeks, and teach the Greeks? What did he mean when he said, 'You will look for me, but you will not find me,' and 'Where I am, you cannot come'?"

On the last and greatest day of the festival, Jesus stood and said in a loud voice, "Let anyone who is thirsty come to me and drink. Whoever believes in me, as Scripture has said, rivers of living water will flow from within them." By this he meant the Spirit, whom those who believed in him were later to receive. Up to that time the Spirit had not been given, since Jesus had not yet been glorified.

Consider This

This was the great Festival of Tabernacles (or Feast of Booths), the celebration of God's faithfulness to the Israelites during the forty years of wandering in the wilderness. He led them with the cloud by day and pillar of fire by night. He faithfully fed them with manna and brought them water from the rock. The Jews would make pilgrimage to Jerusalem, where they would set up booths, or makeshift huts, where they would spend the nights throughout the festival—remembering those years of dwelling in tents.

As God had tabernacled in their midst through those forty years, now God tabernacled among these present generations as they remembered. I get the sense that Jesus could no longer contain himself. Remember, he hadn't planned to go at all. His visit was in secret. He had done a little teaching here and there but maintained a low profile for the most part.

On the last and greatest day of the festival, Jesus stood and said in a loud voice, "Let anyone who is thirsty come to me and drink. Whoever believes in me, as Scripture has said, rivers of living water will flow from within them."

The fiery pillar now shed its light on the Light of the World. The manna in the wilderness formed a bread crumb trail leading to the Bread of Life. The water that once gushed from the rock now flowed like a river of living water forever quenching the thirsty souls of a parched people.

Miracle of miracles—the ancient festival now unfolded in real time in a kind of cosmic fusion of horizons, in a wedding of time and eternity. In one hand, he held the horizon of all history past, and, in the other, he held the horizon of all eternity to come.

When a moment opens up to eternity it can never close again but remains forever open, radiant with revelation like a portal into a reality that never stops happening.

Holy ground. Shoes off. Face down. Listen to him.

His voice still speaking, not as echoes but living words ever asking, "Is anyone thirsty?" And ever pleading, "Come to me!" And always promising "rivers of living water" flowing from within you and me.

The Prayer

Abba Father, we thank you for your Son, Jesus, who has revealed himself to us in a way we can barely comprehend. Come, Holy Spirit, and hold us in these mysteries. Let our thinking give way to awestruck beholding where deep speaks to deep and we can never be the same. We pray in Jesus' name, amen.

The Questions

- Are you thirsty? What is your experience of "rivers of living water flowing from within" you? Could there be something you are missing? Let me ask again—are you thirsty?

44 Why Sometimes the Cost of Peace Is Division

JOHN 7:40–52 ESV | When they heard these words, some of the people said, "This really is the Prophet." Others said, "This is the Christ." But some said, "Is the Christ to come from Galilee? Has not the Scripture said that the Christ comes from the offspring of David, and comes from Bethlehem, the village where David was?" So there was a division among the people

over him. Some of them wanted to arrest him, but no one laid hands on him.

The officers then came to the chief priests and Pharisees, who said to them, "Why did you not bring him?" The officers answered, "No one ever spoke like this man!" The Pharisees answered them, "Have you also been deceived? Have any of the authorities or the Pharisees believed in him? But this crowd that does not know the law is accursed." Nicodemus, who had gone to him before, and who was one of them, said to them, "Does our law judge a man without first giving him a hearing and learning what he does?" They replied, "Are you from Galilee too? Search and see that no prophet arises from Galilee."

Consider This

Never mind Jesus' historic birth in Bethlehem. That's beside the point at this juncture. The point was division, and whether it be over his birthplace or his takes on Mosaic law or his claims to messianic activity, his very presence created controversy.

So there was a division among the people over him.

Why should this surprise us? We were warned. Remember this bit from his first trip to the temple (at eight days old)?

> Then Simeon blessed them and said to Mary, his mother: "This child is destined to cause the falling and rising of many in Israel, and to be a sign that will be spoken against, so that the thoughts of many hearts will be revealed. And a sword will pierce your own soul too." (Luke 2:34–35)

Or how about that time in Matthew when he dropped this bomb?

> "Do not suppose that I have come to bring peace to the earth. I did not come to bring peace, but a sword. For I have come to turn 'a man against his father, a daughter against her mother, a daughter-in-law against her mother-in-law—a man's enemies will be the members of his own household.'" (Matt. 10:34–36)

Though he is the Prince of Peace, Jesus divides people. What if sometimes it takes division to get to peace? Why do we think peace is an easy thing? Is it because of its association with tie-dyed T-shirts and free love? Everyone is fine talking about God until the name of Jesus enters the conversation. Something about Jesus can either start the conversation or stop it in its tracks. Could it be because his very presence causes "the thoughts of many hearts [to] be revealed" (Luke 2:35)?

If we are looking for cheap unity and an easy peace, we should probably move on from Jesus. His peace is costly, and his brand of union is all-consuming.

Something about us wants to believe peace and unity are possible without Jesus. Something about us wants to have the peace of Jesus without going the way of Jesus. It's too costly. It's easier to paper over our conflicts (or worse, deny them) and settle for the superficial harmony of getting along, with a little Jesus sprinkled over the top.

The hardest thing we will ever do is to settle our undivided allegiance to Jesus. It will cost us our idealism, our idolatries, and our ideologies. Until we do, everything about us, including our relationships, will be divided.

Jesus is Lord! Though it cost everything, that's the only peace on the planet.

The Prayer

Abba Father, we thank you for your Son, Jesus, who reveals the thoughts of all of our hearts. He is indeed our peace. Forgive us for settling for less and doing so in his name. Come, Holy Spirit, and awaken our allegiance to the lordship of Jesus in every way. We pray in Jesus' name, amen.

The Questions

- Do you see how our idealism and our ideologies get in the way of our allegiance to Jesus? Why do we have such an aversion to the kind of division Jesus brings? What if that is part of his plan to get to peace? Have you ever been in a situation where Jesus brought division? What happened?

The Lawyers, the Law, and the Lawgiver

45

JOHN 7:53–8:11 | Then they all went home, but Jesus went to the Mount of Olives.

At dawn he appeared again in the temple courts, where all the people gathered around him, and he sat down to teach them.

The teachers of the law and the Pharisees brought in a woman caught in adultery. They made her stand before the group and said to Jesus, "Teacher, this woman was caught in the act of adultery. In the Law Moses commanded us to stone such women. Now what do you say?" They were using this question as a trap, in order to have a basis for accusing him.

But Jesus bent down and started to write on the ground with his finger. When they kept on questioning him, he straightened up and said to them, "Let any one of you who is without sin be the first to throw a stone at her." Again he stooped down and wrote on the ground.

At this, those who heard began to go away one at a time, the older ones first, until only Jesus was left, with the woman still standing there. Jesus straightened up and asked her, "Woman, where are they? Has no one condemned you?"

"No one, sir," she said.

"Then neither do I condemn you," Jesus declared. "Go now and leave your life of sin."

Consider This

The sun was hardly up and the Pharisees were holding court. Let's try to make sense out of this trial.

For starters, we have the law. The Pharisees and teachers of the law came as the prosecutors. They brought a woman, the accused, whom they intended to bring to judgment. Or did they?

"In the Law Moses commanded us to stone such women. Now what do you say?" They were using this question as a trap, in order to have a basis for accusing him.

No, these lawyers cared nothing for this woman, a mere pawn in their chess game. They were going for the Lawgiver. Whose side would he take? Would he set the law aside and grant her immunity from prosecution, or would he permit them to throw the book at her? If ever he had a chance to win points with the powerful, this was it. Let's be clear: he gained nothing by taking her case.

In this classic no-win situation, Jesus searched for the third way and chose to compromise. Are you kidding me? Jesus called a play no one knew was in the playbook. He turned the lawyers into the accused, put them on trial, and compelled them to testify against themselves:

"Let any one of you who is without sin be the first to throw a stone at her."

So how can there ever be any sense of justice in this high court? Why not just throw open the prison doors and let them all go free? Isn't that what the gospel does? The gospel does not do away with justice and judgment; rather, it crushes condemnation. Watch this:

Jesus straightened up and asked her, "Woman, where are they? Has no one condemned you?"

"No one, sir," she said.

"Then neither do I condemn you," Jesus declared.

There's guilt and then there's shame. Guilt can be punished or pardoned. Shame must be crushed—yes, even crucified.

Shaming is our twisted sense of justice whereby we hide from our own unresolved guilt while projecting it onto another person and then condemn them for it. In doing so, we heap condemnation on ourselves and the cycle endlessly repeats itself.

Remember, in the garden, Adam and Eve knew they were guilty, and, rather than abandon themselves to the mercy of God, they covered themselves, hid from God, and prepared their defense (see Genesis 3:7–13). See how it works? Rather than confessing their guilt, they concealed it, and in concealing it they condemned themselves, swallowing their shame. Those who have swallowed shame cannot help but to throw it up onto others. A person who feels condemnation will unwittingly do anything to transfer it to someone else.

That's why we did it. That's why we crucified Jesus. We were there. In fact, we are there.

Now, about the matter of Jesus' words to the woman. Everyone likes to make such a big deal of this, noting that Jesus didn't let her off the hook without a parting stinging rebuke—to show that he was still a hard-liner against sin.

"Go now and leave your life of sin."

Maybe so. Note this: Jesus was not talking to us; he said this to her. No one else was even around to hear it. Our tendency is to take what Jesus said to her and make it our moralistic message to the masses.

I must stand before Jesus, pardon in hand, and hear these merciful words spoken directly to me and no one else but me. I'm the murderer. I'm the adulterer. I'm the thief. I'm the idolater.

I see another truth hiding in this last phrase: "Go now and leave your life of sin." Jesus sets us free from the penalty of sin, and, even better, he sets us free from the power of sin. That's the rest of the gospel—we can actually leave our life of sin.

The Prayer

Lord Jesus Christ, Son of God, have mercy on me, a sinner. Amen.

The Questions

- What do you make of this distinction between guilt and shame and how they work together? Have you given Jesus your shame yet? What are you waiting for?

The Gospel from Fifty Thousand Feet

46

JOHN 8:12–18 ESV | Again Jesus spoke to them, saying, "I am the light of the world. Whoever follows me will not walk in darkness, but will have the light of life." So the Pharisees said to him, "You are bearing witness about yourself; your testimony is not true." Jesus answered, "Even if I do bear witness

about myself, my testimony is true, for I know where I came from and where I am going, but you do not know where I come from or where I am going. You judge according to the flesh; I judge no one. Yet even if I do judge, my judgment is true, for it is not I alone who judge, but I and the Father who sent me. In your Law it is written that the testimony of two people is true. I am the one who bears witness about myself, and the Father who sent me bears witness about me."

Consider This

It's important, even essential, in studying the Bible to stay mindful of our location in any given story or book of the Bible. As we are now into the eighth chapter, let's get some altitude so we can see where we've been and where we are headed.

There are two mega movements at play in John's gospel: darkness to light and death to life. Look back over the journey so far. Water to wine. Paralyzed man walks. Jesus heals the son of the Roman overlords of darkness. He walks into the darkness of the Samarian wilderness and into the life of a woman gripped by the shadows of shame. Don't forget Nicodemus who came to Jesus secretly in the dark of night as a sign of his nascent readiness to break ranks with the darkness of religious control, break free from the death grip of legalism, and walk into the light of life.

Gaining yet more altitude, let's look down on the bigger story of the rise and fall of Israel. We see God's people dwelling once again in the promised land, yet this land now looks more like a desert expanse. Jesus, the God of the promise, enters into the wilderness night of this promised land as the Bread of Life, the Living Water, and the human tabernacle of the presence of almighty God.

Now, from the highest vantage point we can see the beginning of all things: "In the beginning . . . the earth was formless and empty, darkness was over the surface of the deep . . . And God said, 'Let there be light,' and there was light" (Gen. 1:1–3).

And, yes, from the highest vantage point we can see the end of all things: "The city does not need the sun or the moon to shine on it, for the glory of God gives it light, and the Lamb is its lamp" (Rev. 21:23).

As we descend back to the ground, let's come back home to these words from the opening sentences of John: "In him was life, and that life was the light of all mankind. The light shines in the darkness, and the darkness has not overcome it" (1:4–5).

Finally, into this profound landscape of history, set in the endless expanse of eternity, we read these words from Jesus in today's text:

"I am the light of the world. Whoever follows me will not walk in darkness, but will have the light of life."

Behold the stunning sweep of the gospel! Darkness and death give way to light and life. This is what God does, because it is who God is. And it's all coming together into the brilliant resplendence of a thousand suns in the face of Jesus Christ.

This is the gospel we must proclaim into the darkness everywhere we find it—starting with our own lives: "Let there be light!" This is the gospel we must declare into the face of death everywhere we see it: "He is risen!"

The Prayer

Abba Father, we thank you for your Son, Jesus, through whom you created all things and in whom you hold all things together. He is our light and our life. We stand in awe of your sovereign genius as you move everything from darkness to light and from death to life. Come, Holy Spirit, and bring these movements into our lives for the sake of your great name being known in all the earth. We pray in Jesus' name, amen.

The Questions

- Darkness to light. Death to life. How have you seen these movements at work in today's world? In your life? How are darkness and death wreaking havoc in your life? Where do you need light and life to break in? What would it mean to declare, "Let there be light!" into this darkness and "He is risen!" into this death?

47 Are We Asleep to the Reality of Supernatural Power?

JOHN 8:19–24 ESV | They said to him therefore, "Where is your Father?" Jesus answered, "You know neither me nor my

Father. If you knew me, you would know my Father also." These words he spoke in the treasury, as he taught in the temple; but no one arrested him, because his hour had not yet come.

So he said to them again, "I am going away, and you will seek me, and you will die in your sin. Where I am going, you cannot come." So the Jews said, "Will he kill himself, since he says, 'Where I am going, you cannot come'?" He said to them, "You are from below; I am from above. You are of this world; I am not of this world. I told you that you would die in your sins, for unless you believe that I am he you will die in your sins."

Consider This

Jesus knew where he had come from, and he knew where he was going. He had come from God, and he was returning to God. He knew he had come into time from eternity and that he would leave the realm of time and return to eternity. Because Jesus knew his history and his destiny, he was able to live fully in the present, as a frail human being filled with all the fullness of God.

To follow Jesus is to live as he lived. Everything Jesus did we can do. In fact, he told us that we will do even greater things than he did because he was going to the Father (see John 14:12). In his famous sermon, John put it like this: "This is how love is made complete among us so that we will have confidence on the day of judgment: In this world we are like Jesus" (1 John 4:17).

We are like Jesus? Unfortunately, this gets translated into the thin ethical framework of W.W.J.D. (What would Jesus do?).

It gets framed as a behavioral-management approach. Jesus cared for the poor, so we should care for the poor. Jesus loved his enemies, so we should love our enemies. While these propositions are true, they miss the bigger point. To be "like Jesus" in this world means to be a frail, weak, and profoundly limited human being who is filled "to the measure of all the fullness of God" (Eph. 3:14–20). This is not about becoming a superhero. This is what it means to become a saint—a holy one.

Being like Jesus doesn't begin with behavior but beholding. It cannot be sustained by mere imitation. It takes impartation. The love of Christ, though it be delivered by ordinary means, is supernatural power. Love makes people powerful. In fact, love is the only source of true power.

When it comes to this love, we live in an age that is quite asleep. This is the awakening we need. This is the awakening we must have.

The Prayer

Abba Father, we thank you for your Son, Jesus, who reveals to us in our own frail frame what divine love looks like in human life. We cannot be like him without his power at work in us. Come, Holy Spirit, and awaken us to this love that can change everything. We pray in Jesus' name, amen.

The Questions

- Have you ever considered that the love of Jesus is actually the power of God? Do you believe it is possible to be "filled to the measure of all the fullness of God" (Eph. 3:19)? What would that be like? What if we are living in an age of great slumber when it comes to this reality of being filled with the fullness of God and living at the level of supernatural love?

It's Not About Me, but We

48

JOHN 8:25–30 ESV | So they said to him, "Who are you?" Jesus said to them, "Just what I have been telling you from the beginning. I have much to say about you and much to judge, but he who sent me is true, and I declare to the world what I have heard from him." They did not understand that he had been speaking to them about the Father. So Jesus said to them, "When you have lifted up the Son of Man, then you will know that I am he, and that I do nothing on my own authority, but speak just as the Father taught me. And he who sent me is with me. He has not left me alone, for I always do the things that are pleasing to him." As he was saying these things, many believed in him.

Consider This

The text begins with the question of all questions: *"Who are you?"*

They'd heard what he had said. They'd seen what he had done. All of it stirred their curiosity to know more. They knew his name. They knew his hometown. In fact, the more they knew, the more they wanted to know. The biggest mystery was this one:

"Who are you?"

Here's what I find most interesting about the way Jesus answered. He told them about his Father. To answer the question about who he was, he told us about someone else, Abba Father. Even more so, he told us about their relationship. It's like he was saying, "I am not merely who I am. Rather, I am who we are. It's not about me, but about we." In fact, later he was so explicit as to say something like, "If you have seen me you have seen him" (John 14:9). Because we know Jesus, we know the Father. He also said we cannot know the Father except by knowing Jesus (John 14:6–7).

This dynamic of knowing the Father by knowing Jesus is the very same dynamic he wants to work through us. What if someone asks me, "Who are you?" What if, in order to really know who I am, they needed to know who Jesus is? What if I were so filled with such an inexplicable love that my life made no sense apart from Jesus? That's my understanding of what a saint (a holy one) is—someone whose ordinary life is so filled with an extraordinary love that to talk about them would require talking about Jesus.

This is what discipleship to Jesus is all about, not tirelessly running around trying to do good things for God but becoming an actual authorized representative (an ambassador) of Jesus to the world. Sure, this involves doing good, but far more it means walking in an abiding relationship with Jesus such that we do what he is doing and say what he is saying. Doing good is the fruit, but if it would represent the work of Jesus, it must come from knowing him, which is the root. Otherwise, it might as well be the United Way—a great organization, mind you, but not the church Jesus is building.

He's praying this for us, such that we might say with integrity, "The only way to know me is to know we."

I think this is precisely what Jesus prayed for in his prayer recorded in John 17—for me to become we: "My prayer . . . [is] that all of them may be one, Father, just as you are in me and I am in you. May they also be in us so that the world may believe that you have sent me" (vv. 20–21).

The Prayer

Abba Father, we thank you for your Son, Jesus, and for making yourself known to us through him. Grant us the grace of relationships with other people that increasingly resemble the nature of your relationship with your Son. We pray in his name, amen.

The Questions

- Upon being asked, "Who are you?" why does Jesus tell us about his Father? How do you see the differences between the work the United Way is doing and the work the church is doing? What do you make of this idea that "to know me is to know we"?

49 How Faith Can Keep Us from Freedom

JOHN 8:31–38 | To the Jews who had believed him, Jesus said, "If you hold to my teaching, you are really my disciples. Then you will know the truth, and the truth will set you free."

They answered him, "We are Abraham's descendants and have never been slaves of anyone. How can you say that we shall be set free?"

Jesus replied, "Very truly I tell you, everyone who sins is a slave to sin. Now a slave has no permanent place in the family, but a son belongs to it forever. So if the Son sets you free, you will be free indeed. I know that you are Abraham's descendants. Yet you are looking for a way to kill me, because you have no room for my word. I am telling you what I have seen in the Father's presence, and you are doing what you have heard from your father."

Consider This

We learn from the text that it is possible to be a devout, committed, faithful adherent to the truth of a religion or faith and be completely and utterly lost. Jesus was talking to Abraham's descendants. These were the insiders, the ones who chaired all the important committees, who taught Sunday school, and who faithfully gave to the mission. They prayed and fasted and shared with the poor. Yes, they knew, revered, and recited the great creeds of the faith. And, of course, they studied and knew the Scriptures.

Who am I talking about? That's the big surprise:

To the Jews who had believed him, Jesus said, "If you hold to my teaching, you are really my disciples. Then you will know the truth, and the truth will set you free."

He wasn't talking to his detractors. No! He was talking "to the Jews who had believed him."

There comes a point in the lives of we who claim to believe where mere belief will no longer suffice (if it ever did). There is a way of believing that leads to more knowledge, and there is a way of believing that leads to knowing. To be clear, knowledge of God can certainly lead to knowing God, but all too often we amass more knowledge about God that does not lead to knowing him. This way of believing leads to a kind of activity that seems like faithfulness (as in faithfulness to what one knows) but only masquerades as obedience to the truth.

Jesus said, "If you hold to my teaching, you are really my disciples. Then you will know the truth, and the truth will set you free."

Jesus said it's not so much belief in the truth but knowing the truth. Truth is a person. Following Jesus, holding to his teaching, leads to knowing him more, and knowing him more leads to real freedom. This is not about belief and unbelief but slavery and freedom. The irony comes in how they responded:

They answered him, "We are Abraham's descendants and have never been slaves of anyone. How can you say that we shall be set free?"

Here's the hard truth. We can be faithful to the forms of faith we have always known, all the while remaining enslaved to sin. Strangely enough, our well-meaning faith can keep us from freedom. We must know Jesus. He said, "I am the way and the truth and the life. No one comes to the Father except through me" (John 14:6). A child of Abraham won't cut it. A Methodist or a Baptist or a Catholic won't cut it. Jesus only. Jesus ever. Jesus always.

This is not an attempt to shake otherwise faithful people into fear. It is meant to awaken us to the freedom we do not yet know.

"So if the Son sets you free, you will be free indeed."

The Prayer

Abba Father, we thank you for your Son, Jesus, who is both our truth and our freedom. Awaken us to the fullness of this one who loves us more than life, that we may follow him into the life we never knew could be possible. Come, Holy Spirit, and stir a holy discontent in us for anything less. We pray in Jesus' name, amen.

The Questions

- Do you see how a well-intended faith can actually keep us from freedom? Do any examples come to mind? How might well-intended Christians today be functioning in the same manner as the children of Abraham were? How does one break free of this shadow of truth and into the real truth? How is your knowledge about God outrunning your knowing Jesus? How can your knowing catch up?

When the Followers of God Become the Spawn of Satan

JOHN 8:39–47 | "Abraham is our father," they answered.

"If you were Abraham's children," said Jesus, "then you would do what Abraham did. As it is, you are looking for a way to kill me, a man who has told you the truth that I heard from God. Abraham did not do such things. You are doing the works of your own father."

"We are not illegitimate children," they protested. "The only Father we have is God himself."

Jesus said to them, "If God were your Father, you would love me, for I have come here from God. I have not come on my own; God sent me. Why is my language not clear to you? Because you are unable to hear what I say. You belong to your father, the devil, and you want to carry out your father's desires. He was a murderer from the beginning, not holding to the truth, for there is no truth in him. When he lies, he speaks his native

language, for he is a liar and the father of lies. Yet because I tell the truth, you do not believe me! Can any of you prove me guilty of sin? If I am telling the truth, why don't you believe me? Whoever belongs to God hears what God says. The reason you do not hear is that you do not belong to God."

Consider This

If he hadn't done it already, we can be sure Jesus just crossed the line with the Jews:

"You belong to your father, the devil, and you want to carry out your father's desires. He was a murderer from the beginning, not holding to the truth, for there is no truth in him. When he lies, he speaks his native language, for he is a liar and the father of lies."

After multiple signs, multiple sermons, and multiple conversations, they still didn't get it. At times he thought they were grasping it, yet every time they turned on him in another way. Then Jesus read them the riot act.

Insiders rarely recognize it when their religion goes off the rails. It's obvious only in hindsight. From the outside the trains seem to be running right on time. The problem is the new destination. They won't know it until it's too late. That's why God sends prophets to warn the people. Nothing is more dangerous than a runaway religion. The quest for God, gone wrong, unwittingly and unknowingly becomes the quest for Satan. Good, God-fearing, misguided people will readily do evil in God's name and have no idea of it.

Lest we too readily summon those radical Islamic terrorists to the stand, we need only look in our own rearview mirror to expose our own train wreck. Does the American slavery project ring a bell? We appealed to the Old Testament to deny the humanity of an entire race of people, and we cited the New Testament to keep them in line. After all, the Bible does say, "Slaves, obey your earthly masters" (Eph. 6:5a), doesn't it?

Yes, indeed, the followers of Jesus can as readily become the spawn of Satan as did the children of Abraham. Doing the work of Satan in the name of God has a long history, and unless we remember it regularly, we will be among those who are destined to repeat it.

The Prayer

Abba Father, we thank you for your Son, Jesus, who is our Prophet, Priest, and King. Save us from the self-deception of thinking we are beyond self-deception. Lead us not into temptation and deliver us from evil. We want to know you, the Truth, who alone can set us free. We pray in Jesus' name, amen.

The Questions

- How do you react to Jesus calling the Jewish people the spawn of Satan in this instance? Why did he do that? Can you think of other examples where well-intentioned people did great wrong in the name of God? In the name of Jesus, even? How do we guard against such things happening in our own time?

51 The Day Jesus Jumped the Shark?

JOHN 8:48–53 | The Jews answered him, "Aren't we right in saying that you are a Samaritan and demon-possessed?"

"I am not possessed by a demon," said Jesus, "but I honor my Father and you dishonor me. I am not seeking glory for myself; but there is one who seeks it, and he is the judge. Very truly I tell you, whoever obeys my word will never see death."

At this they exclaimed, "Now we know that you are demon-possessed! Abraham died and so did the prophets, yet you say that whoever obeys your word will never taste death. Are you greater than our father Abraham? He died, and so did the prophets. Who do you think you are?"

Consider This

The phrase "jump the shark" has come to be identified with a particular episode in the fifth season of the popular fifties-themed television show *Happy Days*, when Fonzie strapped on a pair of water skis and did a ski jump over a live shark. The phrase has come to represent the point at which a television series crosses the line from reasonable to ridiculous. The Fonz wears leather jackets and rides motorcycles. He doesn't water ski, and, for crying out loud, he doesn't jump sharks!

It strikes me, from the perspective of the Jews, this was the day Jesus jumped the shark.

"Very truly I tell you, whoever obeys my word will never see death."

Really, Jesus? From Adam to Abraham to Elijah to Ezekiel, everybody dies. Okay, well there was that chariot of fire thing with Elijah, but still. This present audience became convinced at this point that Jesus had gone stark raving mad. Sure, they believed in the resurrection of the dead, but that would not happen until the end of the age. Jesus clearly meant something beyond that. He just said his followers would not die. He skipped right over impossible and landed on incredulous.

Then there was Lazarus. Sure, Jesus raised him from the dead, but in order to be raised from the dead, you must be dead first. Then there's that little problem of resuscitation where you have to die yet again later.

Jesus was talking about resurrection here, as in, "I am the resurrection and the life. The one who believes in me will live, even though they die; and whoever lives by believing in me will never die. Do you believe this?" (John 11:25–26).

He wasn't talking in general about the resurrection of the dead. Neither was he talking about not physically dying. So, what was he talking about? "Very truly I tell you, whoever hears my word and believes him who sent me has eternal life and will not be judged but has crossed over from death to life" (John 5:24).

Jesus was talking about the crossing over from death to life—now. He meant something happens to those who believe in him that renders death dead. It's called eternal life—which means, in essence, one dies to death before they die, which awakens them to life while they are alive—never to die again! It means we are already raised from the dead. It's why Paul said, "Wake up, sleeper, rise from the dead, and Christ will shine on you" (Eph. 5:14).

Real Christianity means awakening to the mysterious reality of being raised from the dead before one actually dies. It is impossible. It is incredulous. It is inconceivable. It is . . . real.

So, did Jesus jump the shark? It's a good question. The only way to find out is to follow him into the jaws of death.

The Prayer

Abba Father, we thank you for your Son, Jesus, who is the death of death and the birth of true life. Come, Holy Spirit, and awaken us to this life in a way we thought we knew but did not. Wake us up. We pray in Jesus' name, amen.

The Questions

- Are you ready to jump the shark—to move beyond the impossible to the incredulous? Could you be yet asleep to the fullness of the life Jesus has for you? Preach Ephesians 5:14 to yourself over and over again. Do you perceive a possibility so rich in the Holy Spirit that it creates a kind of holy discontent within you? Is that holy discontent on its way to desperation?

Why the Glory of God Is Not What We Think It Is

52

JOHN 8:54–59 | Jesus replied, "If I glorify myself, my glory means nothing. My Father, whom you claim as your God, is the one who glorifies me. Though you do not know him, I know him. If I said I did not, I would be a liar like you, but I do know him and obey his word. Your father Abraham rejoiced at the thought of seeing my day; he saw it and was glad."

"You are not yet fifty years old," they said to him, "and you have seen Abraham!"

"Very truly I tell you," Jesus answered, "before Abraham was born, I am!" At this, they picked up stones to stone him, but Jesus hid himself, slipping away from the temple grounds.

Consider This

If in the kingdom of God the least is greatest, the last is first, the servant is honored, and the way up is the way down, it would stand to reason that glory might be something completely different than what we think it is.

We think of glory as something reserved for the champion, the greatest, and the hero. When we think of glory, we think of Olympic athletes poised on stands bending over to receive their gold medals as they bask in the glow of exultant fanfare. Glory is the stuff of Super Bowl champions and Little League victors. Something in all of us craves this kind of adulation. We have from the very start. Why? Because we equate glory with godlikeness. We equate glory with sovereignty and power.

It is quite natural for us to project our grandiose notions of glory onto God. We love singing of the glory of God as though it were a celestial light show magnifying our concept of power into exponential infinity and projecting it onto God. And then Jesus walked onto the stage of human history and completely upended our rarified conception of glory:

Jesus replied, "If I glorify myself, my glory means nothing. My Father, whom you claim as your God, is the one who glorifies me."

Remember these words in the opening line of John's gospel? "The Word became flesh and made his dwelling among us. We have seen his glory, the glory of the one and only Son, who came from the Father, full of grace and truth" (1:14).

Now we are getting somewhere. Wouldn't it stand to reason that the glory of God might mean something like "full of grace and truth"? So, what does this idea of the fullness of grace and truth remind us of? How about divine love?

To be sure, the glory of God is the sovereignty and power of God; however, Jesus revealed to us the nature of the sovereignty and power of God. God's sovereign power is not a divine version of human sovereignty and power raised to the nth degree. It is altogether different. Jesus called for "on earth as it is in heaven" (Matt. 6:10). As fallen human beings, we get it precisely backward. When it comes to sovereignty and power, we think it must be in heaven as it is on earth.

The glory of God is the love of God, which we see in its fullest expression on divine display at the cross of Jesus—unfathomably full of grace and truth. While his entire life was the cross, Jesus' finest hour came on Good Friday. In the hour of his greatest glory, he wore human sovereignty as a crown of thorns. On the darkest day of human history, the Light of the World shone brightest. On the day when the Son of God was emptied of his life, grace and truth were poured out in their fullest measure. In the hour when all of the hatred of the human race was unleashed on this sinless Suffering Servant, the love of God revealed itself as the very essence of divine sovereignty.

The Prayer

Abba Father, we thank you for your Son, Jesus, who reveals to us what divine sovereignty and power look like. Thank you for showing us the fullness of your glory in the radiance of his merciful face, full of grace and truth. Come, Holy Spirit, and open the eyes of our hearts that we might see God, high and lifted up, the train of his robe—the cross—filling up all the earth. We pray in Jesus' name, amen.

The Questions

- What do you think of this tendency we have to think of God's sovereignty and power through the lens of "in heaven as it is on earth"? How do you define divine glory? How do you contrast that with earthly glory? What are the implications of the way Jesus revealed the truth of the glory of God? What will it mean to share in this glory, as he wills to share it with us?

53 Why Do Good Things Happen to Bad People?

JOHN 9:1–7 | As he went along, he saw a man blind from birth. His disciples asked him, "Rabbi, who sinned, this man or his parents, that he was born blind?"

"Neither this man nor his parents sinned," said Jesus, "but this happened so that the works of God might be displayed in him. As long as it is day, we must do the works of him who sent me. Night is coming, when no one can work. While I am in the world, I am the light of the world."

After saying this, he spit on the ground, made some mud with the saliva, and put it on the man's eyes. "Go," he told him, "wash in the Pool of Siloam" (this word means "Sent"). So the man went and washed, and came home seeing.

Consider This

Who sinned?

Newton's third law of motion states that for every action there is an equal and opposite reaction. We know it as the law of cause and effect. There's another interesting word to describe this universal law: *karma*.

"Rabbi, who sinned, this man or his parents, that he was born blind?"

Something about our own insecurity demands we ask the question, whether we are conscious of asking it or not. "I wasn't born blind," the disciples reasoned, "either me or my parents must have done something right along the way. We are good people."

These days, we don't so much think this way about people who have a physical or mental disability. When it comes to the poor or the imprisoned, it's a different story. We tend to think people are living in poverty or are in jail because of their own fault or the fault of their parents. After all, the thinking goes, one reaps what they sow.

Jesus dealt a death blow to this whole system and approach to life:

"Neither this man nor his parents sinned," said Jesus, "but this happened so that the works of God might be displayed in him."

So, was Jesus saying just the opposite, as in, this tragedy is not a result of someone's sin; rather, God caused this to happen for a reason—and that was so God could get glory from what Jesus was about to do? This would make God out as some kind of monster, wouldn't it? God caused this man to be born blind so he could suffer untold hardship and constant community shame for forty years or so until Jesus arrived on the scene. . . . Does this sound like God?

What if it's more like this? Every broken place in every broken life holds the possibility for the glorious works of God to be put on display. Everything that happens in life does not happen as a consequence of some prior choice or action. Nor does God plant every tragedy and hardship in the world because he has a reason for it. At the risk of oversimplification, let me state it simply: everything that happens is not God's will, but God has a will in and through everything that happens.

How about cancer? Who sinned? Was it the genetic code of his parents, or was it because he was a chain-smoker? That's the wrong question. Cancer is not bad karma. Cancer, in the hands of God, can become one of two things: (1) it could provide an opportunity for the demonstration of the miraculous healing power of the Holy Spirit to eradicate cancer, or (2) it could provide an opportunity for the demonstration of the miraculous healing power of the Holy Spirit to transform the life, character, faith, and even the family and friends of the sick person who is given the extraordinary gift of faith in the face of fear—come what may. In either instance, cancer always creates the opportunity for the display of the works of God through the ordinary yet supernatural conspiracy of the love of God for a person through his people, the church.

The cross crushed karma, fatalism, and fear. As they looked upon Jesus on the cross on that Good Friday so long ago, so many were asking the question: "Who sinned?" After all, doesn't the Bible say everyone who is hanged on a tree "is cursed by God" (Deut. 21:22–23 ESV)?

As we look upon Jesus on the cross, we know the answer to the question, "Who sinned?" It was me and you. In an act that forever crushed karma, fatalism, fear, and, yes, the curse, Jesus held out healing for all who will receive it: "Christ redeemed us from the curse of the law by becoming a curse for us—for it is written, 'Cursed is everyone who is hanged on a tree'" (Gal. 3:13 ESV).

We are all pretty sure why bad things happen to bad people. Allow me to turn this equation on its side just a bit. This whole system of thinking has compounded over the centuries to culminate in the question of all questions of the modern age: Why do bad things happen to good people? It is yet another misguided question, pointing to the epic fail of karma. The real question we must all come to grips with is this one: Why do good things happen to bad people (a.k.a. sinners)?

Answer: grace.

The Prayer

Abba Father, we thank you for your Son, Jesus, who is beyond amazing grace. How can we fathom this love who would take our place and crush our curse and redeem our lives? Come, Holy Spirit, and heal our blindness, that we might see Jesus and, so, see ourselves. We pray in Jesus' name, amen.

The Questions

- How do you see the difference between karma and grace? Do you tend to always look for the reason for a particular hardship or tragic situation? Do you think God caused it? Is there a situation in your own life that could be a place for the demonstration of the works of God? Are you open to whatever form that might take?

54 Would the True Blind Man Please Come Forward?

JOHN 9:8–15 | His neighbors and those who had formerly seen him begging asked, "Isn't this the same man who used to sit and beg?" Some claimed that he was.

Others said, "No, he only looks like him."

But he himself insisted, "I am the man."

"How then were your eyes opened?" they asked.

He replied, "The man they call Jesus made some mud and put it on my eyes. He told me to go to Siloam and wash. So I went and washed, and then I could see."

"Where is this man?" they asked him.

"I don't know," he said.

They brought to the Pharisees the man who had been blind. Now the day on which Jesus had made the mud and opened the man's eyes was a Sabbath. Therefore the Pharisees also asked him how he had received his sight. "He put mud on my eyes," the man replied, "and I washed, and now I see."

Consider This

Would the true blind man please come forward? Are you catching the splendid irony unfolding in this story?

His neighbors and those who had formerly seen him begging asked, "Isn't this the same man who used to sit and beg?" Some claimed that he was.

There was the blindness of the man born blind, but there was a greater blindness afoot. It was the blindness of the people to the man born blind. Here were "his neighbors and those who had formerly seen him begging," and they were in a debate as to whether he was the blind man. He had become like furniture to his own neighbors. No one seemed to know his name. He was like that guy I see standing on the side of the freeway off-ramp with a sign in his hand that says: "I need food." I am effectively blind when it comes to seeing him.

Several years ago, I was invited to preach at a church on St. Thomas Island. Like so many other places, the contrast between the rich and the poor was staggering, and yet they lived in such close proximity to each other. They had asked me to preach on this very text. I made a comment about this egregious disparity between the rich and the poor and how the longer we see it, the more blind to them we become. At that point, a woman abruptly stood up in the congregation about seven rows from the front. She began shouting at me, "I reject what you are saying. You are wrong! There are no poor people on this island! This is a lie you are speaking about us!" I had never encountered anything like this before or since. I didn't know what to do. The woman went on shouting, and the pastor called her to cease. She sat down reluctantly, and I did my best to finish the message. As I stood in stunned silence, it hit me that the text I was preaching was actually unfolding before our very eyes. Her blindness to the unseen poor all around us was now on full display. It unfolded into a powerful revelatory moment of grace and truth.

Like a kid running out of class at the instant the bell rings, I ran out of the church as the service ended. I have never been so glad to get out of a church before in my life. I'm told something of an awakening happened in the church in the wake of this shocking Sunday.

Honestly, in the many times I read John 9 prior to that occasion, I had never even seen this ironic blindness of everyone around to the man born blind. In fact, I had been blind to him too.

The Prayer

Abba Father, we thank you for your Son, Jesus, who sees us all and who sees us as having the very same worth. Thank you that net worth means nothing in the kingdom of God and that your worth means everything. Open our eyes to see one another in the way you see us. We pray in Jesus' name, amen.

The Questions

- Have you ever noticed this feature in the text—of the blindness of the people to the blind man? Do you still see the poor in your midst, or has your life become so insulated from their presence that you don't have occasion to even look? Have you ever wondered why we aren't told the blind man's name?

How to Make Sense of a Situation That Does Not Make Sense

55

JOHN 9:16–23 ESV | Some of the Pharisees said, "This man is not from God, for he does not keep the Sabbath." But others said, "How can a man who is a sinner do such signs?" And there was a division among them. So they said again to the blind man, "What do you say about him, since he has opened your eyes?" He said, "He is a prophet."

The Jews did not believe that he had been blind and had received his sight, until they called the parents of the man who had received his sight and asked them, "Is this your son, who you say was born blind? How then does he now see?" His parents answered, "We know that this is our son and that he was born blind. But how he now sees we do not know, nor do we know who opened his eyes. Ask him; he is of age. He will speak for himself." (His parents said these things because they feared the Jews, for the Jews had already agreed that if anyone should confess Jesus to be Christ, he was to be put out of the synagogue.) Therefore his parents said, "He is of age; ask him."

Consider This

When you are out to get someone, you are going to find a way to get them. Throughout John's gospel, there were multiple situations where we were told that the Pharisees and religious leadership were looking for a way to kill Jesus. They picked up stones on one occasion. They constantly sought to catch him in some kind of policy loophole. In today's text, in response to the sensational healing of the man born blind, they alleged he was a Sabbath-breaker.

Was this really all about the law? It seems a bit much. In situations like these, where things are hard to understand, there is a simple rule to apply: look around and see who is benefitting most from the status quo, or the way things are. Another way is to ask the question: If things dramatically changed, who stands to lose the most?

This holds true in every organization, from local churches to multinational corporations. The reason things remain the way they are and always have been is because someone or some group is benefitting from them remaining that way. The other interesting question to ponder is this one: Who stands to benefit the most from change?

So how do you assess that in the present situation? How do you assess it in the organizations of which you are a part?

The Prayer

Abba Father, we thank you for your Son, Jesus, who brings to the world the great reversal of love, where the proud are brought down and the humble are lifted up. Open our eyes to corrupt systems of power, especially the ones that bring us gain, and give us the courage to stand up for what is right, even if it is against our self-interest. We pray in Jesus' name, amen.

The Questions

- Analyze the situation from today's text. Who does the status quo benefit? Who loses? What do the losers stand to gain if things change? How does the present state of affairs in your own church benefit you? What most needs to change? What would you lose as a consequence of change? Who loses as a result? What would change mean for the losers?

When Testimony Trumps Theology

56

JOHN 9:24–34 | A second time they summoned the man who had been blind. "Give glory to God by telling the truth," they said. "We know this man is a sinner."

He replied, "Whether he is a sinner or not, I don't know. One thing I do know. I was blind but now I see!"

Then they asked him, "What did he do to you? How did he open your eyes?"

He answered, "I have told you already and you did not listen. Why do you want to hear it again? Do you want to become his disciples too?"

Then they hurled insults at him and said, "You are this fellow's disciple! We are disciples of Moses! We know that God spoke

to Moses, but as for this fellow, we don't even know where he comes from."

The man answered, "Now that is remarkable! You don't know where he comes from, yet he opened my eyes. We know that God does not listen to sinners. He listens to the godly person who does his will. Nobody has ever heard of opening the eyes of a man born blind. If this man were not from God, he could do nothing."

To this they replied, "You were steeped in sin at birth; how dare you lecture us!" And they threw him out.

Consider This

They would not stop. Their power had been challenged to the core by one of the most marginalized people in town. A blind beggar held court with the religious leaders of the nation. They brought him in for questioning, and he wound up interrogating them. He even had the audacity to ask them, "Do you want to become his disciples too?"

This is a picture of catastrophic reversal. Now the blind man lectured the teachers:

"We know that God does not listen to sinners. He listens to the godly person who does his will."

Sin theology abounds in this story. Remember how it began? "Who sinned, this man or his parents?" (v. 1). If you will trace it through, it goes all the way to the end.

Jesus is not bringing more sin theology. To be sure, he takes sin quite seriously, but he does not allow sin to set the frame.

Jesus brings the theology of grace. Recall the conventional theology of the day: "We know that God does not listen to sinners. He listens to the godly person who does his will." Now consider what just happened. Jesus (a.k.a. God) listened to a sinner, the blind man, and lavished grace upon him. Jesus might reframe it like this: "We know that God only listens to sinners, and he transforms them by grace into godly people who do his will."

In the midst of all these social subplots and heated theological debates, we can easily forget what the whole thing is about. It can be like that all too often for us Christians. We can debate the meaning of this text or that one and parse our theology ninety-nine ways to one, and all of that can be a good thing—until we lose sight of the main thing. So, what is the main thing? The man formerly known as the blind man said it best:

"Whether he is a sinner or not, I don't know. One thing I do know. I was blind but now I see!"

The Prayer

Abba Father, we thank you for your Son, Jesus, who disarms our defenses, cuts through our pretense, arrests our avoidance tactics, and takes us to the place of our real testimony. Come, Holy Spirit, and deepen our own experience of grace, that we might stand with the blind beggar and tell the truth, even in the face of great opposition. We pray in Jesus' name, amen.

The Questions

- Do you see how Jesus will not allow the conversation to be framed by sin but, instead, frames it by grace? What difference does this make? Would you say that you are more aware of the power of sin or the power of the grace of God in Jesus Christ? How might this change? Do you have a testimony, perhaps not as dramatic as the blind man's, but that might be framed as, "I once was ________ but now I ________"?

57 The Reason We Are Blind

JOHN 9:35–41 ESV | Jesus heard that they had cast him out, and having found him he said, "Do you believe in the Son of Man?" He answered, "And who is he, sir, that I may believe in him?" Jesus said to him, "You have seen him, and it is he who is speaking to you." He said, "Lord, I believe," and he worshiped him. Jesus said, "For judgment I came into this world, that those who do not see may see, and those who see may become blind." Some of the Pharisees near him heard these things, and said to him, "Are we also blind?" Jesus said to them, "If you were blind, you would have no guilt; but now that you say, 'We see,' your guilt remains.

Consider This

We have just witnessed the ultimate table-turning moment of the gospel of John so far. We began with a man born blind.

We end with the sons of Abraham and the followers of Moses, the ones who came from the womb seeing God, called out as blind guides.

We began with the assumption that the blind man was the sinner (or his parents). We end with the so-called righteous ones being called out as the guilty sinners. The irony is so thick that it approaches satire.

If I could draw one application from this whole affair, it would be this: don't make assumptions about people. Everyone assumed the man born blind was blind for some good reason—because either he or his parents were sinners. Everyone assumed the religious leaders were not sinners but righteous ones, because of their standing in the community. Everyone had some kind of assumption about Jesus. Some thought he was demon-possessed. Others thought he was a prophet. Still others were assured he was a sinner. After all, "Can anything good come out of Nazareth?" (John 1:46 ESV).

Don't make assumptions. So, what is an assumption? An assumption is my hidden assessment of a person or situation raised to the level of established truth. The problem with assumptions is the way we hold these often untested assessments as truth when they may actually be far from the truth. It's our assumptions that fuel our prejudices. When we make decisions about people based on untested assumptions, it's a short step to the trinity of community killers—gossip, judgment, and condemnation.

If you are anything like me, you already have a ton of them. Ask the Holy Spirit to increase your awareness of the assumptions you didn't even know you had. It's a mark of maturity, and it is the pathway toward love.

In the end, our assumptions are the source of our blindness. What we are sure we see clearly keeps us from seeing what is most clearly there.

The Prayer

Abba Father, we thank you for your Son, Jesus, who shatters our unspoken and untested assumptions and replaces them with humble truth. Increase our awareness of the assumptions we hold about one another and give us grace to question them. We pray in Jesus' name, amen.

The Questions

- How do you go about surfacing and questioning your assumptions about people and situations? How do you understand that assumptions can be dangerous? How can we help one another in grace-filled ways to surface and test our assumptions?

58 How to Know If You Really Believe the Gospel

JOHN 10:1–6 ESV | "Truly, truly, I say to you, he who does not enter the sheepfold by the door but climbs in by another way, that man is a thief and a robber. But he who enters by

the door is the shepherd of the sheep. To him the gatekeeper opens. The sheep hear his voice, and he calls his own sheep by name and leads them out. When he has brought out all his own, he goes before them, and the sheep follow him, for they know his voice. A stranger they will not follow, but they will flee from him, for they do not know the voice of strangers." This figure of speech Jesus used with them, but they did not understand what he was saying to them.

Consider This

I once heard a preacher opine in a sermon about how to tell the difference between a shepherd and a butcher. The shepherd leads the sheep to green pastures from the front. The butcher drives the sheep to the slaughter from behind. Whether accurate or not I do not know, but I do know it makes the point for our text.

"But he who enters by the door is the shepherd of the sheep."

There is only one way in for the sheep: follow the Shepherd through the gate. The Pharisees assumed they were already in. Jesus told them otherwise. He invited them in, but mercifully told them that all of the other efforts to gain access were futile. There is only one gate. They must enter in through that way.

Sure, people try all sorts of ways to get in. They climb over or blast through by way of their own righteous efforts or religious systems. While they think they are inside, they remain outside. The danger they pose is the way they try to lead other sheep to follow them in their futile ways of salvation (i.e., perfect observance of the Sabbath and the hundreds of other laws). This effectively steals people's freedom, destroys their faith, and otherwise enslaves them to an idol or false god.

Why does it bother people that there is only one way into the sheepfold? Why is that unfair? What if it is a simple fact? What if it is the truth? Why would we be angry at the truth? What might underly this anger? Might it be a sense of entitlement that we deserve to be on the inside? What if we don't deserve to be on the inside? That would mean something like grace was at work—getting what we don't deserve.

Wouldn't it be a really good thing that there was even a single way to salvation? What if there were no way in? Wouldn't it actually be an amazing thing that this single way of salvation was open to absolutely anyone and everyone who would enter in through this gracious gate? And wouldn't it be the most extraordinary thing in the universe that this access to the sheepfold was not based on our own merits but was a free gift—that no one is entitled yet everyone is invited?

You want to know the gospel truth? This gospel is true. If you don't believe it, don't say it's not fair. Just own that you don't believe it. The amazing thing about this gospel is Jesus still believes in you. He wants you in the fold. He has done everything he can, to the point of laying down his life, so you could be included. He will not decide for you. Only you can do that.

If all of this were true, wouldn't it make sense that we would want to share this with the whole world? I'm starting to finally understand the obvious: the only sign that I believe the gospel is true is that I share it with others.

The Prayer

Abba Father, we thank you for your Son, Jesus, who is himself the brilliance of your grace. Awaken us to the truth about our own faith and make us gracious agents of awakening to others. We pray in Jesus' name, amen.

The Questions

- Why do people consider it unreasonable that God would provide only one way of eternal salvation? Shouldn't that actually be good news? Do you believe Jesus is the only way into the sheepfold of the kingdom of God? If not, why not? Do you actively share this incredible truth with others? If not, why not? And what might your unwillingness to share with others tell you about what you really believe?

Why We Need a Good Shepherd

59

JOHN 10:14–21 ESV | "I am the good shepherd. I know my own and my own know me, just as the Father knows me and I know the Father; and I lay down my life for the sheep. And I have other sheep that are not of this fold. I must bring them also, and they will listen to my voice. So there will be one flock,

one shepherd. For this reason the Father loves me, because I lay down my life that I may take it up again. No one takes it from me, but I lay it down of my own accord. I have authority to lay it down, and I have authority to take it up again. This charge I have received from my Father."

There was again a division among the Jews because of these words. Many of them said, "He has a demon, and is insane; why listen to him?" Others said, "These are not the words of one who is oppressed by a demon. Can a demon open the eyes of the blind?"

Consider This

Sometimes the more familiar we are with a particular Scripture text, the less we understand it. We can know something by heart yet not really know it at all. The Lord's Prayer falls into this category for many. Even more so, the Twenty-Third Psalm also comes to mind. I'm not sure I have ever officiated or been to a funeral where we didn't recite Psalm 23. In fact, that's about where I had this text filed: funerals. I guess that "valley of the shadow of death" (v. 4 ESV) line does it.

I'm not sure why, but this psalm has risen to prominence in my life of late. I'm overwhelmed every time I work my way through it. Far from a death psalm, it is a life psalm. Green pastures, still waters, paths of righteousness, feasting in the presence of enemies, cups of blessing running over, and on the psalm goes.

"The LORD is my shepherd; I shall not want" (v. 1 ESV). When we are well shepherded, we need not worry about anything because the shepherd provides everything. In today's text, Jesus drew water from this ancient well of divine revelation when he said, "I am the good shepherd." Think back through John's gospel. Jesus sat us down in the vast green pasture where he fed us with fish and loaves. He took us to the deep waters of Jacob's well and introduced us to living water. His presence, countenance, and words have restored our souls every step of the way.

The Prayer

Abba Father, we thank you for your Son, Jesus, our Good Shepherd. Because he takes care of everything, we need not worry about anything. Thank you for this gift of perfect security. Come, Holy Spirit, and bring this word to life for us. We pray in Jesus' name, amen.

The Questions

- What is your history with Psalm 23? Spend a few minutes meditating on it each day this week. Do you know Jesus as your Good Shepherd? Does this remain a high ideal, or is it becoming a reality in your life? What connections are you making between Jesus and the gospel of John and Psalm 23?

60 Does Jesus Talk to You?

JOHN 10:22–30 ESV | At that time the Feast of Dedication took place at Jerusalem. It was winter, and Jesus was walking in the temple, in the colonnade of Solomon. So the Jews gathered around him and said to him, "How long will you keep us in suspense? If you are the Christ, tell us plainly." Jesus answered them, "I told you, and you do not believe. The works that I do in my Father's name bear witness about me, but you do not believe because you are not among my sheep. My sheep hear my voice, and I know them, and they follow me. I give them eternal life, and they will never perish, and no one will snatch them out of my hand. My Father, who has given them to me, is greater than all, and no one is able to snatch them out of the Father's hand. I and the Father are one."

Consider This

"My sheep hear my voice, and I know them, and they follow me."

What does it mean to listen to the voice of Jesus? On the one hand, I know a lot of people who consider it ridiculous that Jesus would actually talk to people today. On the other hand, I know a lot of people who insist Jesus talks to them constantly and about everything from what to wear to where to go on vacation.

What do you think? Does Jesus speak to people today? Does he speak to you? Here's my understanding: Jesus speaks through his Word and Jesus speaks through the Holy Spirit. So how do we know if what we are hearing is actually from Jesus and not just what we want to believe Jesus is saying to us? Here are a few guidelines to consider.

First, is what you are hearing consistent with what Jesus has already said as recorded in the Gospels? If what you are hearing is inconsistent with the revelation of Scripture, then you are probably not hearing from Jesus. One of the great gifts of the Gospels is we are given a trustworthy record from which to understand the kinds of things Jesus says. Does what you are hearing sound like what Jesus might say? Second, does what you are hearing create anxiety within you? If so, you might want to question it. The words of Jesus carry peace. They do not create confusion and anxiety. In fact, a sign that Jesus is speaking to us may well be an abiding sense of peace that doesn't even make sense to us. Third, does what you are hearing from Jesus find resonance with the discernment of other believers whom you trust?

In my own experience, this conviction is ever deepening: Jesus is always speaking. Why do I believe this? Because every time I manage to get really still and attentive and find myself humbly submitted to him, I hear his voice. Here's what I don't understand about myself: Why am I not constantly finding this place and posture of listening? I don't have a good answer.

The great Methodist missionary to India E. Stanley Jones often referenced his practice of going to his "listening post." Here's what I like about that: it demonstrates expectation. I find the more I actually expect to hear from Jesus, the more I hear from him.

The Prayer

Abba Father, we thank you for your Son, Jesus, whose word is truth. Thank you that he continues to speak through his recorded words, and thank you that he speaks to us through the gift of the Holy Spirit. Increase our expectation of hearing his voice. We pray in Jesus' name, amen.

The Questions

- What do you think? Does Jesus speak to people today? How are you cultivating the practice of listening to Jesus? What is he saying to you these days?

61 The Difference between a Retreat and Retreating

JOHN 10:31–42 | Again his Jewish opponents picked up stones to stone him, but Jesus said to them, "I have shown you many good works from the Father. For which of these do you stone me?"

"We are not stoning you for any good work," they replied, "but for blasphemy, because you, a mere man, claim to be God."

Jesus answered them, "Is it not written in your Law, 'I have said you are "gods"'? If he called them 'gods,' to whom the

word of God came—and Scripture cannot be set aside—what about the one whom the Father set apart as his very own and sent into the world? Why then do you accuse me of blasphemy because I said, 'I am God's Son'? Do not believe me unless I do the works of my Father. But if I do them, even though you do not believe me, believe the works, that you may know and understand that the Father is in me, and I in the Father." Again they tried to seize him, but he escaped their grasp.

Then Jesus went back across the Jordan to the place where John had been baptizing in the early days. There he stayed, and many people came to him. They said, "Though John never performed a sign, all that John said about this man was true." And in that place many believed in Jesus.

Consider This

Then Jesus went back across the Jordan to the place where John had been baptizing in the early days. There he stayed . . .

He was now in full retreat. He went back to the Jordan River, where it all got started, where the prophetic voice cried out in the wilderness, "Prepare the way for the LORD" (Isa. 40:3; see John 1:23). Something tells me he longed for those earlier days, when life was simpler and the future flashed bright on the horizon. Even so, this place must have stirred enormous grief in him as he remembered John's incredible beginning and tragic end.

It's one thing to know you will ultimately win. That does not change the reality of experiencing real losses.

Here he was, the Son of God, the Word made flesh, the Light of the World, the Bread of Life, the Good Shepherd, the Gate to the Kingdom, and at the same time, the most despised and rejected man in the land. He'd healed the sick, driven out demons, and was on the eve of raising the dead. Still, they (and I should say, we) wanted him dead. In exchange for his unwavering love, he received unmitigated hate: "He came to that which was his own, but his own did not receive him. Yet to all who did receive him, to those who believed in his name, he gave the right to become children of God" (John 1:11–12).

And many were taking him up on the offer.

. . . and many people came to him. They said, "Though John never performed a sign, all that John said about this man was true." And in that place many believed in Jesus.

All of this has me rethinking the whole idea of what *retreat* means. To date, the word *retreat* calls to mind the idea of going away for the weekend with a church group and doing spiritual things—sort of like a spa for the soul. It occurs to me now the connection of the word *retreat* with the idea of running from a fight when you are losing. It's the pathway to surrender. What if retreating were no longer thought of as an optional excursion? What if we began to see retreating as essential for our survival?

There comes a point in the life of every disciple where, in order to go forward, you must retreat; where, in order to win, you must surrender. This is a hard lesson. Let's pay close attention.

The Prayer

Abba Father, we thank you for your Son, Jesus, who though being God, retreats in the face of impending loss. Give us the grace to follow him in this unconventional way. Teach us that retreat is the pathway to surrender and surrender is the path to glory. We pray in Jesus' name, amen.

The Questions

- Why do you think Jesus retreated to the Jordan River? In a world that teaches us to never back down, how can we learn the way of retreating? What might retreat look like for you at the present moment?

Why Jesus Wants Loyal Friends—Not Worshipful Fans

62

JOHN 11:1–7 ESV | Now a certain man was ill, Lazarus of Bethany, the village of Mary and her sister Martha. It was Mary who anointed the Lord with ointment and wiped his feet with her hair, whose brother Lazarus was ill. So the sisters sent to him, saying, "Lord, he whom you love is ill." But when Jesus heard it he said, "This illness does not lead to death. It is for the glory of God, so that the Son of God may be glorified through it."

Now Jesus loved Martha and her sister and Lazarus. So, when he heard that Lazarus was ill, he stayed two days longer in the place where he was. Then after this he said to the disciples, "Let us go to Judea again."

Consider This

Let's call this the conundrum of Bethany. Mary, Martha, and Lazarus made their home in Bethany. They enjoyed a deep friendship with Jesus. In fact, their home in Bethany seems to have been a place of refuge for him. I think of it as a place where he could be off duty, in a sense. It's almost impossible for famous people to have friends. Once a person is put on a stage like that, it's difficult for people to see beyond it.

It's interesting how the gospel writers take us on the inside of these relationships. There was that time in the early days when Martha drove herself mad trying to get everything just so for Jesus and his disciples. You remember, the time Mary broke with all social convention and sat at his feet listening to him (Luke 10:38–42). Then she did it again later, pouring the expensive perfume on his feet (John 12:1–8).

Now Jesus loved Martha and her sister and Lazarus.

They were friends—not fans. It brings me to say something you may consider controversial: Jesus is not looking for worshipful fans. He longs for intimate friends. We will see this a few chapters later when he tells his disciples, "I no longer call you servants . . . Instead, I have called you friends, for everything that I learned from my Father I have made known to you" (John 15:15). Jesus did not come to us to be worshipped like a celebrity but to be known as a friend.

Many are content to know Jesus as Savior; fewer are willing to know him as Lord. Not many, however, will become his friends. Many are content to worship him like a loyal subject who bows low before a king. Fewer still are willing to approach him as the son or daughter of a loving Father. Not many will walk with him as friend.

To be sure, becoming a friend of Jesus doesn't happen all at once. It's not the starting place. We must know him as Savior first, then as a disciple. Discipleship must lead to knowing him as Lord. And here is where we get off track. Our rightful worship of Jesus will lead us down one of at least two paths. Will we become fans (even superfans), arrested in discipleship development, or will we become his friends?

It's costly to become his friend. It will mean being disappointed by him at times. He may even be a couple of days late for your funeral. But at other times, it's for his friends that he raises the dead.

That's the conundrum of Bethany.

The Prayer

Abba Father, we thank you for your Son, Jesus, our Savior, our Lord, and, yes, who would be our friend. Reveal to us where we stand with him and open the path for us to go further. Come, Holy Spirit, and make us into the abiding friends of Jesus. It is in his name we pray, amen.

The Questions

- Where do you find yourself on the path? Do you know Jesus as Savior? Lord? Friend? What do you think of this notion of getting stuck in discipleship, arrested in fandom, instead of progressing into friendship? Do you want to become a better friend to Jesus? What step might you take in that direction?

63 How to Move from Being Loved to Becoming Love

JOHN 11:8–16 ESV | The disciples said to him, "Rabbi, the Jews were just now seeking to stone you, and are you going there again?" Jesus answered, "Are there not twelve hours in the day? If anyone walks in the day, he does not stumble, because he sees the light of this world. But if anyone walks in the night, he stumbles, because the light is not in him." After saying these things, he said to them, "Our friend Lazarus has fallen asleep, but I go to awaken him." The disciples said to him, "Lord, if he has fallen asleep, he will recover." Now Jesus had spoken of his death, but they thought that he meant taking rest in sleep. Then Jesus told them plainly, "Lazarus has died, and for your sake I am glad that I was not there, so that you may believe. But let us go to him." So Thomas, called the Twin, said to his fellow disciples, "Let us also go, that we may die with him."

Consider This

This thing was coming apart at the seams. No one wanted to go anywhere near Jerusalem. It was probably not the wisest choice for Jerusalem's most wanted to show his face even as near as the next town over.

Jesus didn't regard the risk. Love does not see risk. Nor does love see reward. Love only sees people and acts with abandon.

"Our friend Lazarus has fallen asleep, but I go to awaken him."

One day Jesus is in full-retreat mode, and the next he is headed right back to the firing range. How do we explain this? "Now Jesus loved Martha and her sister and Lazarus" (v. 5).

Soon we will hear Jesus distill all of the truth and wisdom of Scripture into a single command—eight words: "Love each another as I have loved you. Greater love has no one than this: to lay down one's life for one's friends" (John 15:12–13). Love does not calculate. Love does not count the risk or weigh the reward. Love pays no attention to self-interest, only the interest of the loved one.

It brings to mind Paul's celebrated word from 1 Corinthians 13: "[Love] always protects, always trusts, always hopes, always perseveres. Love never fails" (vv. 7–8).

We likely know John 3:16. Chances are we don't know 1 John 3:16. It reads: "This is how we know what love is: Jesus Christ laid down his life for us. And we ought to lay down our lives for our brothers and sisters."

How can we do this? We can't. That's where the gospel comes in. Jesus can and he will and he does—through us—if only we will yield our lives to him.

John 3:16 reminds me I am loved; 1 John 3:16 reminds me I am love.

Come, Holy Spirit!

The Prayer

Abba Father, we thank you for your Son, Jesus, who calls us beyond ourselves, challenges us beyond our ability, and changes our nature to be like him, who is love. And all of this by the power of your Spirit for the glory of your name and for the sake of your people. We pray in Jesus' name, amen.

The Questions

- How often do you come to the end of your capacity to love? Where does your love for others go? Ruin your self-interest? Are you ready and willing for your capacity to love to be expanded by Jesus' capacity to love through you?

64 Why the Resurrection Is Not Our Hope

JOHN 11:17–27 | On his arrival, Jesus found that Lazarus had already been in the tomb for four days. Now Bethany was less than two miles from Jerusalem, and many Jews had come to Martha and Mary to comfort them in the loss of their brother. When Martha heard that Jesus was coming, she went out to meet him, but Mary stayed at home.

"Lord," Martha said to Jesus, "if you had been here, my brother would not have died. But I know that even now God will give you whatever you ask."

Jesus said to her, "Your brother will rise again."

Martha answered, "I know he will rise again in the resurrection at the last day."

Jesus said to her, "I am the resurrection and the life. The one who believes in me will live, even though they die; and whoever lives by believing in me will never die. Do you believe this?"

"Yes, Lord," she replied, "I believe that you are the Messiah, the Son of God, who is to come into the world."

Consider This

The stage was set for another sign. Lazarus had been in the tomb four days. As Jesus approached Bethany, Martha went out to meet him. She immediately let Jesus know it was his fault, but there was still time for him to act. That is the real faith of a true friend.

Jesus said to her, "Your brother will rise again."

Martha answered, "I know he will rise again in the resurrection at the last day."

It's like Martha understood Jesus to say something akin to what we so often say in times like these, "Well, you know, Lazarus is in a better place now." She didn't want to hear it. She wanted him back yesterday! She says, in effect, "He's gone! That doesn't help me now." Then Jesus speaks what are perhaps the most revolutionary words ever spoken:

Jesus said to her, "I am the resurrection and the life. The one who believes in me will live, even though they die; and whoever lives by believing in me will never die."

Jesus was not speaking of resurrection in future tense. Well, he was, but not like this is somewhere over the rainbow. The resurrection is not a future event. Neither is it a present event. He was saying, "I am the resurrection." The resurrection is not an event; it is a person. Jesus is the resurrection. Jesus is the life. Jesus was not asking Martha to believe in something that will happen in the future. He wanted her to know, by believing in him now, the future had already happened.

With the resurrection of Jesus, the last day is now brought into the present. This is why we don't hope in the future, as British theologian Jeremy Begbie put it, "we hope from the future." Because Jesus Christ is risen from the dead, we who believe in him, who are baptized into his life, have already died to death and are risen to life. Did you get that? We are dead to death.

"The one who believes in me will live, even though they die; and whoever lives by believing in me will never die."

It's why Paul wrote these words: "'Death has been swallowed up in victory. Where, O death, is your victory? Where, O death, is your sting?'" (1 Cor. 15:54–55).

Because of the resurrection of Jesus, though we die, we do not taste death. It's why Paul said, "For to me, to live is Christ and to die is gain" (Phil. 1:21) and, again, to be absent from the body is to be at home with the Lord (2 Corinthians 5:8).

The resurrection is not our hope. It is our reality. It is our life.

Maybe the most important words from today's text are in the piercing question Jesus asked Martha:

"Do you believe this?"

The Prayer

Abba Father, we thank you for your Son, Jesus, who is the resurrection and the life. Help us grasp this stunning mysterious truth that the resurrection is a person—Jesus. Come, Holy Spirit, and gift us with comprehension of the eternal scope of the resurrection and the life who is Jesus and that this unthinkable gift is ours. We pray in his name, amen.

The Questions

- How do you understand this notion that we do not hope *in* the future, but we hope *from* the future? Do you believe the resurrection is not the future reality of a present event, but the present reality of a future event? Do you believe that, though we die, we live and that, in fact, we have already died to death and are alive in the resurrection and the life now?

Why Jesus Was Not Crying for Lazarus

65

JOHN 11:28–37 ESV | When she had said this, she went and called her sister Mary, saying in private, "The Teacher is here and is calling for you." And when she heard it, she rose quickly

and went to him. Now Jesus had not yet come into the village, but was still in the place where Martha had met him. When the Jews who were with her in the house, consoling her, saw Mary rise quickly and go out, they followed her, supposing that she was going to the tomb to weep there. Now when Mary came to where Jesus was and saw him, she fell at his feet, saying to him, "Lord, if you had been here, my brother would not have died." When Jesus saw her weeping, and the Jews who had come with her also weeping, he was deeply moved in his spirit and greatly troubled. And he said, "Where have you laid him?" They said to him, "Lord, come and see." Jesus wept. So the Jews said, "See how he loved him!" But some of them said, "Could not he who opened the eyes of the blind man also have kept this man from dying?"

Consider This

The poet J. L. McCreery wrote:

> There is no death! the stars go down
> To rise upon some other shore,
> And bright in heaven's jewelled crown
> They shine forever more.*

Unfortunately, the poet was wrong. Death is real. Lazarus was as dead as a hammer.

---

* J. L. McCreery, "There is No Death," in *The World's Best Poetry, Volume III: Sorrow and Consolation*, ed. Bliss Carman et al. (Philadelphia: J. D. Morris and Company, 1904), n.p. Public domain.

So, if Jesus means what he says—that when a person who believes in him suffers death, they do not die—why is he crying at Lazarus's tomb? Read the text carefully on this point:

When Jesus saw her weeping, and the Jews who had come with her also weeping, he was deeply moved in his spirit and greatly troubled.

Jesus wept, not because Lazarus died, but because of the bitter pain this loss inflicted on Mary, Martha, and their friends. To be sure, the text informs us that the Jews interpreted Jesus' tears as an expression of his love for Lazarus. I don't think Jesus was sad about the death of Lazarus. He was sad about the suffering of Lazarus's family and friends.

Jesus hated death not so much for the sake of the one who died but because of the way death devastated those left behind. Jesus knew that through his death and resurrection, he would destroy death with life. Death was not a problem for him. The problem was the depth of human grief over the loss of a loved one.

Because of Jesus, those who die believing in him are actually more alive on the other side of death than they were in their lives beforehand. The grief of the survivors is not so easily solved. In fact, it can only be comforted. The deeper we love in life, the greater our loss in the wake of death. This will not change until Jesus returns and wipes away every tear (see Revelation 7:17, 21:4). The gospel truth is that the greater reality has already changed. Death has been defeated.

The Prayer

Abba Father, we thank you for your Son, Jesus, who has defeated death. Thank you that he comforts us in the wake of our losses with the gift of the gospel. Thank you that, though we mourn, we can dance at funerals. Come, Holy Spirit, strengthen us in these bedrock truths. We pray in Jesus' name, amen.

The Questions

- Why do you think Jesus wept at the tomb of Lazarus? Do you think you protect yourself from loss by not taking the risk of loving others deeply? Are you afraid of death? Do you live in a lot of fear over the possible deaths of others?

66 The Problem behind All Our Problems

JOHN 11:38–44 ESV | Then Jesus, deeply moved again, came to the tomb. It was a cave, and a stone lay against it. Jesus said, "Take away the stone." Martha, the sister of the dead man, said to him, "Lord, by this time there will be an odor, for he has been dead four days." Jesus said to her, "Did I not tell you that if you believed you would see the glory of God?" So they took away the stone. And Jesus lifted up his eyes and said, "Father, I thank you that you have heard me. I knew that you always hear me, but I said this on account of

the people standing around, that they may believe that you sent me." When he had said these things, he cried out with a loud voice, "Lazarus, come out." The man who had died came out, his hands and feet bound with linen strips, and his face wrapped with a cloth. Jesus said to them, "Unbind him, and let him go."

Consider This

My friend Matt LeRoy, who helps lead an amazing church in Chapel Hill, North Carolina, tells a bit of an unconventional Lazarus story. Taz, one of the homeless men who participated in their church, turned up missing and, by all accounts, was presumed dead. The church went into their signature extravagant love mode and held a powerful celebration of life for Taz. Imagine their surprise when, a few weeks later, Taz showed up at church! From that point on, they called him Tazarus!

Death was not part of God's plan for his creation. It was a consequence of human sin—not a consequence as in punishment, but as in irrevocable laws of the universe, like gravity. If sin, then death. It turns out the law of sin and death was not so irrevocable after all. In fact, it's not really accurate to call it a law. It's an aberration. The only true and real law is the law of the spirit of life. The law of sin and death merely describes the outcome of rebellion against the law of the spirit of life.

The law of the spirit of life is profoundly creative. The law of sin and death is pure destruction. The ultimate destruction is the death of a human being, and death seems to get the clear win. The story of the gospel of John so far is the story of the law of the spirit of life reversing the effects of the law of sin and death. Paraplegics walk again. The blind see again. Discarded women thrive again. And, yes, in today's text we see a dead man live again. Death may seem to win the battle, but life wins the war. Love overcomes sin, and life overwhelms death.

The question is: Do we wholeheartedly believe it or do we just nod in casual assent? This is the big *if*.

Jesus said to her, "Did I not tell you that if you believed you would see the glory of God?"

Too many of us live somewhere between true belief and disavowal. Our faith is tentative. We want to be all in, but something causes us to hold out. We can't not believe, yet we can't seem to go all in either. We are like those ancient Laodiceans in the book of Revelation to whom the Spirit speaks these words: "I know your deeds, that you are neither cold nor hot. I wish you were either one or the other! So, because you are lukewarm—neither hot nor cold—I am about to spit you out of my mouth" (Rev. 3:15–16).

I mean, what would it take for us to believe? Would Jesus need to raise someone from the dead? Let's be honest. It doesn't come down to what Jesus does or does not do. It comes down to what is broken in the deepest place in us. Our lack of belief is not because of our obstinance; it's because of our brokenness. Our biggest problem is not sin; it's our broken ability to trust. That's why we sinned in the first place—we didn't trust in the goodness of God. The healing we most need is the healing of our broken capacity to trust. That's the problem behind all of our problems.

Isn't that what it all comes down to? Trusting Jesus. He intends every sign, every saying, and every sermon to call us into an ever-deepening relationship with himself and with each other.

Jesus said to her, "Did I not tell you that if you believed you would see the glory of God?"

We want to see in order to believe. Jesus says it's just the opposite.

The Prayer

Abba Father, we thank you for your Son, Jesus, who heals the most devastating disease we have—our broken ability to trust. Come, Holy Spirit, and open us up to this brokenness within us all and lead us toward healing. Thank you for your utter trustworthiness. We pray in Jesus' name, amen.

The Questions

- Where do you find yourself on the spectrum between all-in belief/trust or disavowed indifference? What keeps you from trusting more? What is it about you, your story, your brokenness that keeps you from growing in trust? Are there relationships, events, or trauma in your past that have broken your ability to trust? Be merciful with yourself; Jesus is. What would pursuing healing look like?

67 On Choosing the Hell of a Predictable Situation

JOHN 11:45–57 ESV | Many of the Jews therefore, who had come with Mary and had seen what he did, believed in him, but some of them went to the Pharisees and told them what Jesus had done. So the chief priests and the Pharisees gathered the council and said, "What are we to do? For this man performs many signs. If we let him go on like this, everyone will believe in him, and the Romans will come and take away both our place and our nation." But one of them, Caiaphas, who was high priest that year, said to them, "You know nothing at all. Nor do you understand that it is better for you that one man should die for the people, not that the whole nation should perish." He did not say this of his own accord, but being high priest that year he prophesied that Jesus would die for the nation, and not for the nation only, but also to gather into one the children of God who are scattered abroad. So from that day on they made plans to put him to death.

Jesus therefore no longer walked openly among the Jews, but went from there to the region near the wilderness, to a town called Ephraim, and there he stayed with the disciples.

Now the Passover of the Jews was at hand, and many went up from the country to Jerusalem before the Passover to purify themselves. They were looking for Jesus and saying to one

another as they stood in the temple, "What do you think? That he will not come to the feast at all?" Now the chief priests and the Pharisees had given orders that if anyone knew where he was, he should let them know, so that they might arrest him.

Consider This

No sooner had Lazarus walked out of the tomb than the religious leaders were trying to put Jesus in it. Finally, they showed their cards:

"If we let him go on like this, everyone will believe in him, and the Romans will come and take away both our place and our nation."

Those who preside over the status quo always stand to lose the most; hence, they most resist change.

Our little fiefdoms are pitiful, but they are ours. We can live the rest of our lives defending the status quo of our fiefdom, or we can let go and open ourselves to something we never imagined possible. My dear friend and mentor Maxie Dunnam says it this way: "Most people will choose the hell of a predictable situation rather than risk the joy of an unpredictable one."

The Prayer

Abba Father, we thank you for your Son, Jesus, who calls us out of the mediocre predictable ways of the status quo and invites us to a great adventure. Give us the grace to say yes. We pray in Jesus' name, amen.

The Questions

- What is the hell of a predictable situation in your own life right now? Are you ready to leave it behind?

68 The Glorious Waste of Worship

JOHN 12:1–11 ESV | Six days before the Passover, Jesus therefore came to Bethany, where Lazarus was, whom Jesus had raised from the dead. So they gave a dinner for him there. Martha served, and Lazarus was one of those reclining with him at table. Mary therefore took a pound of expensive ointment made from pure nard, and anointed the feet of Jesus and wiped his feet with her hair. The house was filled with the fragrance of the perfume. But Judas Iscariot, one of his disciples (he who was about to betray him), said, "Why was this ointment not sold for three hundred denarii and given to the poor?" He said this, not because he cared about the poor, but because he was a thief, and having charge of the moneybag he used to help himself to what was put into it. Jesus said, "Leave her alone, so that she may keep it for the day of my burial. For the poor you always have with you, but you do not always have me."

When the large crowd of the Jews learned that Jesus was there, they came, not only on account of him but also to see Lazarus, whom he had raised from the dead. So the chief priests made

plans to put Lazarus to death as well, because on account of him many of the Jews were going away and believing in Jesus.

Consider This

There's so much that could be said about today's text with Mary and the perfume. Get in your mind the amount of money you made last year. Go to the bank and withdraw it in cash. Now go out into your backyard and make a fire. Is it burning? Take one bill at a time and throw this money into the fire as an act of sacrificial worship to Jesus—a burnt offering, if you will. It's not exactly analogous, but you get the point.

That would be insane, wouldn't it? I mean, why wouldn't you just give that money to people who needed it, right? Disingenuous or not, Judas did make a valid point—even if only a pragmatic one. There's a problem, though, with this kind of thinking: worship is not practical.

Mary's act of worship cannot live in a category anywhere remotely near to helping the poor. Mary was not pouring out her perfume. She was pouring out herself. This was neither calculated nor strategic. Mary was singing the song Isaac Watts would write almost two millennia later: "Were the whole realm of nature mine, that were an offering far too small. Love so amazing, so divine, demands my soul, my life, my all."*

* Isaac Watts, "When I Survey the Wondrous Cross," 1707. Public domain.

Someone is sure to say, "But Jesus said as we did it for the least of these, we would be doing it for him (Matt. 25:40). That makes helping the poor an act of worship to Jesus." To that I would say, "That's a good point. However, in this case, it misses the point entirely."

One more point: there's something to be said for doing extravagant things for the people we love while they are still alive.

"Leave her alone, so that she may keep it for the day of my burial. For the poor you always have with you, but you do not always have me."

It seems to have pleased Jesus that Mary did this for him on that day rather than saving it until his burial. It's probably not a legitimate takeaway from today's text, but I think it is wisdom nonetheless—don't wait to pour out love on people after they die. Do it now.

Finally, the beautiful, impractical thing about Mary's unthinkable act of worship all those years ago is that we can still smell the perfume today.

The Prayer

Abba Father, we thank you for your Son, Jesus, who alone is worthy of our most extraordinary, extravagant, impractical, and even nonsensical acts of worship. Save us from our calculators when it comes to pouring out our gifts on him. Come, Holy Spirit, and lead us in the way of the cross, pouring out our whole lives for Jesus. We pray in Jesus' name, amen.

The Questions

- How did you react to the opening example of getting the equivalent of your income last year in cash and burning it as an offering to Jesus? What would inspire Mary to do what she did? What would inspire you to do something like this? So, where do you fall on the extravagantly wasteful versus practical giving continuum? Judas or Mary?

Have Mercy on Me, a Sinner

69

JOHN 12:12–19 | The next day the great crowd that had come for the festival heard that Jesus was on his way to Jerusalem. They took palm branches and went out to meet him, shouting,

> **"Hosanna!"**
> **"Blessed is he who comes in the name of the Lord!"**
> **"Blessed is the king of Israel!"**

Jesus found a young donkey and sat on it, as it is written:

> **"Do not be afraid, Daughter Zion;**
> **see, your king is coming,**
> **seated on a donkey's colt."**

At first his disciples did not understand all this. Only after Jesus was glorified did they realize that these things had been written about him and that these things had been done to him.

Now the crowd that was with him when he called Lazarus from the tomb and raised him from the dead continued to spread the word. Many people, because they had heard that he had performed this sign, went out to meet him. So the Pharisees said to one another, "See, this is getting us nowhere. Look how the whole world has gone after him!"

Consider This

Finally, we come to Jerusalem, the city of kings, the city who stones the prophets and those sent to her. Into the city of kings, the King of all kings now comes.

"Do not be afraid, Daughter Zion; see, your king is coming, seated on a donkey's colt."

The text affords us an opportunity to get to a high place where we can remember the larger span of the story and try to fathom the future while beholding the one who holds it all together.

Something tells me Jesus was remembering that fateful day when the people of Israel asked the prophet Samuel to appoint for them a king so they could be like the other nations around them. I wonder if he remembered the word of God to Samuel concerning this request: "And the Lord said to Samuel, 'Obey the voice of the people in all that they say to you, for they have not rejected you, but they have rejected me from being king over them'" (1 Sam. 8:7 ESV).

Now, King Jesus, the one who was born a King, in the city of David no less, comes into Jerusalem, the city of kings. The significance of this moment is as thick as the irony. The kingship of God's people, Israel, was being restored to its rightful owner, and no one had any idea of it—but not before the great and final rejection.

Within days we will hear the ruler of Israel, Pontius Pilate, presenting Jesus to the people with these fateful words: "Here is your king" (John 19:14). Then he will ask: "Shall I crucify your king?" (v. 15b). And the chief priests will shout their incredible verdict: "We have no king but Caesar" (v. 15c).

As Jesus dies on the cross a sign will be posted over his head: "JESUS OF NAZARETH, THE KING OF THE JEWS" (v. 19). It will be a final sign, yet one that never stops speaking, written in three languages—Aramaic, Latin, and Greek. Today, this sign is translated into thousands of languages all over the world, and, one day, every nation, tribe, and tongue will together make the confession, "Jesus Christ is Lord!" (see Revelation 7:9–12).

And he shall reign forever and ever!

The Prayer

Abba Father, we thank you for your Son, Jesus, who is our King, high and holy, meek and lowly. Open the eyes of our hearts to behold this scene, this triumphal entry that turned tragic. Come, Holy Spirit, and turn it to our transformation. We reject the ways of this world, and we embrace the ways of your kingdom, which is the royal way of the holy cross. We pray in Jesus' name, amen.

The Questions

- How will you posture your heart as a participant in this unfolding passion story as we enter Jerusalem? How will you move beyond passive observation? As we proceed, bring this ancient prayer to the forefront of your praying. It's called the Jesus Prayer: "Lord Jesus Christ, Son of God, have mercy on me, a sinner." Over and over and over. How does that sit with you?

70 Why Sharing Is Not the Answer—and What Is

JOHN 12:20–26 | Now there were some Greeks among those who went up to worship at the festival. They came to Philip, who was from Bethsaida in Galilee, with a request. "Sir," they said, "we would like to see Jesus." Philip went to tell Andrew; Andrew and Philip in turn told Jesus.

Jesus replied, "The hour has come for the Son of Man to be glorified. Very truly I tell you, unless a kernel of wheat falls to the ground and dies, it remains only a single seed. But if it dies, it produces many seeds. Anyone who loves their life will lose it, while anyone who hates their life in this world will keep it for eternal life. Whoever serves me must follow me; and where I am, my servant also will be. My Father will honor the one who serves me."

Consider This

I call them the twenty-three most challenging words in the Bible:

"Anyone who loves their life will lose it, while anyone who hates their life in this world will keep it for eternal life."

We so want the Christian life to be reasonable, but it is not. To give a little or even a lot is the same as giving nothing at all. The life hid with Christ in God will be everything or it will be nothing. Think about it. Jesus will either give all of himself or he will give nothing. There is no halfway with Jesus.

The powerful thing is that, in exchange for my everything, Jesus will give me his everything. It's hardly an even trade. After all, my everything is not actually that much. Sure, it's a lot to me, but in the grand scheme of things it's five loaves and two fish. On the other hand, Jesus' everything is more than can be comprehended or even imagined. Jesus' everything is the very fullness of almighty God.

It's a very good deal. In exchange for my smallness, I am given his greatness. In exchange for my weakness, I am given his strength. In exchange for my selfishness, I am given his selflessness. In exchange for my extreme limitations, I am given his extraordinary capacities. Who wouldn't take this offer?

"Very truly I tell you, unless a kernel of wheat falls to the ground and dies, it remains only a single seed. But if it dies, it produces many seeds."

The unsurrendered life is the same thing as the unplanted seed—a waste. Why on earth would we go another day holding on to the tiny seed of our lives? It's time to sow our small, fragile selves into the field of God's dream for our lives.

What if the little boy had shared his five loaves and two fish with the crowd? How far would it have gone? Exactly nowhere. Instead, look what happened when he surrendered all he had to Jesus. Precisely unimaginable. We think the gospel is about sharing our lives with others, as though a seed could be shared. No, it's about surrendering our lives to Jesus, who will make of our lives an unending, unimaginable gift to the world. Sharing will never get it done, only surrender will.

This is not unreasonable. It's absurd—that God could be this good. I mean, are we holding out for a better deal? If not you, then who? If not now, then when?

The Prayer

Abba Father, we thank you for your Son, Jesus, who would not take us to the cross, but through it, and into a world beyond our imagining. Thank you that, though it cost us our everything, it returns your everything to us. Come, Holy Spirit, and awaken us to the magnitude of this offer of life. We pray in Jesus' name, amen.

The Questions

- What are the implications of your life as a seed sown into the ground of God's kingdom? What are the implications of not sowing it? What do you make of this notion of Jesus' offer being all or nothing? Is that unreasonable to you? Why do we cling to ourselves? What keeps us from surrendering it all to Jesus?

What to Pray When the Darkness Overwhelms

71

JOHN 12:27–33 | "Now my soul is troubled, and what shall I say? 'Father, save me from this hour'? No, it was for this very reason I came to this hour. Father, glorify your name!"

Then a voice came from heaven, "I have glorified it, and will glorify it again." The crowd that was there and heard it said it had thundered; others said an angel had spoken to him.

Jesus said, "This voice was for your benefit, not mine. Now is the time for judgment on this world; now the prince of this world will be driven out. And I, when I am lifted up from the earth, will draw all people to myself." He said this to show the kind of death he was going to die.

Consider This

Today we come to the crux of the gospel. It's the literal turning point. It happens in this prayerful declaration:

"Now my soul is troubled, and what shall I say? 'Father, save me from this hour'? No, it was for this very reason I came to this hour. Father, glorify your name!"

The hour has come. The die has been cast. With these words, Jesus crosses the proverbial Rubicon. The cross, though it be in Jesus' future, is now behind him—a fait accompli. Note, however, this is not Jesus' reluctant acceptance of his fate:

"Father, glorify your name!"

It is critical for us to grasp the difference between resignation and surrender. Four words make all the difference:

"Father, glorify your name!"

To resign is to turn back, give up, and admit defeat. To surrender means to abandon oneself not to circumstance but to God and to embrace the glorious future of his making. Surrender is not the acceptance of defeat but the declaration of victory, no matter how dark the future may appear.

I've always appreciated the Serenity Prayer, yet often felt it carried something of a spirit of resignation. You know the prayer: "God, grant me the serenity to accept the things I cannot change, the courage to change the things I can, and the wisdom to know the difference."

Honestly, I often felt it a bit platitudinous. Recently, a friend shared the full version of the prayer with me, and now I see it in a whole new light. Here's the rest of the story, if you will:

Living one day at a time,
enjoying one moment at a time;
accepting hardship as a pathway to peace;
taking, as Jesus did,
this sinful world as it is,
not as I would have it;
trusting that You will make all things right
if I surrender to Your will;
so that I may be reasonably happy in this life
and supremely happy with You forever in the next.

Amen.*

Far from weak resignation, the full prayer is one of bold surrender. Many who are reading will undoubtedly face their own hour of unbearable suffering. Don't turn back. Don't give up. Allow what may seem a senseless and needless situation to be turned into a cross-bearing crucible. Do not resign yourself to it. Surrender your life to God through it. While what you are facing may seem the furthest thing from God's will, God has a will in the midst of it. Seize the moment to size up this suffering with a bigger picture. For certain, it is a picture we cannot presently understand. We can only see the frame of this in praying this prayer: "Father, glorify your name!"

---

* Reinhold Niebuhr, "Prayer for Serenity," Celebrate Recovery, accessed January 2, 2021, https://www.celebraterecovery.com/resources/cr-tools/serenityprayer.

The Prayer

Abba Father, we thank you for your Son, Jesus, who showed us what it looks like to walk through an hour of great darkness with the confidence "that though the wrong seems oft so strong, God is the Ruler yet."* Come, Holy Spirit, and grace us even to mouth the words "Father, glorify your name!" as we surrender to your goodness in all things. We pray in Jesus' name, amen.

The Questions

- Do you know someone facing an unthinkable hour at this time? Pray about sharing today's entry with them. How do you see the difference between weak resignation and bold surrender? Which is your tendency? What holds you back from praying a prayer like "Father, glorify your name!" in untenable circumstances?

72 Why People Have Hard Hearts and How to Help Them

JOHN 12:34–41 ESV | So the crowd answered him, "We have heard from the Law that the Christ remains forever. How can you say that the Son of Man must be lifted up? Who is this Son

* Maltbie D. Babcock, "This is My Father's World." Public domain.

of Man?" So Jesus said to them, "The light is among you for a little while longer. Walk while you have the light, lest darkness overtake you. The one who walks in the darkness does not know where he is going. While you have the light, believe in the light, that you may become sons of light."

When Jesus had said these things, he departed and hid himself from them. Though he had done so many signs before them, they still did not believe in him, so that the word spoken by the prophet Isaiah might be fulfilled:

> "Lord, who has believed what he heard from us,
> and to whom has the arm of the Lord been revealed?"

Therefore they could not believe. For again Isaiah said,

> "He has blinded their eyes
> and hardened their heart,
> lest they see with their eyes,
> and understand with their heart, and turn,
> and I would heal them."

Isaiah said these things because he saw his glory and spoke of him.

Consider This

The hardest thing about a hard-hearted person is that they are the last to know. Have you ever known anyone who set out to be a hard-hearted person or who considers themselves as such? I haven't either. So how do people become hard-hearted? I have a working theory.

Hard-hearted people are typically the way they are because something happened in their past that made them brokenhearted people. They risked vulnerability, trust, or relationship, and they were hurt, betrayed, or rejected. In such circumstances, in an effort to protect themselves from such pain, people tend to vow to themselves they will never let anything like that happen again. In many cases, bitterness will take root and eventually hardness will begin to set in. They become invulnerable, untrusting, and isolated (even if they seem to remain relational people). Unbelief does not so much come from a willful choice to not believe but from a broken heart that has become hardened. Signs and wonders can have surprisingly little effect on such people.

Such people are often described as jaded or cynical. Their way of hearing and seeing people and life in general gets distorted. It is a self-fulfilling, self-perpetuating reality. Hard-hearted people have an insatiable need to be right and are often perceived as self-righteous. And let's be clear: hard-hearted people are not bad people; they are broken people. The problem is this condition of hard-heartedness is impervious to healing. Unfortunately, the various ways and means they deploy to protect themselves from pain also shield them from healing. Walling others out has the unfortunate side effect of walling themselves in.

". . . lest they see with their eyes, and understand with their heart, and turn, and I would heal them."

How does a hard-hearted person escape this condition? They get out of it in the same way they got into it—a broken heart. Just as the unhealed broken heart became hardened, so the hardened heart must become broken again in order to be healed. That's why we use the term "hardened." A fiercely protected, hardened heart does not easily break. The only hope: love them anyway.

The Prayer

Abba Father, we thank you for your Son, Jesus, who heals the brokenhearted. Give us eyes to see the hidden brokenheartedness of those whose hearts have become hardened. We know only your love heals, and so make us vessels of this love for others. We pray in Jesus' name, amen.

The Questions

- Have you ever thought of a hard-hearted person as a brokenhearted person? Why or why not? How do you tend to protect yourself from being hurt by others? Could that have resulted in developing any hardness in your heart? Do you know any people you would consider to be hard-hearted at the present time? What would it look like for you to step up your love for them?

The Big Problem with People Pleasers

73

JOHN 12:42–50 | **Yet at the same time many even among the leaders believed in him. But because of the Pharisees they would not openly acknowledge their faith for fear they would** be put out of the synagogue; for they loved human praise more than praise from God.

Then Jesus cried out, "Whoever believes in me does not believe in me only, but in the one who sent me. The one who looks at me is seeing the one who sent me. I have come into the world as a light, so that no one who believes in me should stay in darkness.

"If anyone hears my words but does not keep them, I do not judge that person. For I did not come to judge the world, but to save the world. There is a judge for the one who rejects me and does not accept my words; the very words I have spoken will condemn them at the last day. For I did not speak on my own, but the Father who sent me commanded me to say all that I have spoken. I know that his command leads to eternal life. So whatever I say is just what the Father has told me to say."

Consider This

The text provides us with a powerful definition of the word *coward*. Did you see it?

Yet at the same time many even among the leaders believed in him. But because of the Pharisees they would not openly acknowledge their faith for fear they would be put out of the synagogue; for they loved human praise more than praise from God.

The old hymn comes to mind, "Stand up, stand up for Jesus." So why wouldn't Jesus' supporters stand up for him?

It's called cowardice. It's because we fear men more than we fear God, or as the text has it, we love the accolades of people more than the affirmation of God.

Did you catch this from the text: "many even among the leaders believed in him"? Why would it say, "even among the leaders," as though that should surprise us? Maybe it's because the leaders weren't leading. Here's the hard truth: they were following. They wavered between two opinions—what the Pharisees thought of them and what Jesus thought of them. There's a word that captures this malady suffered by so many leaders: *people-pleasing*. Here's the surprising truth: at the heart of people-pleasing is the fear of people. The proverb says it well: "Fear of man will prove to be a snare, but whoever trusts in the LORD is kept safe" (Prov. 29:25).

People pleasers tend to rise quickly in the ranks because they curry favor with those who can help them advance. As a result, the higher they rise, the greater their cowardice. It's why people tend to loathe politicians. And, yes, this is particularly acute in the church. The great irony of people pleasers is that they aren't really loyal to the people they are trying to please; their loyalty is to themselves. It's why often the greatest leaders aren't found in positions of leadership.

The desire to please people is not a bad thing, just deceptive. It can come from a heart of deep love. We just need to take care that our interest in pleasing people is not our own interest in protecting ourselves. And, of course, the goal is not to be a people offender. The aim is to be true to God.

The Prayer

Abba Father, we thank you for your Son, Jesus, who shows us what it looks like to perfectly love people and love God at the same time. Thank you for showing us this way of serving people, not in order to please them, but in order to love you and, in loving you, to become vessels of your love for them. Come, Holy Spirit, and lead us in this way. We pray in Jesus' name, amen.

The Questions

- Do you struggle with being a people pleaser? Why do you think this is the case? What would happen if you were suddenly freed from the need (and even compulsion) to please people? Why do we tend not to respect people-pleasing leaders? How can we help them (us)?

74 When Washing Feet Is More Than Washing Feet

JOHN 13:1–5 | It was just before the Passover Festival. Jesus knew that the hour had come for him to leave this world and go to the Father. Having loved his own who were in the world, he loved them to the end.

The evening meal was in progress, and the devil had already prompted Judas, the son of Simon Iscariot, to betray Jesus.

Jesus knew that the Father had put all things under his power, and that he had come from God and was returning to God; so he got up from the meal, took off his outer clothing, and wrapped a towel around his waist. After that, he poured water into a basin and began to wash his disciples' feet, drying them with the towel that was wrapped around him.

Consider This

Why so much detail here?

So he got up from the meal, took off his outer clothing, and wrapped a towel around his waist. After that, he poured water into a basin and began to wash his disciples' feet, drying them with the towel that was wrapped around him.

Why couldn't John have just written: "He washed his disciples' feet"? Would that not have been enough? Apparently not.

John wanted us to see something. Actually, I am convinced he wanted us to *behold* something. I think the Holy Spirit inspired John to give this account in such detail because he wanted us to see the exquisite nature of extraordinary love poured into the lowliest, ordinary, undignified act of service.

It has me asking myself: *Does anything I do for another person come anywhere close to this exquisite nature of extraordinary love poured into the lowliest, ordinary, undignified act of service? Further, is there anything I have ever done, great or small, that would merit this granular level of description?* It's just so easy to get caught up in the undertow of oughts and shoulds and duty-bound obligatory service. On the other hand, it's easy to be sucked into the seduction of wanting to do something extraordinary and grandiose. What slays me about this story is the way Jesus takes the most menial ordinary and unmentionable act of service and fills it with such love that, two thousand years later, we still can't get over it.

I think this must have been something of what Mother Teresa meant when she said, "We can do no great things—only small things with great love."

The good news. These opportunities present themselves every single day.

The Prayer

Abba Father, we thank you for your Son, Jesus, who takes an unmentionable and undignified act of service and makes it something we can't stop speaking of. Lead me in this way of living today. We pray in Jesus' name, amen.

The Questions

- Why such detail in this description? What's your take? How do you observe the difference between duty-bound service and love-empowered service? What holds you back from pouring your very best into the most menial and ordinary acts?

Jesus Loves You, but I'm His Favorite

75

JOHN 13:6–11 | He came to Simon Peter, who said to him, "Lord, are you going to wash my feet?"

Jesus replied, "You do not realize now what I am doing, but later you will understand."

"No," said Peter, "you shall never wash my feet."

Jesus answered, "Unless I wash you, you have no part with me."

"Then, Lord," Simon Peter replied, "not just my feet but my hands and my head as well!"

Jesus answered, "Those who have had a bath need only to wash their feet; their whole body is clean. And you are clean, though not every one of you." For he knew who was going to betray him, and that was why he said not every one was clean.

Consider This

It was a small circle of people. Jesus had a method here. He was going one by one—person to person—washing their feet. What was not computing for Peter here? Did he have feet issues? Did he think his feet didn't stink? It didn't occur to Peter that he was just like everyone else in the circle. He thought he was somehow different from the rest.

He came to Simon Peter, who said to him, "Lord, are you going to wash my feet?"

It wasn't so much, "Are *you* going to wash my feet?" but, "Are you going to wash *my* feet?" Jesus had long been preparing the disciples for passion—his and theirs. The disciples were preparing for position. In the understatement of the first century, Jesus responded:

"You do not realize now what I am doing, but later you will understand."

"No," said Peter, "you shall never wash my feet."

It is reminiscent of an earlier occasion where, in response to Jesus predicting his passion, Peter rebuked him, "Never, Lord! This shall never happen to you!" Remember Jesus' stunning response? "Get behind me, Satan! You are a stumbling block to me; you do not have in mind the concerns of God, but merely human concerns" (see Matthew 16:22–23).

Jesus answered, "Unless I wash you, you have no part with me."

In case you weren't convinced of Peter's strategy, check out his response:

"Then, Lord," Simon Peter replied, "not just my feet but my hands and my head as well!"

Peter was desperate to be distinguished from his peers. He wanted to be distinguished as the one Jesus didn't wash or the one Jesus really washed. He needed to stand out, to rise above, to be set apart and distinct from the rest.

Our pride craves more and more status, more and more recognition, more and more accolades. We need to be better, stronger, and more important—and we need others to know it. Peter had been there, done that, and he had the T-shirt: "Jesus loves you, but I'm his favorite."

This seeking after status distinction is at the heart of jealousy and envy. It fuels the constant comparing of ourselves with others. Bottom line: if the unmerited love of God is not enough for us, it's a sign that we don't know the unmerited love of God.

The Prayer

Abba Father, we thank you for your Son, Jesus, who confers upon us the only status that matters: recipient of the love of God. Take us to the place in our inmost person where our identity and security comes from you alone. We pray in Jesus' name, amen.

The Questions

- How do you try to distinguish yourself from others? Why? Is your core identity anchored in the love of God for you, or are you still building another system of self-worth? Is the unmerited love of God enough for you? What would need to change for this to be the case?

Why Did Jesus Wash Our Feet?

76

JOHN 13:12–20 | When he had finished washing their feet, he put on his clothes and returned to his place. "Do you

understand what I have done for you?" he asked them. "You call me 'Teacher' and 'Lord,' and rightly so, for that is what I am. Now that I, your Lord and Teacher, have washed your feet, you also should wash one another's feet. I have set you an example that you should do as I have done for you. Very truly I tell you, no servant is greater than his master, nor is a messenger greater than the one who sent him. Now that you know these things, you will be blessed if you do them.

"I am not referring to all of you; I know those I have chosen. But this is to fulfill this passage of Scripture: 'He who shared my bread has turned against me.'

"I am telling you now before it happens, so that when it does happen you will believe that I am who I am. Very truly I tell you, whoever accepts anyone I send accepts me; and whoever accepts me accepts the one who sent me."

Consider This

What a question! Let's read this text as addressed to us.

"Do you understand what I have done for you?"

The short answer: Yes, Jesus, you washed our feet.

On the surface, yes. Something much deeper happened beneath the surface. Jesus all at once acknowledged the power dynamics and differentials in human relationships while collapsing status distinctions within them.

Watch how it worked. He acknowledged the power dynamics:

"You call me 'Teacher' and 'Lord,' and rightly so, for that is what I am. . . . Very truly I tell you, no servant is greater than his master."

Jesus was the Rabbi; the disciples were the students. Jesus was the Master; the disciples were the followers. There was a clear differential here, and Jesus had the power. Now, watch what he did with it.

"Now that I, your Lord and Teacher, have washed your feet, you also should wash one another's feet. I have set you an example that you should do as I have done for you."

Jesus did not divest himself of his power, nor did he try to pretend there was no power differential between him and his disciples. He collapsed the power dynamics and the status-based relationships by reversing them. The greatest actually made himself the least, and so revealed true greatness.

It's not about people in power giving lip service to equality. This is not about equality. It's far more radical than that. It's about identity. Jesus showed us his identity is not shaped by his role. It's just the opposite. His role is shaped by his identity. That's why he washed our feet.

The Prayer

Abba Father, we thank you for your Son, Jesus, who, being in very nature God, did not consider equality with God something to be grasped, but made himself nothing; and taking on the very nature of a servant, being made in human likeness and found in the appearance of a man, he humbled himself and became obedient to death, even death on a cross (see Philippians 2:5–11). Come, Holy Spirit, and form this very mind in us. We pray in Jesus' name, amen.

The Questions

- How do you understand what Jesus did for us in washing our feet? Do you see how doing acts of service is quite possibly a very different thing than taking on the nature of a servant? Why? Do you see the critical distinction between our identity being determined by our activity versus our activity being determined by our identity? Why does this matter?

77 The Ultimate Failure of Love

JOHN 13:21–27A ESV | After saying these things, Jesus was troubled in his spirit, and testified, "Truly, truly, I say to you, one of you will betray me." The disciples looked at one another, uncertain of whom he spoke. One of his disciples, whom Jesus loved, was reclining at table at Jesus' side, so Simon Peter motioned to him to ask Jesus of whom he was speaking. So that disciple, leaning back against Jesus, said to him, "Lord, who is it?" Jesus answered, "It is he to whom I will give this morsel of bread when I have dipped it." So when he had dipped

the morsel, he gave it to Judas, the son of Simon Iscariot. Then after he had taken the morsel, Satan entered into him.

Consider This

"Truly, truly, I say to you, one of you will betray me."

Why do you think Jesus said this to his disciples? Did he think Judas might change his mind? Did he want each of the disciples to search their own soul? Did he just want to put everyone on notice that things were about to go bad?

The biblical meaning of betrayal is something like "to be handed over to the authorities." We see the word back in Matthew 5 when Jesus said, "Settle matters quickly with your adversary who is taking you to court. Do it while you are still together on the way, or your adversary may hand you over to the judge, and the judge may hand you over to the officer, and you may be thrown into prison" (v. 25).

To be handed over to the judge or the court means to be betrayed. It means to be abandoned. In Matthew 5 we see an instance of being betrayed by an adversary or an enemy. Jesus seemed to say that can be expected, so be prepared to settle with them to avoid this outcome.

It's when betrayal comes at the hand of a friend that it is so painful. Betrayal is the ultimate breach of relationship and the most devastating failure of love. While the betrayer may be forgiven, they never get over it. If you've ever betrayed someone, you know what I mean. While the victim of betrayal may get over it, the pain never goes away. If you've suffered betrayal, you know what I'm talking about.

While Jesus holds endless grace for both the betrayer and the betrayed, the consequences of betrayal never end.

The Prayer

Abba Father, we thank you for your Son, Jesus, who submitted himself to betrayal, enduring its pain, taking it to the cross, and leaving it behind in the grave. Have mercy on us who have betrayed and who have been betrayed. We pray in Jesus' name, amen.

The Questions

- Have you ever betrayed another person? Have you ever been betrayed by another person? Betrayal, on either end, is indeed a cross to bear. Are you ready to allow Jesus to bear it with and for you?

78 Why Love Must Be More Than Love

JOHN 13:27B–38 ESV | Jesus said to him, "What you are going to do, do quickly." Now no one at the table knew why he said this to him. Some thought that, because Judas had the moneybag, Jesus was telling him, "Buy what we need for the feast," or that he should give something to the poor. So, after receiving the morsel of bread, he immediately went out. And it was night.

When he had gone out, Jesus said, "Now is the Son of Man glorified, and God is glorified in him. If God is glorified in him, God will also glorify him in himself, and glorify him at once. Little children, yet a little while I am with you. You will seek me, and just as I said to the Jews, so now I also say to you, 'Where I am going you cannot come.' A new commandment I give to you, that you love one another: just as I have loved you, you also are to love one another. By this all people will know that you are my disciples, if you have love for one another."

Simon Peter said to him, "Lord, where are you going?" Jesus answered him, "Where I am going you cannot follow me now, but you will follow afterward." Peter said to him, "Lord, why can I not follow you now? I will lay down my life for you." Jesus answered, "Will you lay down your life for me? Truly, truly, I say to you, the rooster will not crow till you have denied me three times."

Consider This

A new command. On the eve of the end, Jesus gave his disciples a new command: "Love one another."

What's new about this? This command is all over the Bible. Jesus had certainly said this kind of thing before. Love one another. Big whoop! We want to say, "But we've already heard that, Jesus."

Jesus meant a different kind of love. He was talking about a love that is more than just love. And isn't that the problem? Love has come to mean so many things that it means little to nothing anymore. The truth? It's always been that way.

Jesus refused to leave it at, "Love one another." He went on to define what he meant when he said "love."

"Just as I have loved you, you also are to love one another."

With six small words, Jesus exploded this tired old word as we understand it: "Just as I have loved you." What if we took these six little words and went back and inscribed them at the top of every page of the gospel of John? That would be a good exercise in interpretation.

There are at least three steps in the progression toward this kind of love. First, we love others for our own sake. Second, we learn to love others for their sake. Third, by the grace and mercy of God alone, we will learn to love others for God's sake. To love another person for God's sake means to love them with the very same love with which Jesus has loved us. In this sense, it is impossible to love another person for God's sake apart from God.

The primary ministry and mission of the Holy Spirit is to inhabit our whole lives to the end that we are given to loving others as Jesus has loved us. This is the entire meaning of sanctification—of being made holy as God is holy—loving others as Jesus has loved us. This is the sum total of the will of God: to love others as Jesus has loved us. Let's give John Wesley the last word on this subject today:

> [One cause of] a thousand mistakes is [this:] . . . not considering deeply, that love is the highest gift of God; humble, gentle, patient love; that all visions, revelations, [or] manifestations whatever, are little things

compared to love; and that all [other] gifts . . . are either the same with or infinitely inferior to it.

[Y]ou should be thoroughly [aware] of this—the heaven of heavens is love. There is nothing higher in religion; there is, in effect, nothing else; if you look for anything but more love, you are looking wide of the mark, you are getting out of the royal way. And when you are asking others, "Have you received this or that blessing?" if you mean anything but more love, you mean wrong; you are leading them out of the way, and putting them [on] a false scent. Settle it then in your heart, that from the moment God has saved you from all sin, you are to aim at nothing more but more of that love described in the thirteenth [chapter] of [First] Corinthians. You can go no higher than this, till you are carried into Abraham's bosom.*

The Prayer

Abba Father, we thank you for your Son, Jesus, who takes us to the next level of love and shows us it is not up but down, at the feet of others. Fill us with this love and train us to love others as you have loved us. Come, Holy Spirit, and reveal to the depths of our souls just how profoundly Jesus has loved us. We pray in Jesus' name, amen.

---

* John Wesley, *A Plain Account of Christian Perfection* (Franklin, TN: Seedbed Publishing, 2014), 93.

The Questions

- Our love for others will not exceed the depths of our knowing of Jesus' love for us. On a scale of 1 to 10, with 10 being the highest, where do you rate your knowing beyond knowledge of the love of God in Jesus Christ? Why is it necessary for Jesus to qualify for us the meaning of love? What holds you back from loving others with this kind of love? What can be done to grow beyond it?

79 The Eternal Mystery of Being in Two Places at One Time

JOHN 14:1–7 ESV | "Let not your hearts be troubled. Believe in God; believe also in me. In my Father's house are many rooms. If it were not so, would I have told you that I go to prepare a place for you? And if I go and prepare a place for you, I will come again and will take you to myself, that where I am you may be also. And you know the way to where I am going." Thomas said to him, "Lord, we do not know where you are going. How can we know the way?" Jesus said to him, "I am the way, and the truth, and the life. No one comes to the Father except through me. If you had known me, you would have known my Father also. From now on you do know him and have seen him."

Consider This

This is the universal go-to text for funerals everywhere. In fact, that's about the only place I ever hear it. While comforting many a soul in the wake of loss, I'm not so sure this is what Jesus had in mind when he spoke these words.

The context here is not a funeral but final preparations for a sequence of cataclysmic events—namely, Jesus' death, burial, resurrection, ascension, sending of the Holy Spirit, and final return. Jesus clearly addressed the living, not about death, but concerning their ongoing relationship with him in the absence of his physical presence.

Bear with me. This is about to get mind-bending. Jesus taught his disciples what it means to dwell in two realms simultaneously—on earth and in heaven. "On earth as it is in heaven" (Matt. 6:10) is not an ethical paradigm but a living mystery.

Stay with me. Because Jesus is physically seated in heaven at the right hand of the Father, he is able to dwell all over the earth in and through his disciples (i.e., the church) via the person and power of the Holy Spirit. In like but opposite fashion, because Jesus' disciples are physically present all over the world, they are also seated in heaven in the presence of Jesus by the person and power of the Holy Spirit. The Holy Spirit mediates the presence of Jesus "on earth as it is in heaven" (Matt. 6:10). And the Holy Spirit mediates the presence of Jesus' disciples (a.k.a. the body of Christ) in heaven as it is on earth.

This is what Jesus meant when he said "that where I am you may be also" (John 14:3). Jesus is here and we are there. Paul was all over this in his letters:

> And God raised us up with Christ and seated us with him in the heavenly realms in Christ Jesus. (Eph. 2:6)

> Since, then, you have been raised with Christ, set your hearts on things above, where Christ is, seated at the right hand of God. Set your minds on things above, not on earthly things. For you died, and your life is now hidden with Christ in God. When Christ, who is your life, appears, then you also will appear with him in glory. (Col. 3:1–4)

This is indeed a profound mystery, and one in which we have scarcely begun to perceive the implications. So, what if we began to apply this text more for our lives than others' deaths?

The Prayer

Abba Father, we thank you for your Son, Jesus, who has prepared a place for us, that where he is, we may also be. Come, Holy Spirit, and help us grasp the reality that he is here with us and we are there with him, and show us all this can mean in our lives. We pray in Jesus' name, amen.

The Questions

- So, does it make more sense to see this text as futuristic or as present? What does it mean that we are "seated . . . in the heavenly realms" (Eph. 2:6)? What are the implications of this way of understanding the presence of Jesus and the presence of his people?

The Secret to Doing Greater Things Than Jesus

80

JOHN 14:8–14 | Philip said, "Lord, show us the Father and that will be enough for us."

Jesus answered: "Don't you know me, Philip, even after I have been among you such a long time? Anyone who has seen me has seen the Father. How can you say, 'Show us the Father'? Don't you believe that I am in the Father, and that the Father is in me? The words I say to you I do not speak on my own authority. Rather, it is the Father, living in me, who is doing his work. Believe me when I say that I am in the Father and the Father is in me; or at least believe on the evidence of the works themselves. Very truly I tell you, whoever believes in me will do the works I have been doing, and they will do even greater things than these, because I am going to the Father. And I will do whatever you ask in my name, so that the Father may be glorified in the Son. You may ask me for anything in my name, and I will do it."

Consider This

I remember the first time I came across this text years ago. I'm sure I had read it before, but for some reason on that occasion it jumped off the page.

"Very truly I tell you, whoever believes in me will do the works I have been doing, and they will do even greater things than these, because I am going to the Father."

I remember filing it into a growing collection of Scripture texts I categorized as follows: "This is either not true or I am not getting it." I believed it then just as I believe it now, and I think I get it more than I got it then, but if I'm honest, I must admit to you I still think I'm missing something here.

How about you? Have you been doing the works of Jesus and even greater works than he did while on earth? I've had people try to let me off the hook by saying Jesus wasn't exactly talking about greater, as in works of greater magnitude. They said he meant greater as in quantity of works. Nice try, but I don't buy it. I'm convinced he meant greater in every respect.

Honestly, I would settle for simply doing the same works Jesus did. Those would be great enough for starters, don't you think? So, what's the problem? Why aren't the uncommon works of Jesus more commonplace in our time? I will risk a diagnosis: we aren't seeing the greater works because we don't yet possess the greater love.

Return again with me to those days when I first discovered this text. I diagnosed my deficit as a power problem, which quickly led me to believe I had a faith problem. I didn't have enough faith. After all, Jesus did say, "whoever believes in me," so I focused on believing more, thinking I would gain more power. It didn't work.

Finally, the obvious occurs to me that John 14 is couched between John 13, of which verses 34–35 read: "A new command I give you: Love one another. As I have loved you, so you must love one another. By this everyone will know that you are my disciples, if you love one another," and John 15, of which verses 12–13 read: "My command is this: Love each other as I have loved you. Greater love has no one than this: to lay down one's life for one's friends."

It's interesting, too, to note this movement between 1 Corinthians 12 and 14. Remember what chapter 13 is all about? You got it: love.

I am convinced love is the power. We will finally see greater things when we learn the ways of greater love. It makes sense, doesn't it? When we finally break into the rarified air of loving others as Jesus has loved us, we will discover the only true power and that it has been waiting on us the whole time.

The Prayer

Abba Father, we thank you for your Son, Jesus, who is the love of God. Thank you that to love as he loves is impossible apart from his presence. Teach us to love his presence more than his power and, in doing so, to discover the power of his love in our presence. We pray in Jesus' name, amen.

The Questions

- Can we really do greater things than even Jesus did? Is it true? Or are we just not getting it? Can you recount a time when you saw greater love lead to greater things? What holds you back from the way of greater love? Will it be worth it in the end to have held back?

81 The Two Most Under-Realized Revolutionary Words in the Bible

JOHN 14:15–21 | "If you love me, keep my commands. And I will ask the Father, and he will give you another advocate to help you and be with you forever—the Spirit of truth. The world cannot accept him, because it neither sees him nor knows him. But you know him, for he lives with you and will be in you. I will not leave you as orphans; I will come to you. Before long, the world will not see me anymore, but you will see me. Because I live, you also will live. On that day you will realize that I am in my Father, and you are in me, and I am in you. Whoever has my commands and keeps them is the one who loves me. The one who loves me will be loved by my Father, and I too will love them and show myself to them."

Consider This

How awesome is this? In this, the final discourse in the fourth gospel, Jesus let us in on everything. The amazing thing is we have it written down.

I don't think I yet grasp the gravity and magnitude of these words. The second person of the Trinity introduced us to the third person of the Trinity. As I read these words, I think I understand them. I've read them many times. I've studied them. I believe them. Sometimes I think my present understanding actually keeps me from a deeper understanding. What will it take for me to wake up to the thinness of my own understanding, become dissatisfied with my shallow faith, and plunge into the depths of this reality Jesus invited us into?

"On that day you will realize that I am in my Father, and you are in me, and I am in you."

This is what the Holy Spirit does. He moves Jesus from being with us to being within us.

"The world cannot accept him, because it neither sees him nor knows him. But you know him, for he lives with you and will be in you."

There they are—the two most under-realized, revolutionary words in the whole Bible: *in you.*

The Prayer

Abba Father, thank you for your Son, Jesus, who wills to live in me by the power of the Holy Spirit. Give me more access to myself, that I might give more of myself to him. Increase my understanding and experience of Jesus being in me. I pray in Jesus' name, amen.

The Questions

- Are you ready for a deeper experience of Christ in you? How would he know this? How do you or would you know that Christ is dwelling in you? How might you cultivate and nourish a growing awareness of this "in you" reality?

82 Why Jesus Doesn't Do Reverse Delegation

JOHN 14:22–27 | Then Judas (not Judas Iscariot) said, "But, Lord, why do you intend to show yourself to us and not to the world?"

Jesus replied, "Anyone who loves me will obey my teaching. My Father will love them, and we will come to them and make our home with them. Anyone who does not love me will not obey my teaching. These words you hear are not my own; they belong to the Father who sent me.

"All this I have spoken while still with you. But the Advocate, the Holy Spirit, whom the Father will send in my name, will teach you all things and will remind you of everything I have said to you. Peace I leave with you; my peace I give you. I do not give to you as the world gives. Do not let your hearts be troubled and do not be afraid."

Consider This

Why do we want Jesus to do what he wants us to do? Isn't that what Judas (not Iscariot) was getting at? Jesus does not do reverse delegation.

"But, Lord, why do you intend to show yourself to us and not to the world?"

Sometimes I think this is how we reason when it comes to the greater works Jesus told us we would be doing. We see signs and wonders as something Jesus drops here and there like glory bombs. We think of them as being the causal agent of people believing in God. Here's my question: What if it's the divinely empowered human love behind the signs and wonders that makes the bigger difference? That would make love the causal agent of faith. It raises my thought again about the lack of greater works being directly related to the lack of greater love.

"But, Lord, why do you intend to show yourself to us and not to the world?"

Isn't that just like us? We want Jesus to show himself to us and to the world. Instead, Jesus intends to show himself to us—and, through us, he intends to show himself to the world. We keep asking Jesus to do something he is asking us to do. It's like we are asking him to write the check, and all the while he is saying to us, "Cash it!"

"My Father will love them, and we will come to them and make our home with them."

Jesus will have no other home, no other temple, than his disciples.

I want to test an idea with you. What if it's like this: For God so loved the world, he gave his one and only Son. For Jesus so loved the world, he gave his one and only church. For the church so loves the world, we give the one and only Spirit.

The Prayer

Abba Father, we thank you for your Son, Jesus, who is himself the great sign and wonder. Thank you that he has chosen to show himself to the world through the church. Awaken us to his readiness to love the world through us. Lead us to the greater love that leads to the greater works. We pray in Jesus' name, amen.

The Questions

- Wouldn't it be easier if Jesus would just show himself to the world directly? Why do we, like Judas, want this? What hinders Jesus showing himself to the world through the church? What hinders Jesus showing himself to the world through you?

83 Why Obedience May Not Mean What You Think It Means

JOHN 14:28–31 ESV | "You heard me say to you, 'I am going away, and I will come to you.' If you loved me, you would have rejoiced, because I am going to the Father, for the Father is

greater than I. And now I have told you before it takes place, so that when it does take place you may believe. I will no longer talk much with you, for the ruler of this world is coming. He has no claim on me, but I do as the Father has commanded me, so that the world may know that I love the Father. Rise, let us go from here."

Consider This

There is a strong theme weaving its way through this closing session between Jesus and his disciples. It can be brought down to one word: *obedience*. Here are a few examples from John's gospel:

"A new command I give you: Love one another. As I have loved you, so you must love one another." (13:34)

"If you love me, keep my commands." (14:15)

"Whoever has my commands and keeps them is the one who loves me." (14:21a)

"Anyone who loves me will obey my teaching." (14:23a)

"Anyone who does not love me will not obey my teaching." (14:24a)

"[H]e comes so that the world may learn that I love the Father and do exactly what my Father has commanded me." (14:31)

"If you keep my commands, you will remain in my love, just as I have kept my Father's commands and remain in his love." (15:10)

English Bible translations bounce around with the underlying Greek word and its meaning. The root Greek term is *tereo*. Sometimes it is translated "keep" and at other times "obey." People tend to resist obedience language because of its association with slavery, oppression, authoritarianism, and, yes, parenting. When one person tells another person to "obey" them, it usually happens in a powering down context.

When Paul tells children to obey parents (Eph. 6:1–3) and slaves to obey masters (Col. 3:22–24), we see a different Greek term: *hupakouo*. Interestingly, this term carries a meaning more like "to hear or to listen intently."

So why all this? We need to grasp the gravity and intensity of Jesus' words. When Jesus told us to keep his words or obey his commands, and when he told us how he obeyed his Father's commands, here's what he meant. Go back to the previous passages, and everywhere we see the term *keep* or *obey*, insert these words: Pay close attention to what I say, keep these words in your mind, impress the teaching on your hearts, guard it with vigilance, give all of your energy to applying it to your life, be careful to put it into practice, and treasure it above everything else.

Let's give this a shot with John 14:23, which says, "Anyone who loves me will obey my teaching . . ."

Anyone who loves me will *pay close attention to what I say, keep these words in your mind, impress the teaching on your hearts, guard it with vigilance, give all of your energy to applying it to your life, be careful to put it into practice, and treasure it above everything else.*

This was how Jesus handled the commands of his Father. This was his instruction to us. I don't know about you, but this both convicts and encourages me. I'm afraid I am a little more casual and too often aloof. I hold Jesus' teaching too much at the aspirational level and not enough at the "I must do this at all costs because my life depends on it" level.

This, my friends, is the sum total of what it means to love Jesus.

Obedience is not blind submission. It's the totalizing attention of love.

The Prayer

Abba Father, we thank you for your Son, Jesus, who not only calls us to obedience but who shows us exactly what it looks like in action. Deliver us from our easy familiarity with his words. Teach us to cherish and to love his words. Open our minds to perceive them afresh and train our hearts to love them with all we are. We pray in Jesus' name, amen.

The Questions

- How have you tended to think about the term *obedience* in the past? How does my amplified take on what the term means help you? Challenge you? Encourage you? How do you push back on it? What would it mean to get the whole notion of obedience out of the category of power and into the category of love? What would be the implications of this for your relationships? Your leadership?

84 When Symbols Obscure the Signs

JOHN 15:1–4 | "I am the true vine, and my Father is the gardener. He cuts off every branch in me that bears no fruit, while every branch that does bear fruit he prunes so that it will be even more fruitful. You are already clean because of the word I have spoken to you. Remain in me, as I also remain in you. No branch can bear fruit by itself; it must remain in the vine. Neither can you bear fruit unless you remain in me."

Consider This

They were walking with the Upper Room in the rearview mirror and the garden of Gethsemane in their sites. As they passed by the temple complex, they looked up at the grand edifice, and, there, at the top of the structure, they saw a vine carved into the stone. This was Israel's great symbol. "I am the true vine," he told them. The whole Israel project had been a failure. Despite every effort of the Father, the vine of this once great nation had failed.

As they crossed the Kidron Valley, I wonder if they passed by an active vineyard. It strikes me that Jesus was setting up a massive contrast for his followers. On the one hand, this incredible institution marked by grand buildings and run by the power structures of a prestigious establishment. On the other hand, this ordinary vineyard flourishing with grapes and yet in need of constant tending and care. The structure depended on its systems. The vineyard depended on its Vinedresser.

When our symbols come to represent our systems and structures instead of the signs for which they stand, it's only a matter of time before the signs disappear. This is why the signs and sayings of Jesus are so critical. Each one of them, in its own way, indicts the system and its hypocrisy and reveals the truth of the true God and all his glory.

We would be well served to go back and reread the Gospels with this in mind. In the very first sign, Jesus—the true vine—turned water into wine. He completed it with the sign in the Upper Room as he lifted up the cup and offered it to his disciples, saying, "This is my blood, the blood of the New Covenant, poured out for you and for many for the forgiveness of sins" (Matt. 26:28).

His very first saying was, "I am the bread of life" (John 6:35). He completed it with the sign in the Upper Room as he broke bread and gave it to his disciples, saying, "This is my body given for you" (Luke 22:19b). The whole thing holds together in such mystical integrity and concrete practicality, only God could have imagined it. In fact, the only way God could reveal it was by coming himself. And isn't that the miracle of it all—how the complexity of it all coheres so simply and comes together so completely in the person of Jesus Messiah?

"He cuts off every branch in me that bears no fruit, while every branch that does bear fruit he prunes so that it will be even more fruitful."

This is the pruning we need, a cutting away and a discarding of all the complexity we have created in our own religious establishments, that we might get back to the piercing simplicity of the True Vine and the God of the garden.

The Prayer

Abba Father, we thank you for your Son, Jesus, who reveals the truth to us in his very personhood. Expose all of the false vines we turn to for the life only Jesus can give. Prune us. Grant us the mercy of showing us what we are really trusting in, and give us the courage to return to you with all of our hearts, to place our trust in you alone, whatever it takes. Come, Holy Spirit! We pray in Jesus' name, amen.

The Questions

- What insight is the Holy Spirit impressing on you through this text? How have our symbols obscured the signs? Are we saluting our symbols? What would it mean to re-embrace the sign who is Jesus? What false vines have you or do you tend to trust in for life? Will you welcome new pruning? It's not something you have to do for yourself. He will do it. Will you let him?

85 Jesus as Life Enhancement vs. Jesus as Life Support

JOHN 15:5–6 | "I am the vine; you are the branches. If you remain in me and I in you, you will bear much fruit; apart from me you can do nothing. If you do not remain in me, you are

like a branch that is thrown away and withers; such branches are picked up, thrown into the fire and burned."

Consider This

Several years ago, a popular author came out with a small book called *The Secrets of the Vine*. While I didn't read it, I'm sure it had some good insights; however, the title is problematic for me. It tells me there are principles that can be extracted from a text like John 15, that there are ways and means and formulas to be distilled for my betterment. Maybe that's true. I guess I just don't see this text as a neat object lesson from Jesus on how to have a better quiet time.

For my money, this text makes plain there are no secrets of the vine. The secret is the Vine. Jesus was not teaching us how to have a closer walk with him. He was sharing his last words with his followers, which have life-and-death consequences. Abiding in Jesus means life. Not abiding in Jesus means death. It's that plain. It's "bear much fruit" on the one hand and "thrown into the fire and burned" on the other. There's no in between. This is not life enhancement; it's life support.

J. Hudson Taylor once famously said, "Christ is either Lord of all, or he is not Lord at all." I used to interpret a saying like this as a matter of personal decision—that Jesus was Lord only to the extent that I decided to make him my Lord. I see it differently now. Jesus is Lord, period, or he is not. If he is not, we of all people are fools and most to be pitied. If he is, and we do not order our whole lives accordingly, we of all people are fools and most to be pitied.

I fear we are all mostly asleep to the totalizing implications of lordship. At least I can say I fear I am. We speak it with our lips, but our lives tell a different story. We hold back and hedge and go along with the easy currents of Christian subculture and reasonable faith. Our children know more about algebra than they know of the Bible. At least this is what we have deemed most essential to measure in their development.

"Apart from me you can do nothing."

These are not the words of a good-to-great life enhancement guru to upper-middle-class minivan and SUV drivers. This is the piercing clarity of the Word of God. Actually, we can do something apart from Jesus. We can do a lot. It will just amount to nothing.

Let's start by saying this over and over and over again, "Apart from you, Jesus, I can do nothing."

The Prayer

Abba Father, we thank you for your Son, Jesus, who always tells the truth, no matter how hard or glorious or beautiful it may be. Bring us into the "I am the vine; you are the branches" real life with him. Come, Holy Spirit, and train us to surrender our whole lives to the lordship of Jesus and to do it until we have done it. We pray in Jesus' name, amen.

The Questions

- Are you sensitized to the totalizing influence of the culture in which we live and the way it constantly forms us in its image? Where do you see it in your life? If Jesus is Lord, what kind of pruning needs to happen in your life? "Apart from me you can do nothing." Do you really believe this statement?

The Reason Our Joy Is Not Complete

86

JOHN 15:7–13 | "If you remain in me and my words remain in you, ask whatever you wish, and it will be done for you. This is to my Father's glory, that you bear much fruit, showing yourselves to be my disciples.

"As the Father has loved me, so have I loved you. Now remain in my love. If you keep my commands, you will remain in my love, just as I have kept my Father's commands and remain in his love. I have told you this so that my joy may be in you and that your joy may be complete. My command is this: Love each other as I have loved you. Greater love has no one than this: to lay down one's life for one's friends."

Consider This

Before the kingdom of heaven is a place, it is a people. And before it is a people, it is a person. In fact, there is no such thing as a person apart from other persons. As the African Ubuntu saying goes, "A person is a person because of other people." Sure, we can be individual human beings in and of ourselves, but to be a real person is another thing altogether.

More than anywhere else in Scripture, this final discourse in John's gospel reveals to us the interrelationship of the persons of the Trinity. There is no Son apart from the Father. There is no Father apart from the Son. And there is no Spirit apart from the Father and the Son. To speak of the interrelatedness of the Father, Son, and Holy Spirit is to speak of love. This is why John declared in his short sermon, "God is love" (1 John 4:8).

The kingdom of heaven is the manifest presence of the interrelated persons of the Trinity. For the kingdom of heaven to be upon the earth, the interrelated persons of the Trinity must manifest their presence through the interrelationships of human beings. The kingdom of heaven does not come through a person, but through persons. There is simply no such thing as love outside of relationship.

"On earth as it is in heaven" (Matt. 6:10) must mean only one thing: the love enjoyed between Father, Son, and Holy Spirit moving, manifesting, and infusing itself in and through the interrelationships of human persons to the end of complete joy. Is this not precisely what Jesus said here?

"As the Father has loved me, so have I loved you. Now remain in my love. If you keep my commands, you will remain in my love, just as I have kept my Father's commands and remain in his love. I have told you this so that my joy may be in you and that your joy may be complete. My command is this: Love each other as I have loved you. Greater love has no one than this: to lay down one's life for one's friends."

This is how Jesus prayed for us two chapters later in John 17:20–21: "My prayer is not for them alone. I pray also for those who will believe in me through their message, that all of them may be one, Father, just as you are in me and I am in you. May they also be in us so that the world may believe that you have sent me."

The love of God is the supernatural logic of the kingdom of heaven. Last will be first, the servant will be greatest, down is the way up, the smallest seed becomes the greatest tree, to give is to receive, losing one's life means finding it, ask and receive, seek and find, knock and the door opens.

"If you remain in me and my words remain in you, ask whatever you wish, and it will be done for you."

The Prayer

Abba Father, we thank you for your Son, Jesus, who has revealed to us everything that matters. Grant that our understanding might become our faith, and that our faith might become our experience. Lord, we must know your love to share it, and yet the more we share, the more we know. Come, Holy Spirit, and bring us into this blessed joy. We pray in Jesus' name, amen.

The Questions

- "A person is a person because of other people." React to that statement. See the difference between a human being and a real person? Why would you say our joy is not complete?

87 Why Jesus Doesn't Need Servants

JOHN 15:14–17 | "You are my friends if you do what I command. I no longer call you servants, because a servant does not know his master's business. Instead, I have called you friends, for everything that I learned from my Father I have made known to you. You did not choose me, but I chose you and appointed you so that you might go and bear fruit—fruit that will last—and so that whatever you ask in my name the Father will give you. This is my command: Love each other."

Consider This

I see a progression of maturity for the followers of Jesus in today's text I have not noted before. It's the movement from servant to friend.

"I no longer call you servants, because a servant does not know his master's business. Instead, I have called you friends . . ."

Up to this point it strikes me Jesus did not look at or consider his disciples as friends. They were servants. He expected them to follow and obey him based on incomplete knowledge and understanding. They did not yet know their master's business. The Greek word for disciple is *mathetes*, and it means a "learner." They had been learning along the way as Jesus' apprentices from his teaching, modeling, demonstration, and debriefing. They made errors and misjudgments and experienced outright failure at times. At other times, their successes fed their ambitions more than their faith. Still, at other points, they hit the bull's-eye and enjoyed the deep fulfillment of life as a servant of Jesus.

It strikes me that this graduation to friendship commenced when Jesus identified himself as their servant by washing their feet. Following this, he brought them into the inner circle, sharing with them the intimate interrelationships of Father, Son, and Holy Spirit, into which they would soon be initiated:

". . . for everything that I learned from my Father I have made known to you."

Many servants of God never graduate to friendship with Jesus. Why? There is a big difference between a servant-master relationship and a friendship relationship. The former is characterized by duty; the latter, by love. Servants do what is required; friends do whatever it takes.

I think there's another reason that many servants of God never graduate to friendship with Jesus. Too many of us fail to grasp that, before we are servants, we are sons and daughters. Our deepest identity is not that of a servant but of a beloved son or daughter of an adoring Father. The gospel begins at the river where we hear our name and receive the pure, unmerited, unchangeable blessing of adoption. We will only receive the gift of friendship with Jesus to the extent we can embrace the blessing of adoption by the Father—and all of this made palpably real in our experience by the Holy Spirit.

Servanthood is neither the beginning of our identity nor the end of it. Servanthood is the essence of our vocation, the character of our love, and the gift of ourselves to one another. Servanthood, in the words of Thomas à Kempis, is the "royal way of the Holy Cross."

The road to friendship with Jesus begins with the gift of adoption as sons and daughters. We are discipled as servants in the way of the cross. We arrive at the gift of friendship, never graduating from servant work, but raised to the level of holy love. We are transformed in our self-understanding from responsibility to a master to the obedience of love. We become the friends of Jesus to find ourselves no longer his servants but the empowered servants of others.

And then there's this word that takes us all the way back to the beginning:

"You did not choose me, but I chose you and appointed you so that you might go and bear fruit—fruit that will last—and so that whatever you ask in my name the Father will give you."

There's only one thing to do now: love each other.

The Prayer

Abba Father, we thank you for your Son, Jesus, apart from whom we can do nothing and without whom we would never find this royal way. Remind us of our baptism—every single day. Train our minds to serve and transform our hearts by the obedience of love. We need you to take us by the hand and lead us step-by-step. We will follow. Come, Holy Spirit. We pray in Jesus' name, amen.

The Questions

- Do you see how we always simultaneously live in all three of these realities: son/daughter, servant, and friend? Where do you find yourself most challenged today? Think through the story of the prodigal son (Luke 15:11–32) and the two brothers and their confused sense of identity and vocation, and process it through our text. Do you have any insights or see any implications? What do you make of this notion of graduating from being a servant of Jesus to a friend of Jesus, and yet fully commissioned to become a servant of other people? Does this resonate with your understanding and experience? Do you have any pushback?

Why a Hater's Gonna Hate and What Can Be Done about It

88

JOHN 15:18–25 ESV | "If the world hates you, know that it has hated me before it hated you. If you were of the world, the world would love you as its own; but because you are not of the world, but I chose you out of the world, therefore the world hates you. Remember the word that I said to you: 'A servant is not greater than his master.' If they persecuted me, they will also persecute you. If they kept my word, they will also keep yours. But all these things they will do to you on account of my name, because they do not know him who sent me. If I had not come and spoken

to them, they would not have been guilty of sin, but now they have no excuse for their sin. Whoever hates me hates my Father also. If I had not done among them the works that no one else did, they would not be guilty of sin, but now they have seen and hated both me and my Father. But the word that is written in their Law must be fulfilled: 'They hated me without a cause.'"

Consider This

Jesus spent the first seventeen verses of the fifteenth chapter talking about love. He devoted the rest of the chapter to talking about hate. I've always loved the first part of chapter fifteen but never paid the least bit of attention to the rest of it. What's going on here?

Jesus was raising the greatest challenge to love—rejection. The great strategy of hatred is to elicit a reciprocal response. The most sinister strategy of hate, however, is to elicit a preemptive response. Jesus knows the pain of rejection, and he wanted to prevent our retaliating against rejection. Jesus also knows our nature and our natural tendency to want to defend ourselves. Even deeper, he knows our natural tendency to want to protect ourselves from pain. We do this by preemptively rejecting anyone who we perceive may reject us. Not only is preemptive rejection at work in our interpersonal relationships, it lives at the very nerve of all prejudice. This is the essence of prejudice—the preemptive rejection (or prejudgment) of entire groups of people.

Instead of retaliation, or returning rejection for rejection, or, worse, instead of prejudice, or preempting being rejected by rejecting first, Jesus gave us another approach. He showed us what love does in these instances.

First, Jesus told us we can't take hatred or rejection personally. It will feel deeply personal, but you can't take it personally. Why? Because it is not about you, Jesus said—it's about him. And the truth is, Jesus seemed to say, it's not about him—it's about them. And, at the deepest level, it's not about them—it's the world. They belong to the world. They didn't choose the world; the world chose them.

Second, Jesus told us what he does want us to take very personally—that he has chosen us.

As it is, you do not belong to the world, but he has chosen you out of the world.

If we can learn to take Jesus' love personally, not only will we be able to respond to rejection with love, we will be empowered to love preemptively. Wow! At the heart of the heart of the gospel of Jesus Christ is the preemptive love of God. In fact, the reason Jesus is able to love his enemies is because he loved them before they were enemies. Remember John 3:16? "For God so *loved* the *world* that he gave his one and only Son, that whoever believes in him shall not perish but have eternal life" (italics mine).

Or how about Romans 5:8? "But God demonstrates his own love for us in this: While we were still sinners, Christ died for us."

The only way we will ever grow to become preemptive lovers is to grow in the understanding and experience that we are preemptively loved, which is to say: chosen.

The Prayer

Abba Father, we thank you for your Son, Jesus, who not only has chosen us, but who chooses us over and over and over again. Awaken us to our chosenness, that our lives might become sources of awakening for others. Remind us not to take rejection personally. Come, Holy Spirit, and fill us with the preemptive love of Jesus. We pray in his name, amen.

The Questions

- Do you struggle with taking things too personally? Why do you think it is about you? Why might it not be about them? What is your experience of preemptively rejecting other people? Do you tend toward this kind of self-protection? What would it mean to become more aware of this tendency in you? What can you do today, right now, that might move you toward becoming a preemptive lover of other people?

89 Why Aren't We Being Persecuted?

JOHN 16:1–6 | "All this I have told you so that you will not fall away. They will put you out of the synagogue; in fact, the time is coming when anyone who kills you will think they are offering a service to God. They will do such things because they have not known the Father or me. I have told you this, so that

when their time comes you will remember that I warned you about them. I did not tell you this from the beginning because I was with you, but now I am going to him who sent me. None of you asks me, 'Where are you going?' Rather, you are filled with grief because I have said these things."

Consider This

Here in the United States, persecution is a concept we understand, yet it is a non-value. On the contrary, Jesus sets the persecution of his followers as one of the highest values in his kingdom: "Blessed are those who are persecuted because of righteousness, for theirs is the kingdom of heaven" (Matt. 5:10).

To follow Jesus means the inevitability of persecution. So why aren't we in the United States persecuted? Could it be because we have established a form of Christianity that doesn't warrant being persecuted? We live in a value system that most highly prizes comfort; anything that disturbs our comfort and security must be put down. Is it any wonder that we react to the persecution of Christians in other parts of the world by thinking we should somehow stop it—effectively trying to make it a non-value for them too?

Notice what Jesus doesn't say. He does not say that when you are persecuted, he will intervene or make sure someone puts a stop to it. No, he says when you are persecuted, you are blessed in the kingdom of God. Really, he's telling us we should expect it and not be surprised when it happens. So, does Jesus want us to sit by idly while our brothers and sisters are being torn to shreds for their faith in him? I think rather than coming to their defense, he would have us come to their side. At least, I can say that's what it looks like he plans to do:

"I have told you this, so that when their time comes you will remember that I warned you about them."

So, is persecution something we should seek out? Heavens no. We probably should be asking the question: "Why is persecution not seeking us out?" I think it's because we are mostly asleep to what the New Testament considers Christianity.

Awakening is coming, and it will be glorious; however, with it will come persecution. Count on it. It's why Jesus instructs us to count the cost, prepare for it, and not be surprised.

The Prayer

Abba Father, we thank you for your Son, Jesus, who endured our persecution all the way to the cross. Thank you for his incredible prayer in the face of persecution: "Father, forgive them, for they do not know what they are doing" (Luke 23:34). Thank you for this gracious warning he gives us and even more for his promised presence in the midst of such trials. Come, Holy Spirit, and increase our courage. We pray in Jesus' name, amen.

The Questions

- Why aren't we being persecuted for our faith? Why do we feel burdened to eradicate the persecution of Christians, as though that were Jesus' instruction to us? What would it mean for you to prepare for persecution?

Why Jesus Is Not Enough

90

JOHN 16:7–11 | **"But very truly I tell you, it is for your good that I am going away. Unless I go away, the Advocate will not come to you; but if I go, I will send him to you. When he comes, he will prove the world to be in the wrong about sin and righteousness and judgment: about sin, because people do not believe in me; about righteousness, because I am going to the Father, where you can see me no longer; and about judgment, because the prince of this world now stands condemned."**

Consider This

What if Jesus is not enough?

If Jesus is not enough, then there must be more. Is this not what he is saying in today's text?

"But very truly I tell you, it is for your good that I am going away. Unless I go away, the Advocate will not come to you . . ."

Jesus, without the Holy Spirit, is not enough. Or am I missing something? Sure, we can talk about the Holy Spirit's role to point to and magnify Jesus, but is it not right to say that, apart from the Holy Spirit, Jesus is not enough?

It reminds me of that occasion in Ephesus, when the apostle Paul asked them: "Did you receive the Holy Spirit when you believed?" Remember what they said? "They answered, 'No, we have not even heard that there is a Holy Spirit'" (Acts 19:2).

So here we have a church who believed in Jesus but who had no idea of the Holy Spirit. The big question is: Were they even the church? Clearly, Paul considered their belief in Jesus as inferior and not enough.

Believing in Jesus is not enough. We must have the Holy Spirit. In the great Apostles' Creed, we affirm, "I believe in the Holy Spirit."* Do we mean by this that we affirm the reality of the Holy Spirit, or we assent to the truth of the Holy Spirit, or are we placing our real trust in the Holy Spirit?

What if Jesus had never gone to the Father? What if he had never ascended? What if he were still here in the same sense that he was on earth following his resurrection and prior to his ascension? Would we not still remain in an inferior and even incomplete state with respect to our relationship to him? He would be with us but not in us. And maybe that's the point I am laboring to make. It is not enough for Jesus to be with us. He must be within us, and without the Holy Spirit, he cannot be within us.

I am coming to believe, as many of you, that the great awakening we long for will not so much be an awakening to Jesus but an awakening to the Holy Spirit, who is the only one who can awaken us to Jesus.

The Prayer

Abba Father, we thank you for your Son, Jesus, who leads us to the Father and who gives us the gift of the Holy Spirit.

---

* Apostles' Creed: Traditional Version, *United Methodist Hymnal*, #881 (Nashville, TN: United Methodist Publishing House, 1989).

Thank you that, without Jesus, we don't know you, and without the Holy Spirit, we don't know Jesus. Bring us into this holy mystery in an ever-deepening way, that our lives might be filled with the Holy Spirit and so witness the reality of Jesus to others. It is in his name we pray, amen.

The Questions

- Jesus is enough, but apart from the Holy Spirit, is he really? Do you believe there is more to knowing Jesus than you presently know? What holds you back from a fuller knowing of and relationship with the Holy Spirit?

The Threefold Movement of Discipleship to Jesus

91

JOHN 16:12–18 | "I have much more to say to you, more than you can now bear. But when he, the Spirit of truth, comes, he will guide you into all the truth. He will not speak on his own; he will speak only what he hears, and he will tell you what is yet to come. He will glorify me because it is from me that he will receive what he will make known to you. All that belongs to the Father is mine. That is why I said the Spirit will receive from me what he will make known to you."

Jesus went on to say, "In a little while you will see me no more, and then after a little while you will see me."

At this, some of his disciples said to one another, "What does he mean by saying, 'In a little while you will see me no more, and then after a little while you will see me,' and 'Because I am going to the Father'?" They kept asking, "What does he mean by 'a little while'? We don't understand what he is saying."

Consider This

"In a little while you will see me no more, and then after a little while you will see me."

There was never going to be an easy way for Jesus to do this—to explain the eternal verities and incomprehensible mysteries of his presence in the midst of his absence to his disciples. I'm convinced it's why he spent the first two years, eleven months, and twenty-seven days (give or take) working to develop them into the kind of people who were capable of friendship with God. It's no small thing—becoming the kind of person who can be a friend of Jesus.

As previously discussed, this is what discipleship is all about—embracing our adoption as sons and daughters and growing to trust in God as our good Father, being trained to imitate Jesus in the humble way of a servant, and learning to walk in friendship with Jesus in the fellowship of the Holy Spirit.

This is the outline of what I'm calling the threefold movement of discipleship to Jesus. It is as comprehensive as it is simple, and yet it inspires a million questions—like these:

At this, some of his disciples said to one another, "What does he mean by saying, 'In a little while you will see me no more, and then after a little while you will see me,' and 'Because I am going to the Father'?"

This is what the disciples of Jesus do. They put down pretense, confess their ignorance, and ask one another questions in order to grow in their faith and understanding.

They kept asking, "What does he mean by 'a little while'?"

Maybe the biggest insight to be had here is this one: we cannot hope to become the friends of Jesus apart from becoming the friends of one another. It takes the context of real friendship to lay aside our need to know it all and to be right and to be someone other than who we really are. Only friends can make this admission to one another:

"We don't understand what he is saying."

The Prayer

Abba Father, we thank you for your Son, Jesus, who trains us as servants and transforms us as friends. Give us the humility to be honest about what we don't understand and the courage to ask one another. Teach us the way of walking in friendship with a few others that we might grow together as disciples in the fellowship of the Holy Spirit. We pray in Jesus' name, amen.

The Questions

- Where do you find yourself in this discipleship journey—trusting the good Father, imitating Jesus the servant, walking in friendship with Jesus in the fellowship of the Holy Spirit? What kind of people must we become to enjoy friendship with Jesus and with one another? Why is it hard for us to admit to one another that we do not understand?

92 Praying in the Name of Jesus Is Not Magic—Just Miraculous

JOHN 16:19–24 ESV | Jesus knew that they wanted to ask him, so he said to them, "Is this what you are asking yourselves, what I meant by saying, 'A little while and you will not see me, and again a little while and you will see me'? Truly, truly, I say to you, you will weep and lament, but the world will rejoice. You will be sorrowful, but your sorrow will turn into joy. When a woman is giving birth, she has sorrow because her hour has come, but when she has delivered the baby, she no longer remembers the anguish, for joy that a human being has been born into the world. So also you have sorrow now, but I will see you again, and your hearts will rejoice, and no one will take your joy from you. In that day you will ask nothing of me. Truly, truly, I say to you, whatever you ask of the Father in my name, he will give it to you. Until now you have asked nothing in my name. Ask, and you will receive, that your joy may be full."

Consider This

Over these past few chapters Jesus has been careful to repeat himself on a particular issue no less than six times. Did you catch it?

"And I will do whatever you ask in my name, so that the Father may be glorified in the Son." (14:13)

"You may ask me for anything in my name, and I will do it." (14:14)

"If you remain in me and my words remain in you, ask whatever you wish, and it will be done for you." (15:7)

"You did not choose me, but I chose you and appointed you so that you might go and bear fruit—fruit that will last—and so that whatever you ask in my name the Father will give you." (15:16)

"Very truly I tell you, my Father will give you whatever you ask in my name." (16:23b)

"Until now you have not asked for anything in my name. Ask and you will receive, and your joy will be complete." (16:24)

These texts might be filed in the folder labeled: "This is either not true or I am not getting it." Of course, we know they are true, so we must try to ascertain why we aren't getting it. I think it must be a deficiency in our discipleship. Is it any wonder Jesus waits until the end to share these teachings?

It's a weak analogy, but think of it like this: I'm not going to give my children a credit card until I am satisfied they have reached such a level of maturity and character that they can be trusted with such responsibility.

The name of Jesus is an enormous power and an even greater stewardship. Our capacity to steward this kind of power will never exceed our capacity to sublimate our self-interest to the interest of Jesus. That's our problem isn't it: the protection of our own self-interest? Discipleship to Jesus is not about having no self-interest; it's about abiding in a state of trusting surrender to Jesus, who alone satisfies our self-interestedness with the interest of his kingdom. Is this not the meaning of, "Seek first his kingdom and his righteousness, and all these things will be given to you as well" (Matt. 6:33)?

I'm pretty sure this is all true, and even more sure I am ready to start getting it at a whole new level. Praying in the name of Jesus is not magic—just miraculous. And there's a world of difference.

The Prayer

Abba Father, we thank you for your Son, Jesus, who teaches us what it means to abide in his name, to ask and seek and knock and to receive and to find and to have the door opened. Disciple us to the kind of maturity that we live in the flow of your kingdom and discover complete joy. We pray in Jesus' name, amen.

The Questions

- Why do you think Jesus was so explicit and so repetitive about our learning to ask in his name? Why is it so difficult to sublimate our own self-interest to the interest of Jesus? Where are you most challenged in your discipleship today?

The Most Under-Recognized Promise of Jesus

93

JOHN 16:25–33 | "Though I have been speaking figuratively, a time is coming when I will no longer use this kind of language but will tell you plainly about my Father. In that day you will ask in my name. I am not saying that I will ask the Father on your behalf. No, the Father himself loves you because you have loved me and have believed that I came from God. I came from the Father and entered the world; now I am leaving the world and going back to the Father."

Then Jesus' disciples said, "Now you are speaking clearly and without figures of speech. Now we can see that you know all things and that you do not even need to have anyone ask you questions. This makes us believe that you came from God."

"Do you now believe?" Jesus replied. "A time is coming and in fact has come when you will be scattered, each to your own home. You will leave me all alone. Yet I am not alone, for my Father is with me.

"I have told you these things, so that in me you may have peace. In this world you will have trouble. But take heart! I have overcome the world."

Consider This

"In this world you will have trouble."

That's the bumper sticker I want to make. Why? Because the followers of Jesus often get it precisely backward at this point. We think trouble should be the exception, not the rule. As a result, trouble all too often surprises us. We are shocked when something bad happens to us, of all people, the followers of Jesus. It leads to one of the most problematic problems of all time—the problem of evil—and one of the most problematic questions of the modern age: Why do bad things happen to good people? Jesus has a ready response to this question:

"In this world you will have trouble."

Why do bad things happen to good people and why do good things happen to bad people? The first problem with the question is the false premise that we are actually good people. Remember that time when the guy approached Jesus and called him "good teacher," to which Jesus replied, "Why do you call me good? . . . No one is good—except God alone" (see Mark 10:17–18). So, there's that. The second problem with the question is the way it affirms the fundamental value system of karma (i.e., that good things happen to good people and bad things happen to bad people). Remember that time Jesus' disciples queried him about the man born blind, asking him, "Who sinned, this man or his parents?" (John 9:2). In other words, this guy's trouble must be explained by someone's bad behavior somewhere in the past. But Jesus replied, "Neither this man nor his parents sinned" (v. 3a).

It may be the most under-recognized promise in the whole Jesus catalog:

"In this world you will have trouble."

Jesus and the church he's building are not interested in developing philosophical constructs and theological explanations concerning the problem of evil to middle- and upper-class people who believe they are entitled to trouble-free lives. No, the church about which Jesus said "the gates of hell shall not prevail against it" (Matt. 16:18 ESV) is all about fighting evil and overcoming it by the supernatural power of the love of God.

Friends in the Lord, we need to get over it. In this world we will have trouble. We will get cancer. Tragedy will strike our families. Untimely deaths will occur. Our children will endure trauma. At the other end of the spectrum, people will be beheaded simply for their faith in Jesus. Trouble is the unfortunate feature and bitter fruit of the insanely complex, compounded brokenness of the whole fallen creation. It is not an indictment on the goodness of God nor on the faith of his followers.

The big difference on this point is not between people who follow Jesus and people who don't. Trouble is our common lot. The big difference is the people who follow Jesus get to add this tiny little hand grenade of a footnote to our bumper sticker:

"But take heart! I have overcome the world."

Forget the bumper sticker. That's our banner and battle cry. This is the very source of the fountain of eternal joy. This is the gospel, and it is not for later. It is for today, right now, this moment. And millions upon millions of people are yearning not just to hear it but to see it in our lives.

The Prayer

Abba Father, we thank you for your Son, Jesus, who has indeed overcome the world. Translate this truth into the depths of our souls. Shake us free from our indulgent enclaves of comfort in this world. Give us the courage to enter into the trouble of others and the grace to lead them to you who overcome. We pray in Jesus' name, amen.

The Questions

- Do you struggle with the problem of evil in the sense that it keeps you from believing in a good God? Have you labored under the false assumption that because you love God, follow Jesus, and serve other people that you have immunity from trouble in your life and family? Are you ready, in a new way, to face the inevitable reality of trouble, to not be surprised by it, and to be so filled by the Holy Spirit that you show the world what it looks like when Jesus overcomes? What's your next step? What will it look like to "take heart"?

94 When an Hour Is More Than Sixty Minutes

JOHN 17:1–5 ESV | When Jesus had spoken these words, he lifted up his eyes to heaven, and said, "Father, the hour has come; glorify your Son that the Son may glorify you, since you have given him authority over all flesh, to give eternal life to

all whom you have given him. And this is eternal life, that they know you, the only true God, and Jesus Christ whom you have sent. I glorified you on earth, having accomplished the work that you gave me to do. And now, Father, glorify me in your own presence with the glory that I had with you before the world existed."

Consider This

We come now to the end; at least, it is the beginning of the end. Perhaps most aptly, we might say it is the end of the beginning. Remember how this gospel began, "In the beginning was the Word . . ." (1:1).

There is the beginning and there is the end. Here's the burning question: What comes in between?

If you answered, "the middle," you are exactly right and yet have missed the point entirely.

The middle is this murky expanse of chronological time in which the world drifts in and out of sleep, tossed to and fro by the waves of political machinations and the ever-shifting tides of the spirit of the age amid the sounds of rising and falling empires. Everything all at once seems so important and urgent and yet so transient and temporary. The middle is a place of vacuous lostness amid the arrogant certainty and searing conviction of an utterly self-righteous generation.

This middle place is exactly the same today as it was on the day when Jesus spoke these immortal words from his longest prayer. In the messy malaise of this middle, Jesus spoke words that forever shift our sense of time and eternity. Into the wandering abyss of the unresolved middle, Jesus declared kairos with these five words:

"Father, the hour has come."

We have come to the moment of the complete and utter unveiling of his eternal destiny. We are about to witness the absolute and unimaginable shift of the center of the gravity of glory.

There are millennia, centuries, months, weeks, days, and hours. And then there is *the hour*.

You have, no doubt, noticed this recurrent theme through the whole gospel. "My hour has not yet come," Jesus said to his mother at the wedding miracle at Cana of Galilee (2:4). "The hour is coming, and is now here," he told the woman at the well, "when true worshipers will worship the Father in spirit and truth" (4:23). Survey the gospel from chapters 2 to 4 to 5 and 7 and 8 and 12 to 13 and 16 and now 17: "the hour" keeps on coming up.

Into the midst of the muddy, miry, slumbering middle of nowhere and no time—when all "the best laid plans of mice and men go oft awry, and leave us nothing but grief and pain, for promised joy"*—Jesus commands the bell tower of eternity to ring out the carillon chorus of this precipitous prelude:

"Father, the hour has come."

---

* Robert Burns, "To a Mouse," 1785. Public domain.

The hour of eternal life has dawned on the faces of our weary clocks. Here is the mystery: this is no sixty-minute hour. It is an eternal hour, an ever-open, right-here, right-now open window into life. Eternal life breaks into ordinary time.

And what is eternal life? Is it the future we await when our bodies are laid in the ground? No!

"And this is eternal life, that they know you, the only true God, and Jesus Christ whom you have sent."

There are only two realities now. We are either asleep in the middle or awake in *the hour*.

The Prayer

Abba Father, we thank you for your Son, Jesus, whom to know is eternal life. Oh, that we might know him. I want to know Jesus, more today than I did yesterday and more tomorrow than even today. Come, Holy Spirit, and remind us, remind me, that the hour is always now—this hour. We pray in Jesus' name, amen.

The Questions

- How is your conception of eternal life growing? Deepening? How are you finding yourself in the miry muck and muddle of the middle at this time in your life? How might you awaken more deeply to the hour in the midst of the middle? Perhaps you might begin by declaring with Jesus, "Father, the hour has come."

95 The Eleven Most Important Words of Prayer

JOHN 17:6–10 | "I have revealed you to those whom you gave me out of the world. They were yours; you gave them to me and they have obeyed your word. Now they know that everything you have given me comes from you. For I gave them the words you gave me and they accepted them. They knew with certainty that I came from you, and they believed that you sent me. I pray for them. I am not praying for the world, but for those you have given me, for they are yours. All I have is yours, and all you have is mine. And glory has come to me through them."

Consider This

Let's remember John 17 is a prayer. It is easy to sidestep this fact in pursuit of learning other dimensions of what Jesus said here. Jesus was a person of prayer. He did not have a prayer life; rather he lived before us a life of prayer. This is the transition we must make—from a prayer life that fits neatly into our compartmentalized days to a life of prayer that flows in unceasing ways, captivating our consciousness and ever charging our imaginations with the power and possibilities of God in this world. It is to this end that we must immerse ourselves in the life of Jesus. We are his apprentices and there is so much to learn.

As I count them, we have nine distinct recorded prayers from Jesus in the Gospels. By my count, this one from John 17, commonly referred to as "Jesus' High Priestly Prayer," is number six of nine. The final three are his prayers from the cross. I call this one "The Lord's Prayer." And for obvious reasons, the one we commonly call "The Lord's Prayer," I call "The Disciples' Prayer."

My big takeaway about prayer from John 17 this time around comes from these words embedded in verse 10 of today's text. Brace for impact . . .

"All I have is yours, and all you have is mine."

Oh, my goodness! Did you hear that?

"All I have is yours, and all you have is mine."

Is not all of the essence and ethos of prayer itself captured in these eleven words? In fact, can we henceforth refer to this text in a kind of shorthand symbol for our lives of prayer—indeed, for our lives, period? Let us call it "Eleven."

"All I have is yours, and all you have is mine."

"But," you say, "this is Jesus talking to his Father. This is their relationship, not ours." To that I say, no, Jesus is talking to *our* Father, and he wants for us to have the same relationship with the Father as he does. In fact, he brings us on the inside of his relationship with the Father. Reread John 15 and you will see the logic clearly.

"All I have is yours, and all you have is mine."

These eleven words must find their way into the depths of our praying hearts and minds. What if I brought these words to the fore of every prayer? What if these words became my simple everyday, walking-around, breathing prayer?

"All I have is yours, and all you have is mine."

Are you grasping the comprehensive vastness of this? This is like a wedding vow, only spoken to the God of heaven and earth.

"All I have is yours, and all you have is mine."

The Prayer

Abba Father, we thank you for your Son, Jesus. We say with him, "All I have is yours, and all you have is mine." Come, Holy Spirit, and emblazon these words on our hearts until they are our hearts' cry. Help us to grasp this and to understand what in us fights against deeply believing it. We pray in Jesus' name, amen.

The Questions

- "All I have is yours." Is this really something you can say to God without reservation? "All you have is mine." Do you really believe this? Are you ready to weave these words, this prayer, into your life of prayer?

96 The Prayer for Holiness

JOHN 17:11–19 | "I will remain in the world no longer, but they are still in the world, and I am coming to you. Holy Father, protect them by the power of your name, the name you gave me, so that they may be one as we are one. While I was with them, I protected them and kept them safe by that name you

gave me. None has been lost except the one doomed to destruction so that Scripture would be fulfilled.

"I am coming to you now, but I say these things while I am still in the world, so that they may have the full measure of my joy within them. I have given them your word and the world has hated them, for they are not of the world any more than I am of the world. My prayer is not that you take them out of the world but that you protect them from the evil one. They are not of the world, even as I am not of it. Sanctify them by the truth; your word is truth. As you sent me into the world, I have sent them into the world. For them I sanctify myself, that they too may be truly sanctified."

Consider This

I'm not sure if we know this definitively, but I believe Jesus prayed this prayer in the presence of his disciples. Otherwise, how could it have ever been written down? I picture the Twelve there with him and agreeing with amens all along the way.

". . . so that they may have the full measure of my joy within them." YES, LORD! AMEN!

". . . for they are not of the world any more than I am of the world." YES, LORD! AMEN!

"My prayer is not that you take them out of the world but that you protect them from the evil one." YES, LORD! AMEN!

"Sanctify them by the truth; your word is truth." YES, LORD! AMEN!

"As you sent me into the world, I have sent them into the world." YES, LORD! AMEN!

It matters because we are them now. We need to bring our agreements alongside this prayer. Petitions and prayers like these, from the heart and mind of Jesus, spoken by us in agreement in the power of the Spirit . . . well, these are the prayers that go places. They create trajectories of movement deep in our spirits, and they become navigational beacons by which Jesus guides our steps to take us places we would have otherwise never gone.

One in particular I would lift out today: "Sanctify them by the truth; your word is truth." I love that this is verse 17:17. I want us to "rememberize" (both remember and memorize) this one. And let's personalize the pronouns.

"Sanctify [us] by the truth; your word is truth."

"Sanctify [me] by the truth; your word is truth."

"Sanctify [insert names of your band members; loved ones] by the truth; your word is truth."

Sanctify. The word is *hagiazo* (pronounced hag-ee-ad-zo). It's the same word that gets translated in the Disciples' Prayer (a.k.a. the Lord's Prayer) as "hallowed" in "hallowed be your name" (Matt. 6:9). It means "make holy," which unfortunately we tend to think of as "make religious." I think of it as asking for the Lord to make me transcendentally translucent with the brightness of the Holy Spirit in a way that the light of God can shine in and through me with the fiery and brilliant radiance of Jesus—through the totality of who I am as an ordinary human being. To ask to be "sanctified" is to ask for one's life to have the effect of a burning bush—on fire but not consumed, a sight that inspires the awe of God in the awakened and evokes a breathtaking curiosity in those yet asleep.

"Sanctify them by the truth; your word is truth."

We are sanctified by the truth, which is the Word of God. Now, this is the work of the Holy Spirit. But the Spirit of God works by, with, and through the Word of God. To equate this with reading one's Bible is to get at it yet still miss it. The notion here of the Word and Truth is revelation. It is not a flat concept of the Bible as a mere document but the revelation of God as a living Word. Jesus is the Word and the Truth. Holy Scripture is the text by and through which he teaches and trains us in the power of the Spirit. We must have a larger, richer, and deeper awe and appreciation for the Word of God, not as a way of increasing our knowledge, but as a way of increasing our sense of knowing God—which, as we saw earlier in the text, is eternal life.

"Sanctify them by the truth; your word is truth."

The Prayer

Abba Father, we thank you for your Son, Jesus, who perfectly brings together Word and Spirit, grace and truth, prayer and faith. Sanctify us by the truth; your word is truth. Come, Holy Spirit, and sanctify me, Lord. Open the eyes of my heart to perceive your vision for my sanctification. Hallow me, Father, until I am like Jesus, at which point I will be most myself. We pray in Jesus' name, amen.

The Questions

- How are you growing in your understanding of what sanctification is? What did you used to think? What do you believe now? How do you perceive you are being sanctified by the Word of God? Who is a person in your life (either now or in the past) that strikes you as a hallowed person? How so?

97 Why Unity May Not Be the Goal

JOHN 17:20–23 | "My prayer is not for them alone. I pray also for those who will believe in me through their message, that all of them may be one, Father, just as you are in me and I am in you. May they also be in us so that the world may believe that you have sent me. I have given them the glory that you gave me, that they may be one as we are one—I in them and you in me—so that they may be brought to complete unity. Then the world will know that you sent me and have loved them even as you have loved me."

Consider This

Unity. Unity. Unity.

Everyone says this passage is about unity. What if it's not?

What if, in fact, unity is not the point? Here's what it says:

". . . that all of them may be one, Father, just as you are in me and I am in you."

Jesus is praying for our relationships with each other to carry the same essence and ethos as his relationship with his Father. There is a word for this: *love*.

> "As the Father has loved me, so have I loved you. Now remain in my love. If you keep my commands, you will remain in my love, just as I have kept my Father's commands and remain in his love." (John 15:9–10)

Jesus brought the entire program down to one command: "Love each other as I have loved you" (John 15:12).

This text is about love. How can I say that?

Here's why:

". . . so that the world may believe that you have sent me."

It takes us back to another familiar text. Rewind the tape about fourteen chapters: "For God so loved the world that he gave his one and only Son, that whoever believes in him shall not perish but have eternal life" (John 3:16).

The Father puts all the freight and weight of his love for the world on his Son. Jesus puts all the freight and weight of the world's faith on his followers' love for each other. It comes down to our relationships, which is why I am fond of saying, "Our relationships are the mission." It's why we are investing ourselves so deeply in what we call banded discipleship.* We believe Jesus' prayer will only be answered in a big way through being answered in millions and millions of small ways.

Unity is not the goal. It is not even the outcome. The goal is love. The outcome is great awakening.

---

* See Seedbed's discipleshipbands.com for more information.

The Prayer

Abba Father, thank you for your Son, Jesus, who shows us what love is by becoming love incarnate in his relationship with us. Come, Holy Spirit, and make real the love of Jesus in my love for others. Lead me into even one relationship where I can become the life-laying-down love of Jesus for another. In Jesus' name, amen.

The Questions

- What do you make of this reading of the text? Why is it that we tend to think of unity as the goal, and why do we think of unity as the outcome of agreeing with one another? Do any of your relationships approach the character of the relationship between the Father and the Son? Are you becoming love? How so? Where?

98 Unity Comes from Union; Union Does Not Come from Unity

JOHN 17:24–26 ESV | "Father, I desire that they also, whom you have given me, may be with me where I am, to see my glory that you have given me because you loved me before the foundation of the world. O righteous Father, even though the world does not know you, I know you, and these know that you have sent me. I made known to them your name, and I will

continue to make it known, that the love with which you have loved me may be in them, and I in them."

Consider This

Unity without union is like ice cream without cream. Unity does not mean mere togetherness. It does not mean getting along with everyone. It does not mean compromising conviction. It does not mean uniformity of thought. Unity is not something people achieve; rather, it is a gift that can only be received.

"I made known to them your name, and I will continue to make it known, that the love with which you have loved me may be in them, and I in them."

Unity is the fruit of union. Union is the fruit of Jesus' brand of love. Jesus' brand of love is the fruit of deep and trusting obedience. As I read it and see it, the New Testament is concerned about two primary matters: (1) establishing the nature, scope, power, and truth of the gospel of Jesus Christ, and (2) dealing with false teaching coming from the spirit of the age.

So, what does this have to do with unity? It is the gospel of Jesus Christ, which brings supernatural love into the world, which manifests itself in a divine unity within human community, which convinces the world of the way and the truth and the life who is Jesus. The strategy of false teaching is to compromise the truth in the name of love (which is not love) in order to maintain a unity (which is not unity).

You see, there is a way of approaching true doctrine that makes it seem false. And there is a way of approaching false doctrine that makes it seem true. The former are legalistic textualists. The latter are licentious heretics. Both miss Jesus and his gospel in very different yet equally self-righteous ways. The former claim the high ground of truth. The latter claim the high ground of grace. In reality, neither has either.

The reality is grace and truth are not two things. They are one thing. They are, in fact, the love of God in Jesus Christ. They are not principles that can be learned or ideals to be held in tension. They will be lived and experienced in union or not at all, which is why they are only experienced in the living person of Jesus Christ and in a shared, loving union with him. Here is the import of this prayer in John 17. It is why the doctrine of the Trinity is the first and ultimate doctrine of the church.

"I made known to them your name, and I will continue to make it known, that the love with which you have loved me may be in them, and I in them."

The true gospel can never be reduced to a flat doctrine. The true gospel will always lead us into doctrine as a multidimensional dwelling place of revelation. The true gospel is an infinite and eternal expanse of union with God. But, remember, unity comes from union—never the other way around.

The Prayer

Abba Father, we thank you for your Son, Jesus, who is the mystery long hidden and now revealed in and through all who would abandon themselves to him in trusting obedience. Oh, how we need Jesus! Oh, how we desire him! Come,

Holy Spirit, and help us to grasp the mystery of true union with one another in Jesus. Bring us on the inside of it. In Jesus' name, amen.

The Questions

- On which side of things do you tend to err—legalistic textualist or licentious heretic? Why might that be? What is it about you that would cause you to miss the mark in this particular way? True gospel and false teaching. Does this help clarify the landscape all around us today on so many fronts?

Why Your Gospel May Be Too Small

99

JOHN 18:1–9 ESV | When Jesus had spoken these words, he went out with his disciples across the brook Kidron, where there was a garden, which he and his disciples entered. Now Judas, who betrayed him, also knew the place, for Jesus often met there with his disciples. So Judas, having procured a band of soldiers and some officers from the chief priests and the Pharisees, went there with lanterns and torches and weapons. Then Jesus, knowing all that would happen to him, came forward and said to them, "Whom do you seek?" They answered him, "Jesus of Nazareth." Jesus said to them, "I am he." Judas, who betrayed him, was standing with them. When

Jesus said to them, "I am he," they drew back and fell to the ground. So he asked them again, "Whom do you seek?" And they said, "Jesus of Nazareth." Jesus answered, "I told you that I am he. So, if you seek me, let these men go." This was to fulfill the word that he had spoken: "Of those whom you gave me I have lost not one."

Consider This

It has been said that the Gospels are passion narratives with long introductions. Let's resist this characterization, as it implies the gospel of Jesus Christ can be reduced to three days of his life—that everything that came before was simply preliminary.

The word *gospel* simply means "good news." When we reduce the gospel to the crucifixion, death, and resurrection of Jesus, we unwittingly reduce the passion of Jesus to a single transactional event. This has the further unintended consequence of reducing salvation to a single transactional experience: (1) Jesus died on the cross for my sins, (2) I accept his gift on my behalf, and (3) I am saved. It's true as far as it goes. It just stops way short of the gospel of Jesus Christ.

How about we frame it a bit larger? What if we thought of the passion of Jesus as the gospel of Jesus? Only, the passion of Jesus was far more than three days in world history. What if the passion of Jesus is as old as the Son of God, which is to say, eternal? After all, doesn't the Bible refer to Jesus as the Lamb slain from before the foundation of the world (Rev. 13:8)? What if our idea of the gospel is just too small? What if the passion of Jesus doesn't begin at John 18:1 but John 1:1? "In the beginning was the Word, and the Word was with God, and the Word was God. He was with God in the beginning" (John 1:1–2).

I have always been intrigued by Paul's way of putting it: "For if, while we were God's enemies, we were reconciled to him through the death of his Son, how much more, having been reconciled, shall we be saved through his life!" (Rom. 5:10).

The Prayer

Abba Father, thank you for your Son, Jesus, whose eternal preexistence, conception, birth, childhood, life, words, deeds, signs, sayings, suffering, death, resurrection, ascension, and return are his passion, which are the gospel. Come, Holy Spirit, and open our hearts and minds to conceive of this in a far deeper way than we have before. We pray in Jesus' name, amen.

The Questions

- Is your gospel too small? The unchanging nature of salvation is by grace through faith (see Ephesians 2:8–9). But what if the scope of salvation is far greater than we have realized? What are the implications of the passion of Jesus being the whole gospel rather than the last few chapters?

100 Why Standing Up for Jesus May Not Be the Right Thing to Do

JOHN 18:10–18 ESV | Then Simon Peter, having a sword, drew it and struck the high priest's servant and cut off his right ear. (The servant's name was Malchus.) So Jesus said to Peter, "Put your sword into its sheath; shall I not drink the cup that the Father has given me?"

So the band of soldiers and their captain and the officers of the Jews arrested Jesus and bound him. First they led him to Annas, for he was the father-in-law of Caiaphas, who was high priest that year. It was Caiaphas who had advised the Jews that it would be expedient that one man should die for the people.

Simon Peter followed Jesus, and so did another disciple. Since that disciple was known to the high priest, he entered with Jesus into the courtyard of the high priest, but Peter stood outside at the door. So the other disciple, who was known to the high priest, went out and spoke to the servant girl who kept watch at the door, and brought Peter in. The servant girl at the door said to Peter, "You also are not one of this man's disciples, are you?" He said, "I am not." Now the servants and officers had made a charcoal fire, because it was cold, and they were standing and warming themselves. Peter also was with them, standing and warming himself.

Consider This

This text presents a fascinating pairing of courage and cowardice in the person of Peter. Peter, who said he would fight to the death with Jesus (John 13:37; Matt. 26:35; Mark 14:31; Luke 22:33), seemed to make good on his promise as he drew his sword to defend him. However, within the hour he would disavow knowing him. What on earth was going on here?

Does this come down to our own self-interest? Peter rose to the occasion as the public hero yet slinked into the shadows when his private loyalty promised no gain. Peter was ready to go all in when he thought he could win, but he folded his cards when he knew defeat was imminent. Why do we defend Jesus when it serves our own interest, yet deny him when it serves only his? It is because we have surrendered to our enemy instead of to our friend.

Do you remember the old hymn "Stand Up for Jesus"?

Stand up, stand up for Jesus,
ye soldiers of the cross;
lift high his royal banner,
it must not suffer loss.
From vict'ry unto vict'ry
his army he shall lead,
till ev'ry foe is vanquished,
*and Christ is Lord indeed.**

---

* George Duffield, "Stand Up, Stand Up, for Jesus, Ye Soldiers of the Cross," 1858. Public domain.

I think our big problem is we think we are the ones to vindicate Jesus, when the truth is he needs no vindication. There is a way of standing up for Jesus wherein we do so to vindicate ourselves. We are not the soldiers of the cross. We are the friends of Jesus. We do not vindicate Jesus when we fight for him; he vindicates us when we suffer loss with him.

The apostle Paul knew this well. He had given his life to be the great vindicator of God. No one stood up for God more than the pre-Paul Saul. His sole ambition? To vanquish the foes of God. Then he met Jesus, who knocked him off his horse. After that, everything changed. Paul went from God's lawyer to Jesus' friend. He did not stand up for Jesus; he laid down his life for him. He did not fight for Jesus; he suffered with him. He did not hate the enemies of God; he loved them to the very end.

In what is perhaps the most glorious expression of holy ambition in the history of the church, Paul put it like this: "I want to know Christ—yes, to know the power of his resurrection and participation in his sufferings, becoming like him in his death, and so, somehow, attaining to the resurrection from the dead" (Phil. 3:10–11).

Jesus didn't need Peter to stand up for him. He needed him to suffer with him. The same is true for us.

The Prayer

Abba Father, thank you for your Son, Jesus, who needs no vindication. Forgive us for standing for him when it serves our self-interest yet failing to suffer with him when it serves him alone. Come, Holy Spirit, and bring us into the fellowship of the cross, which is the friendship of Jesus. We do not grasp this. Give us the courage to get off our high horse and come low to the ground before you. We pray in Jesus' name, amen.

The Questions

- Ruminate on Paul's words. Personalize them as your own prayer. As we proceed to the cross, let them become the royal banner we lift high. What is "participation in his sufferings," in your understanding? What holds you back from this? Do you feel like you need to vindicate Jesus? Are you ready and willing to be vindicated by Jesus? Are you ready to take truer steps toward "becoming like him in his death"?

Method Acting vs. Role Play and the Call to Discipleship

101

JOHN 18:19–27 ESV | The high priest then questioned Jesus about his disciples and his teaching. Jesus answered him, "I have spoken openly to the world. I have always taught in synagogues and in the temple, where all Jews come together. I have said nothing in secret. Why do you ask me? Ask those who have heard me what I said to them; they know what I said." When he had said these things, one of the officers standing by

struck Jesus with his hand, saying, "Is that how you answer the high priest?" Jesus answered him, "If what I said is wrong, bear witness about the wrong; but if what I said is right, why do you strike me?" Annas then sent him bound to Caiaphas the high priest.

Now Simon Peter was standing and warming himself. So they said to him, "You also are not one of his disciples, are you?" He denied it and said, "I am not." One of the servants of the high priest, a relative of the man whose ear Peter had cut off, asked, "Did I not see you in the garden with him?" Peter again denied it, and at once a rooster crowed.

Consider This

Let's begin today where we ended yesterday, with Paul's declaration of intent: "I want to know Christ—yes, to know the power of his resurrection and participation in his sufferings, becoming like him in his death, and so, somehow, attaining to the resurrection from the dead" (Phil. 3:10–11).

Jesus will always be betrayed. Jesus will always be ambushed. Jesus will always be dragged before the authorities. Jesus will always be slapped around by the officials. Jesus will always be questioned by the establishment. Jesus will always be condemned by the crowd. And, yes, Jesus will always be denied by his disciples. This passion of Jesus is not the drama of a long time ago in a galaxy far, far away. The names have changed, but all of these players are still on the stage.

There are many roles to be occupied and parts to be played, but there is only one script for the friends of Jesus. Paul captures it in his declaration, "I want to know Christ" (Phil. 3:10a).

While the world around us plays its various parts, the friends of Jesus are not role-playing at all. They are method actors. Method acting is not about role-playing but identity formation. The method actor literally takes on the identity of the character. Reminiscent of Paul's exhortation to have the same mind in you that was in Christ Jesus (see Philippians 2:5), method actors take on the minds of the characters they are playing. As we continue this slow walk to the cross with Jesus, let's dwell together in this declaration until we have made it our own: "I want to know Christ—yes, to know the power of his resurrection and participation in his sufferings, becoming like him in his death, and so, somehow, attaining to the resurrection from the dead" (Phil. 3:10–11).

The Prayer

Abba Father, thank you for your Son, Jesus, who disciples us until we share in his very character. Shatter the thin role-playing exercises we have settled for and mistaken as our faith. Take us deep into the fellowship of his sufferings. Lead us to become like him in his death, that we might truly live. We pray in Jesus' name, amen.

The Questions

- What do you think of this concept of method acting as a model for discipleship? What might it mean for you to become like Jesus in his death at this point in your life? Where is that place of struggle right now? Are you working to internalize Paul's declaration of intent? Dwell on it. Immerse yourself in it.

102 When Religion Is the Problem

JOHN 18:28–36 | Then the Jewish leaders took Jesus from Caiaphas to the palace of the Roman governor. By now it was early morning, and to avoid ceremonial uncleanness they did not enter the palace, because they wanted to be able to eat the Passover. So Pilate came out to them and asked, "What charges are you bringing against this man?"

"If he were not a criminal," they replied, "we would not have handed him over to you."

Pilate said, "Take him yourselves and judge him by your own law."

"But we have no right to execute anyone," they objected. This took place to fulfill what Jesus had said about the kind of death he was going to die.

Pilate then went back inside the palace, summoned Jesus and asked him, "Are you the king of the Jews?"

"Is that your own idea," Jesus asked, "or did others talk to you about me?"

"Am I a Jew?" Pilate replied. "Your own people and chief priests handed you over to me. What is it you have done?"

Jesus said, "My kingdom is not of this world. If it were, my servants would fight to prevent my arrest by the Jewish leaders. But now my kingdom is from another place."

Consider This

Jesus is a problem for religious people. He is a nuisance, an irritant, in the way, a problem. He does not fit because he will not get with the program. He is a threat to the status quo, not because of anything he does, but by the sheer fact of being who he is. This is why the seven "I Am" declarations of Jesus figure so prominently in John's gospel.

Religious people want Jesus to fit into and serve their religion, which is to say the particular set of beliefs, values, practices, and programs to which they turn to bring order to their chaos, make sense of their existence, and otherwise enhance their lives. Religion and religious systems have a way of fitting God into the boxes and spaces we create in our lives to contain him—only God will not be contained.

We see this at work in one of the supreme ironies in Scripture in today's text:

Then the Jewish leaders took Jesus from Caiaphas to the palace of the Roman governor. By now it was early morning, and to avoid ceremonial uncleanness they did not enter the palace, because they wanted to be able to eat the Passover.

It didn't start this way. It never does. We are talking about the Passover, for crying out loud, which, prior to the resurrection of Jesus, was the single most cataclysmic, defining event in the history of the world: the miraculous deliverance of the households marked by the blood of the lamb; the enormity of Egyptian agony over the defeat of Pharaoh and the death of the firstborn; the frantic, panicked escape in the middle of the night, only to meet their apparent end with their backs against the wall of the sea.

By now it was early morning, and to avoid ceremonial uncleanness they did not enter the palace, because they wanted to be able to eat the Passover.

Sometimes, in order to have a nice Passover party we need to get Jesus out of the way.

Sometimes profundity can only be expressed through profanity. It's why I'm stopping now. This is one of those times.

The Prayer

Abba Father, thank you for your Son, Jesus, who is not only our Passover, but who is *the* Passover. Deliver us from the vanity of our rites and rituals, that we might be awakened to the vileness in our souls which led to the violence of the cross. We pray in Jesus' name, amen.

The Questions

- How does this strike you . . . dispensing with Jesus in order to get to the Passover celebration? Can you see how our own religious ceremony can actually obscure Jesus? Has faith become a project for you? A life-enhancement or self-improvement program? What will it take to break free from this? Has church and the way you do church become something of a box or compartment for God in your life? What can be done about this?

The Right Side of History or the Right Side of Truth?

103

JOHN 18:37–40 ESV | Then Pilate said to him, "So you are a king?" Jesus answered, "You say that I am a king. For this purpose I was born and for this purpose I have come into the world—to bear witness to the truth. Everyone who is of the truth listens to my voice." Pilate said to him, "What is truth?"

After he had said this, he went back outside to the Jews and told them, "I find no guilt in him. But you have a custom that I should release one man for you at the Passover. So do you want me to release to you the King of the Jews?" They cried out again, "Not this man, but Barabbas!" Now Barabbas was a robber.

Consider This

I grew up thinking Barabbas was a bad guy. You know, just another garden-variety criminal. I thought the people hated Jesus so much they would rather let a convicted murderer go free than save him. It turns out Barabbas was more of a freedom-fighter type, an insurrectionist, a hero who had taken one for the team. The people loved Barabbas. He was probably something of a minor celebrity among them. He would make an excellent Passover gift.

And isn't it interesting how the Roman governor had a custom of observing the Jewish Passover by releasing one of their prisoners? It's kind of like he was the agent of the Passover, pardoning a criminal in celebration. It's all such a joke. Did Pilate have any idea what the Passover meant? Did he know it was the downfall of Pharaoh? He couldn't have cared less. The Jews were nothing to Pilate and less than nothing to Caesar. Releasing Barabbas was like throwing them a bone to get them out of his hair.

Meanwhile, back at the palace, Pontius Pilate, mid-level political appointee that he was, engaged in what must have seemed like yet another of the most inconsequential conversations of his career. Little did he know this interaction with another convicted criminal would ultimately make him more famous than Caesar. Pilate patronized him:

"So you are a king?"

Listen to what Jesus said to him:

"You say that I am a king. For this purpose I was born and for this purpose I have come into the world—to bear witness to the truth. Everyone who is of the truth listens to my voice."

Pilate said to him, "What is truth?"

My translation of Pilate's retort: "Whatever!"

Isn't that always the world's posture toward the truth? Whatever!

"Everyone who is of the truth listens to my voice."

Truth has a side. These days everybody wants to be on the right side of history. No one seems to care too much about being on the right side of the truth.

Truth has a side. We must find our way there.

The Prayer

Abba Father, thank you for your Son, Jesus, who not only teaches us the truth, but who is, himself, the Truth. Grant us the humility to love the Truth and the courage to stand by his side no matter what. We pray in Jesus' name, amen.

The Questions

- How would we know we were on the side of Truth? How do you respond to the question "What is truth?" Is it possible to be on the right side of history without being on the right side of Truth?

Pontius Pilate and the Politician in Us All

104

JOHN 19:1–11 ESV | Then Pilate took Jesus and flogged him. And the soldiers twisted together a crown of thorns and put it

on his head and arrayed him in a purple robe. They came up to him, saying, "Hail, King of the Jews!" and struck him with their hands. Pilate went out again and said to them, "See, I am bringing him out to you that you may know that I find no guilt in him." So Jesus came out, wearing the crown of thorns and the purple robe. Pilate said to them, "Behold, the man!" When the chief priests and the officers saw him, they cried out, "Crucify him, crucify him!" Pilate said to them, "Take him yourselves and crucify him, for I find no guilt in him." The Jews answered him, "We have a law, and according to that law he ought to die because he has made himself the Son of God." When Pilate heard this statement, he was even more afraid. He entered his headquarters again and said to Jesus, "Where are you from?" But Jesus gave him no answer. So Pilate said to him, "You will not speak to me? Do you not know that I have authority to release you and authority to crucify you?" Jesus answered him, "You would have no authority over me at all unless it had been given you from above. Therefore he who delivered me over to you has the greater sin."

Consider This

Why do we love to hate Pontius Pilate? He didn't start anything. He had no dog in the fight. It actually seemed like he wanted to help Jesus. Peter, Jesus' number-one disciple, denied him three times. Pontius Pilate, who didn't know Jesus from Adam and who stood to gain nothing from releasing him, tried to save him three times. Everything was perfectly backward.

Pilate is a case study on why people disdain politicians. He was a man who was long on conviction and short on courage. He wanted to stand on principle, yet he wanted to please people. His ultimate interest, however, was in protecting himself by preserving his power.

Have you ever noticed how what we most despise in others is what we hate most about ourselves?

The Prayer

Abba Father, thank you for your Son, Jesus, whose character is the union of conviction and courage. Make it so with us. We pray in Jesus' name, amen.

The Questions

- What do you think of Pontius Pilate? Does your courage measure up to your convictions?

I Pledge Allegiance to the . . .

105

JOHN 19:12–22 ESV | From then on Pilate sought to release him, but the Jews cried out, "If you release this man, you are not Caesar's friend. Everyone who makes himself a king opposes Caesar." So when Pilate heard these words, he brought Jesus out and sat down on the judgment seat at a place called The Stone Pavement, and in Aramaic Gabbatha. Now it was the

day of Preparation of the Passover. It was about the sixth hour. He said to the Jews, "Behold your King!" They cried out, "Away with him, away with him, crucify him!" Pilate said to them, "Shall I crucify your King?" The chief priests answered, "We have no king but Caesar." So he delivered him over to them to be crucified.

So they took Jesus, and he went out, bearing his own cross, to the place called The Place of a Skull, which in Aramaic is called Golgotha. There they crucified him, and with him two others, one on either side, and Jesus between them. Pilate also wrote an inscription and put it on the cross. It read, "Jesus of Nazareth, the King of the Jews." Many of the Jews read this inscription, for the place where Jesus was crucified was near the city, and it was written in Aramaic, in Latin, and in Greek. So the chief priests of the Jews said to Pilate, "Do not write, 'The King of the Jews,' but rather, 'This man said, I am King of the Jews.'" Pilate answered, "What I have written I have written."

Consider This

"We have no king but Caesar."

We might expect to hear this in the courts of Rome but not in the streets of Jerusalem.

How many times that very day had they uttered the words they prayed every day?

Barukh ata Adonai Eloheinu, melekh ha`olam, which means, "Blessed are you, Lord our God, the King of the universe."

Yet when it mattered most, they declared their allegiance to Caesar.

They might as well have been saying, "We have no king but Pharaoh."

Later that night they would sing the songs of Passover: "It is better to take refuge in the Lord than to trust in humans. It is better to take refuge in the Lord than to trust in princes" (Ps. 118:8–9).

"We have no king but Caesar."

Their conversion to the dark side was now complete—they had gone from God as their King to God granting their wishes for a king and, finally, to pledging their allegiance to Caesar as their king.

Meanwhile, the King of kings was being led to slaughter.

That night, those same devout voices would close their prayers, captaining their praise with these fateful words of ironic prophecy: "The stone the builders rejected has become the cornerstone; the Lord has done this, and it is marvelous in our eyes" (Ps. 118:22–23).

The Prayer

Blessed are you, O Lord our God, the King of the universe, for you have given us in your own Son, the King of kings and the Lord of lords, the stone the builders rejected—indeed, the chief cornerstone. You have done this, and it is marvelous in our eyes. We pray in his name, amen.

The Questions

- Do you find all of this as incredulous as I do—the leaders of God's own people giving allegiance to Caesar as king while crucifying the King of kings? Does this have any influence or sense of warning about our own relationship to the secular power of the state and its leaders? Did you realize the common pledge of allegiance in those days was "Caesar is Lord"? How does that impact your understanding of the claim "Jesus is Lord"?

106 It Is Finished! What Is "It"?

JOHN 19:23–30 | When the soldiers had crucified Jesus, they took his garments and divided them into four parts, one part for each soldier; also his tunic. But the tunic was seamless, woven in one piece from top to bottom, so they said to one another, "Let us not tear it, but cast lots for it to see whose it shall be." This was to fulfill the Scripture which says,

> **"They divided my garments among them,**
> **and for my clothing they cast lots."**

So the soldiers did these things, but standing by the cross of Jesus were his mother and his mother's sister, Mary the wife of Clopas, and Mary Magdalene. When Jesus saw his mother and the disciple whom he loved standing nearby, he said to

his mother, "Woman, behold, your son!" Then he said to the disciple, "Behold, your mother!" And from that hour the disciple took her to his own home.

After this, Jesus, knowing that all was now finished, said (to fulfill the Scripture), "I thirst." A jar full of sour wine stood there, so they put a sponge full of the sour wine on a hyssop branch and held it to his mouth. When Jesus had received the sour wine, he said, "It is finished," and he bowed his head and gave up his spirit.

Consider This

What, exactly, is finished? Listen to the inspired witnesses and writers of Scripture. Read very slowly that you might listen very carefully:

> When you were dead in your sins and in the uncircumcision of your flesh, God made you alive with Christ. He forgave us all our sins, having canceled the charge of our legal indebtedness, which stood against us and condemned us; he has taken it away, nailing it to the cross. And having disarmed the powers and authorities, he made a public spectacle of them, triumphing over them by the cross. (Col. 2:13–15)

> "He himself bore our sins" in his body on the cross, so that we might die to sins and live for righteousness; "by his wounds you have been healed." For "you were like sheep going astray," but now you have

returned to the Shepherd and Overseer of your souls. (1 Peter 2:24–25)

God made him who had no sin to be sin for us, so that in him we might become the righteousness of God. (2 Cor. 5:21)

Therefore, there is now no condemnation for those who are in Christ Jesus, because through Christ Jesus the law of the Spirit who gives life has set you free from the law of sin and death. For what the law was powerless to do because it was weakened by the flesh, God did by sending his own Son in the likeness of sinful flesh to be a sin offering. And so he condemned sin in the flesh, in order that the righteous requirement of the law might be fully met in us, who do not live according to the flesh but according to the Spirit. (Rom. 8:1–4)

But because of his great love for us, God, who is rich in mercy, made us alive with Christ even when we were dead in transgressions—it is by grace you have been saved. (Eph. 2:4–5)

The Prayer

Abba Father, we thank you for your Son, Jesus, who is the author, the pioneer, and the perfecter of our faith. Thank you for finishing what we could never complete and for opening this door for us that can never be closed. We pray in Jesus' name, amen.

The Questions

- How could something so cosmically significant as Jesus' death on the cross be so completely invisible to those gathered at the scene? Choose a verse or phrase from the highlighted Scriptures and focus on it, dwell on it, meditate on it. Which one will you choose? "It is finished!" What is the significance of these words of Jesus for you today?

The Problem with Our Crosses

107

JOHN 19:31–37 | **Now it was the day of Preparation, and the next day was to be a special Sabbath. Because the Jewish leaders did not want the bodies left on the crosses during the Sabbath, they asked Pilate to have the legs broken and the bodies taken down. The soldiers therefore came and broke the legs of the first man who had been crucified with Jesus, and then those of the other. But when they came to Jesus and found that he was already dead, they did not break his legs. Instead, one of the soldiers pierced Jesus' side with a spear, bringing a sudden flow of blood and water. The man who saw it has given testimony, and his testimony is true. He knows that he tells the truth, and he testifies so that you also may believe. These things happened so that the scripture would be fulfilled: "Not one of his bones will be broken," and, as another scripture says, "They will look on the one they have pierced."**

Consider This

"They will look on the one they have pierced."

When is the last time you looked upon the one we have pierced?

We Protestants are big on the cross but not so much on the crucifix. Why is that? For a faith built around the blood of Christ, we like our crosses pretty clean. The trouble is, this scene was anything but clean.

Instead, one of the soldiers pierced Jesus' side with a spear, bringing a sudden flow of blood and water.

We gladly sing of surveying "the wondrous cross,"* but when it comes down to it, there's not a lot of surveying going on.

The empty cross declares life and resurrection. The crucifix declares suffering and death. Don't we need both? Is this not at least part of the reason the gospel writers gave us such graphic details? It brings us back to Paul's declaration of longing we visited earlier: "I want to know Christ—yes, to know the power of his resurrection and participation in his sufferings, becoming like him in his death, and so, somehow, attaining to the resurrection from the dead" (Phil. 3:10–11).

Might it not aid us to share in the fellowship of his sufferings to, at minimum, be intimately familiar with them? Might we be well served to embrace the painful blessing of looking

---

* Isaac Watts, "When I Survey the Wondrous Cross," 1707. Public domain.

on the one we have pierced? Might it be time for the Protestant part of the church to learn to behold the Pierced One?

Years ago, when my oldest son was young, I kept a small statue of Jesus on the cross on my desk. One day he picked up the little crucifix, and as he pondered it with his small fingers, he asked me, "Daddy, what is this for? How do we use this?" The question arrested me. As I began to respond—probably with some ridiculous answer—he interrupted me, saying, "Or, Daddy, is this for looking at?"

Abandoning my Sunday school answer, I replied to him, "Yes, David. That's exactly right. This is for looking at."

The Prayer

Abba Father, we thank you for your Son, Jesus, who endured the cross as the supreme act of love for us. Grant us fresh eyes to look upon the one we have pierced, to behold him in his suffering, that we might somehow become like him in his death. Come, Holy Spirit, and lead us in this way that leads to real resurrection power. We pray in Jesus' name, amen.

The Questions

- Do you own a crucifix? If not, why not? If so, how do you relate to/handle it? Why do we resist the sign of the crucifix? Is it latent (or active) anti-Catholic bias? Is that a good reason? Will you develop a practice of looking on the one we have pierced? Do you see the importance of this? Why or why not?

108 The Difference between Respectable and Respect

JOHN 19:38–42 | Later, Joseph of Arimathea asked Pilate for the body of Jesus. Now Joseph was a disciple of Jesus, but secretly because he feared the Jewish leaders. With Pilate's permission, he came and took the body away. He was accompanied by Nicodemus, the man who earlier had visited Jesus at night. Nicodemus brought a mixture of myrrh and aloes, about seventy-five pounds. Taking Jesus' body, the two of them wrapped it, with the spices, in strips of linen. This was in accordance with Jewish burial customs. At the place where Jesus was crucified, there was a garden, and in the garden a new tomb, in which no one had ever been laid. Because it was the Jewish day of Preparation and since the tomb was nearby, they laid Jesus there.

Consider This

We don't know a lot about Joseph of Arimathea, but we tend to like him. I wonder, though, would we like him if he hadn't shown up at the cross and taken care of the body of Jesus?

It seems up to that point Joseph had a lot of "want to" when it came to doing the right thing, but he had a lot more "need for" when it came to being recognized for doing the respectable thing. Joseph, like so many men (and women) was more interested in being respectable than actually being respected:

Now Joseph was a disciple of Jesus, but secretly because he feared the Jewish leaders.

It's interesting how living in fear of other people creates this condition. We conform to the expectations of others in order to maintain our respectability with them. We don't respect them; we fear them. And the truth is, they don't respect us either. Meanwhile, we live in the shared self-deception of respectability. One doesn't receive respect from working to be respected; one gets respectability.

Truth be told, we don't really know too many Peter, James, and John characters. We know tons of Joseph and Nicodemus types. They run our towns, our local governments, and civic organizations. They usher at church, teach Sunday school, and generally do what is expected of them. We are good, God-fearing, respectable people. Our respectability gives us access to both the chief priest and the chief justice. We are as at home in the chamber of commerce as we are in the church. And all of this can be quite good.

I'm trying to point out a critical distinction between crowd-level churchmanship and courage-based discipleship. The difference is respectability versus real respect. We will never stop talking about Joseph of Arimathea and Nicodemus—not because of their high standing in the community, but because they stepped out of the shadows of their secret discipleship and comfortable reputations and did something courageous.

This was not a self-interested act of community service. They had no notion of any impending resurrection. Because they broke ranks with respectable religion and associated themselves with a crucified Messiah, they will live in the eternal respect of the risen Lord (and ours).

The Prayer

Abba Father, we thank you for your Son, Jesus, who walked into the world of respectable religion and called us to follow him into courageous discipleship. Awaken us to this opportunity and let us never look back. We pray in Jesus' name, amen.

The Questions

- Why is respectability so seductive? What is the difference between wearing your religion on your sleeve and being publicly associated with Jesus? What do you think of this distinction between respectability and respect? What are we afraid of?

109 Why the Resurrection Must Mean More

JOHN 20:1–7 ESV | Now on the first day of the week Mary Magdalene came to the tomb early, while it was still dark, and saw that the stone had been taken away from the tomb. So she ran and went to Simon Peter and the other disciple, the one whom Jesus loved, and said to them, "They have taken the Lord out of the tomb, and we do not know where they

have laid him." So Peter went out with the other disciple, and they were going toward the tomb. Both of them were running together, but the other disciple outran Peter and reached the tomb first. And stooping to look in, he saw the linen cloths lying there, but he did not go in. Then Simon Peter came, following him, and went into the tomb. He saw the linen cloths lying there, and the face cloth, which had been on Jesus' head, not lying with the linen cloths but folded up in a place by itself.

Consider This

We miss the shocking surprise of the resurrection of Jesus because our hindsight will not allow us to linger in the stunning sting of his death. I mean, just when you thought things could not get any worse, they get worse.

We don't commonly make this connection, but Easter actually began with more bad news. Mary Magdalene left her home in the darkness of Sunday morning to meet the dawn of a new day of grief. She found the tomb, but Jesus' body was gone.

Where did we get the idea that Mary was going to the first Easter sunrise service? It never dawned on her (or anyone else) that Jesus was alive. Clearly someone had stolen his body. The ultimate insult now followed the ultimate injury.

For us, the resurrection of Jesus is like being in on the surprise of our surprise birthday party. It's hard to be surprised when you know it is going to happen. There's just no way to un-know it.

On the other hand, we have all lived through or are living in situations that keep getting worse. I'm trying to ask a question here I can hardly even understand. What if the resurrection of Jesus actually creates the possibility for an alternate reality just on the other side of any hopeless situation? We think we are on the way to the grief of a grave, but what if we are seeing the situation all wrong? What if the resurrection of Jesus doesn't just defeat death; what if it reverses it? In other words, where sin and death once ruled, love and life would now reign. It would mean no situation or scenario would be too difficult for God—that nothing would be impossible.

The gospel must mean more than the indefinite extension of one's life beyond their physical death. After all, death is more than the event at the end of your life. Death is the pervasive force of darkness that, as the poet Tom Hennen says, "sticks to everything."

In the resurrection of Jesus Christ, the power of the gospel has unleashed the reality of eternity from the future, restoring it to the present into the lives of all who will not just believe and walk over the line, but who will live over the line—who won't just be born again, but who will grow up into this new life. This is the life Jesus came to reveal and now lives to release into all creation.

The Prayer

Abba Father, we thank you for your Son, Jesus, who has defeated death, not just the finality of the event of death, but the very principality of death. Enlarge our understanding of his resurrection, that we might not just hope for it but live into it. Come, Holy Spirit, and awaken us anew. We pray in Jesus' name, amen.

The Questions

- How does the advantage of historical hindsight prove a disadvantage for us when approaching the tomb of Jesus? What do you think? Is the gospel more than the indefinite extension of life beyond the grave? If so, what? What does it mean that death, beyond just the event of death, is defeated?

Why the Empty Tomb Is Not Enough

110

JOHN 20:8–14 | **Finally the other disciple, who had reached the tomb first, also went inside. He saw and believed. (They still did not understand from Scripture that Jesus had to rise from the dead.) Then the disciples went back to where they were staying.**

Now Mary stood outside the tomb crying. As she wept, she bent over to look into the tomb and saw two angels in white, seated where Jesus' body had been, one at the head and the other at the foot.

They asked her, "Woman, why are you crying?"

"They have taken my Lord away," she said, "and I don't know where they have put him." At this, she turned around and saw Jesus standing there, but she did not realize that it was Jesus.

Consider This

They came. They saw. *[They] went back to where they were staying.*

Over the centuries we have developed the impression that Easter was a slam-dunk reality. Everyone woke up early. Someone said, "He is risen," and everyone else responded, "He is risen indeed." And then everyone went to the country club for lunch.

It was not that way.

Finally the other disciple, who had reached the tomb first, also went inside. He saw and believed.

I always read this verse to mean the disciple believed Jesus was raised from the dead. It means he believed someone had taken Jesus' body from the tomb. Look what happened next.

Then the disciples went back to where they were staying.

They came. They saw. They went back home.

Though the resurrection happened suddenly, Easter itself is a slow-rising reality. It's one thing to believe the tomb is empty, yet quite another to believe Jesus is risen from the dead.

The question we must ask ourselves is this one: Is our faith built on an empty tomb or on a risen Lord? That the tomb is empty is not an article of faith; it is a fact of history. We can go and see it today. The empty tomb was enough to get the disciples to come and see and go back home. Neither is the resurrection of Jesus a spiritual phenomenon—something that must be experienced to be believed.

The circumstantial evidence of the empty tomb is good but inadequate. The inner experience of a spiritual resurrection is nice but not enough. The Christian faith is built on nothing more and nothing less than the physical, bodily resurrection of Jesus Christ from the dead. It either happened or it did not. If it did, the implications are mind-bogglingly unfathomable. If it did not, we are fools.

This is not my truth or your truth. It is either *the* truth or it is not true at all.

The Prayer

Abba Father, we thank you for your Son, Jesus, who is risen from the dead. Bring us to an unshakable clarity of conviction around this eternal reality. Bring us to this reckoning of believing or not, and give us the courage to land on one side or the other. Save us from the mushy middle ground of maybe. We pray in Jesus' name, amen.

The Questions

- Do you believe Jesus is physically, bodily raised from the dead? Why or why not? Do you believe it by a preponderance of the evidence or beyond a reasonable doubt? Why do you think it is so critical to be clear on this singular point? Or don't you?

111 Meet Mary—the Glass Ceiling Crusher

JOHN 20:15–18 | He asked her, "Woman, why are you crying? Who is it you are looking for?"

Thinking he was the gardener, she said, "Sir, if you have carried him away, tell me where you have put him, and I will get him."

Jesus said to her, "Mary."

She turned toward him and cried out in Aramaic, "Rabboni!" (which means "Teacher").

Jesus said, "Do not hold on to me, for I have not yet ascended to the Father. Go instead to my brothers and tell them, 'I am ascending to my Father and your Father, to my God and your God.'"

Mary Magdalene went to the disciples with the news: "I have seen the Lord!" And she told them that he had said these things to her.

Consider This

She thought he was the gardener.

And perhaps, in the biggest sense, he was. Remember the beginning of John's gospel? "In the beginning was the Word . . . " (1:1a). The world began in a garden. Did it ever occur to you that the resurrection of Jesus happened in a garden? This is no accident.

It is as though this first day of the week is the first day of the new creation. The Gardener is in his garden.

Again, Easter is a slow-rising reality. The question for us: Have we reduced it to a doctrinal declaration, or is the reality still rising?

Mary's first communication to the disciples was concerning the empty tomb: Jesus was gone. Her next message to them was quite different:

"I have seen the Lord!"

This, my friends, is eyewitness testimony—direct evidence. And it won't be the last. If they had wanted to bolster the story, they would have made Peter the star witness. Problem is, he wasn't. John simply told us the truth. He gave us an unlikely witness to an unbelievable event, and, in the most interesting way, she became the most credible character on the planet.

If anyone wants to challenge the veracity and legitimacy of women serving at both the highest and lowest levels in the kingdom of God, they will have to deal with Mary. Okay, even better, they will have to deal with Jesus. Full stop.

Mary . . . the surprise witness . . . the apostles' apostle.

The Prayer

Abba Father, we thank you for your Son, Jesus, who, with you, created the whole world by speaking words and who is himself the Word made flesh. Thank you that, by his death, you planted the new creation, and, by his resurrection, you brought it forth from the ground. Shake us from our slumber and awaken us to the fullness of the new creation. We pray in Jesus' name, amen.

The Questions

- What do you think of Mary's mistaking Jesus for the gardener? Do you believe Mary's direct eyewitness testimony about her seeing Jesus? What is the significance of Mary being a woman in this instance? What would it mean to be awakened to the resurrection as more than a single event in history, but as the redefining of everything past and going forward?

112 Why You Should Stop Smoking

JOHN 20:19–25 | **On the evening of that first day of the week, when the disciples were together, with the doors locked for fear of the Jewish leaders, Jesus came and stood among them and said, "Peace be with you!" After he said this, he showed them his hands and side. The disciples were overjoyed when they saw the Lord.**

Again Jesus said, "Peace be with you! As the Father has sent me, I am sending you." And with that he breathed on them and said, "Receive the Holy Spirit. If you forgive anyone's sins, their sins are forgiven; if you do not forgive them, they are not forgiven."

Now Thomas (also known as Didymus), one of the Twelve, was not with the disciples when Jesus came. So the other disciples told him, "We have seen the Lord!"

But he said to them, "Unless I see the nail marks in his hands and put my finger where the nails were, and put my hand into his side, I will not believe."

Consider This

As this first week of the new creation continues to unfold, we come to another very significant moment.

And with that he breathed on them and said, "Receive the Holy Spirit."

Let's remember again those first words from this gospel account: "In the beginning was the Word, and the Word was with God, and the Word was God. He was with God in the beginning. Through him all things were made; without him nothing was made that has been made" (John 1:1–3).

Now go with me back to the beginning, when the Word made man: "Then the LORD God formed a man from the dust of the ground and breathed into his nostrils the breath of life, and the man became a living being" (Gen. 2:7).

One more stop as we develop this biblical theology of breath: Ezekiel 37 and the valley of dry bones.

> Then he said to me, "Prophesy to the breath; prophesy, son of man, and say to it, 'This is what the Sovereign LORD says: Come, breath, from the four winds and breathe into these slain, that they may live.'" So I prophesied as he

> commanded me, and breath entered them; they came to life and stood up on their feet—a vast army. (vv. 9–10)

Word and Spirit. Body and breath. Death and resurrection.

I remember as a kid the first time I saw an older person wheeling around an oxygen tank behind them. My parents explained to me they had a disease called emphysema, which meant they couldn't breathe well, necessitating their breathing in oxygen through the tube from the tank. And, yes, it provided the first golden opportunity to instruct us on the perils of smoking cigarettes. I remember how slow and cumbersome it was for these people to get around. It was like they were already on life support.

As I studied this verse about Jesus breathing on his disciples, I discovered the Greek term behind "breathe": *emphusao* (pronounced em-phoo-sah-o). See the connection? Because of sin, our spiritual breathing has been constricted. We all wheel around our little oxygen tanks to get us through our days, compensating for our perennial shortness of breath, breathing in whatever we think will do the trick. Meanwhile, Jesus stands by, ready to breathe into us the very breath of life—the Holy Spirit—filling our lungs with the breath of God.

E. Stanley Jones said it best: "Unless the Holy Spirit fills, the human spirit fails."

The Prayer

Abba Father, thank you for your Son, Jesus, who breathes into us the breath of life—the Holy Spirit. I believe in the Holy Spirit. Thank you for this inestimable gift of your life into my life, like breath. I want to breathe deeper, Jesus. Open up my lung capacity. Make me one who is able to breathe life into others. We pray in Jesus' name, amen.

The Questions

- What would it have been like to stand before Jesus with the disciples and hear him say, "Receive the Holy Spirit"? Is the Holy Spirit more of a concept to you that you believe or a reality that you experience? Do you have spiritual emphysema? What can be done to let go of the counterfeit breathing tank and begin breathing life from the Spirit of God?

The Gift of Doubters to the Faith of Us All

113

JOHN 20:26–31 | A week later his disciples were in the house again, and Thomas was with them. Though the doors were locked, Jesus came and stood among them and said, "Peace be with you!" Then he said to Thomas, "Put your finger here; see my hands. Reach out your hand and put it into my side. Stop doubting and believe."

Thomas said to him, "My Lord and my God!"

Then Jesus told him, "Because you have seen me, you have believed; blessed are those who have not seen and yet have believed."

Jesus performed many other signs in the presence of his disciples, which are not recorded in this book. But these are written that you may believe that Jesus is the Messiah, the Son of God, and that by believing you may have life in his name.

Consider This

I remember as a kid a commercial advertising my favorite breakfast cereal, Frosted Flakes. Tony the Tiger, the cartoon spokesperson for the sugary treat, was trying to get a reluctant young boy to taste the cereal. He called the boy "Doubting Thomas." Though hard to imagine such a thing happening now, the biblical reference made perfect sense to us kids back then. It brings to mind the now immortal words of Dorothy to her sidekick dog, Toto, after being dislocated by the tornado to the land of Oz: "I've got a feeling we're not in Kansas anymore."*

In an approaching age where the story of Jesus will be all but forgotten by the post-Christian culture around us, Doubting Thomas will play an increasingly important role. In a post-rational world, people will believe everything under the sun on the thinnest shreds of personal experience alone, but when it comes to the Bible, they will demand proof worthy of the rules of evidence.

---

* Quoted from *The Wizard of Oz* 1939 film adaptation of L. Frank Baum, *The Wonderful Wizard of Oz* (Chicago: George M. Hill Company, 1900).

This is where Thomas comes in. Thomas needed proof. In response to the eyewitness testimony of his friends, "We have seen the Lord" (v. 25a), Thomas replied, "Unless I see the nail marks in his hands and put my finger where the nails were, and put my hand into his side, I will not believe" (v. 25b).

Thomas is the star witness for an age of would-be believers who need more data. The point of Thomas is not to press doubters to hold out for their own proof. His point is to say to doubters, "I see you. I get you. I am you. You can trust me. The deal is real."

Many would-be followers of Jesus may not resonate with Peter or trust Mary. They may be looking for ancient skeptics in their own image like Thomas. We must not despise their press for more data. In the end, Thomas's doubt leads to the strongest declaration of faith in all of Scripture:

Thomas said to him, "My Lord and my God!"

It's strangely and deeply satisfying to behold the way a former skeptic's doubt-turned-faith bolsters the courage of us all.

The Prayer

Abba Father, thank you for your Son, Jesus, who is risen from the dead and who lives to give us resurrection faith. Awaken the remaining doubt within my soul, that I might become more alive to the faith yet waiting to arise in me. I will not fear my doubt but bring it before you, where it might be transformed into declarative faith. Jesus, you are my Lord and my God. I pray in your name, amen.

The Questions

- What do you think of this notion of those who are like Thomas being able to more easily trust Thomas? Do you identify with Thomas? What do you think of the strength of the confession "My Lord and my God!"? Are you ready to make this confession? What would it take for this declaration to deepen in you?

114 On Not Getting Back to Normal

JOHN 21:1–5 ESV | After this Jesus revealed himself again to the disciples by the Sea of Tiberias, and he revealed himself in this way. Simon Peter, Thomas (called the Twin), Nathanael of Cana in Galilee, the sons of Zebedee, and two others of his disciples were together. Simon Peter said to them, "I am going fishing." They said to him, "We will go with you." They went out and got into the boat, but that night they caught nothing.

Just as day was breaking, Jesus stood on the shore; yet the disciples did not know that it was Jesus. Jesus said to them, "Children, do you have any fish?" They answered him, "No."

Consider This

It doesn't take long to get back to normal. Three years of life completely turned upside down by Jesus, a shocking death, a stunning resurrection—and back to normal:

Simon Peter said to them, "I am going fishing." They said to him, "We will go with you." They went out and got into the boat, but that night they caught nothing.

There's another way of saying "get back to normal." It's called "going back to sleep." It doesn't take long to go back to sleep. Waking up can be the hardest thing in the world, and going back to sleep can be the easiest. The old life, the old normal, has deep grooves and holds enormous gravity.

"Give them a break," some say, "let them go fishing." How can I make such a judgment? For me, it comes down to how Jesus addressed them. The Greek word is *paidion*. Most translations use the word "children" because it means a young child. He didn't use the terms *doulos* ("servants") or *philos* ("friends"), which he had used before. He called them little children. They were in active regression, going back to the old normal, drifting back into sleep.

Though John's gospel opens with the invitation to become children of God (John 1:12–13), the goal of the gospel is to grow us up in the grace and truth of Jesus (2 Peter 3:18). We are about to witness a reset.

Remember days back when Jesus brought his disciples into friendship with him? Remember in particular what he told them at that time, "I no longer call you servants, because a servant does not know his master's business. Instead, I have called you friends, for everything that I learned from my Father I have made known to you" (John 15:15).

Jesus awakens us. Jesus disciples us. Jesus bands us together. He doesn't intend for us to go back to normal, to drift back to sleep. He has plans and purposes for us: "You did not choose me, but I chose you and appointed you so that you might go and bear fruit—fruit that will last—and so that whatever you ask in my name the Father will give you" (John 15:16).

Many of us find ourselves in a state of heightened awakening these days. For all the havoc brought on by COVID-19, it has given many the gifts of awakening. Our arrested development has been . . . well . . . arrested. We are at a different place with Jesus now, a new place. This global pandemic will end, and life will go back to normal. The piercing question we must prepare to answer: Will we go back to normal?

The Prayer

Abba Father, we thank you for your Son, Jesus, who is risen from the dead and ascended at your right hand. Thank you, Jesus, for sharing everything with us that you learned from your Father. Thank you for calling us your friends. Thank you for choosing us and appointing us to go and bear much lasting fruit. Thank you for the gift of the Holy Spirit, who is bringing it all to pass—right here and right now. We don't want to go back to normal. Show us the way forward. We are with you now. We pray in your name, amen.

The Questions

- Paul wrote: "When I was a child, I talked like a child, I thought like a child, I reasoned like a child. When I became a man, I put the ways of childhood behind me" (1 Cor. 13:11).

How are you growing up into maturity in Jesus Christ? Do you realize the power of the gravity of the old normal, the old life? How will you withstand it? Do you realize the power of the gravity of Jesus is greater than the gravity of the world? The Spirit is willing. What will be the cost of abandoning your life and will to Jesus? What will be the cost of not doing so?

Our Lives as Fishing Stories

115

JOHN 21:6–11 ESV | He said to them, "Cast the net on the right side of the boat, and you will find some." So they cast it, and now they were not able to haul it in, because of the quantity of fish. That disciple whom Jesus loved therefore said to Peter, "It is the Lord!" When Simon Peter heard that it was the Lord, he put on his outer garment, for he was stripped for work, and threw himself into the sea. The other disciples came in the boat, dragging the net full of fish, for they were not far from the land, but about a hundred yards off.

When they got out on land, they saw a charcoal fire in place, with fish laid out on it, and bread. Jesus said to them, "Bring some of the fish that you have just caught." So Simon Peter went aboard and hauled the net ashore, full of large fish, 153 of them. And although there were so many, the net was not torn.

Consider This

"Follow me," he told them in those earliest days, "and I will make you fishers of people" (Matt. 4:19). In a stunning flash of déjà vu, Jesus did the miracle of the great catch of fish yet again. He completed the cycle. First-century fishermen fished at night because the fish could see the nets in the light of day. No one catches fish in the daylight—except Jesus.

No one turns water into wine—except Jesus. No one feeds five thousand people with five loaves and two fish—except Jesus. No one raises a man from the dead after four days in the tomb—except Jesus. And we could do this all day.

Still, we are so bent on doing our own thing our own way. We love church consultants and missional strategies and worship styles and biblical frameworks and our endless, exhausting ideas. We will fish for people all night long, repeatedly come up empty—and call it faithfulness. When will we finally realize Jesus plus zero equals everything? When will we start with Jesus? When will we humbly renounce our grandiose plans and dare to believe the impracticality of impossible things in Jesus' name alone? When will we finally risk our reputation on Jesus alone, which is another way of asking: When will we become fools for his sake?

We are at the end of the fourth and final gospel and still fishing and still catching nothing. When will we give up on all our best plans and risk everything on Jesus alone?

These are the painful questions of holy discontent, the path of the long journey to the end of ourselves—the way of the cross. That's the journey where we learn to trade in our love of results for love of people.

Jesus said it so plainly: "Greater things will you do than these because I go to the Father" (see John 14:12b). After thirty years on the job, I still believe him, and yet I want to ask, "Jesus, when do we get to do the greater things?"

Maybe I've got thirty years left; maybe only three. Only he knows. I do know this. Whatever time I have left, I am going to go all in and risk it all on Jesus, which means risking it all on loving those he came to save. He's worth it. They are worth it. After all, at the end of a long night of trying everything you know to do and coming up empty—that's when he strides onto the shoreline of our lives and turns it all around.

The Prayer

Abba Father, thank you for your Son, Jesus, who is risen from the dead and ascended at your right hand. Thank you for this great fishing story. That's what I want you to make of my life—a great fishing story. Come, Holy Spirit, and bring me to the end of myself, the letting go of all I think I have to offer, where I find the only thing worth offering is Jesus himself. I pray in his name, amen.

The Questions

- How do you evaluate the investment of the rest of your life in league with Jesus? What would you trade for some real fishing stories? When they are standing around at your graveside service, what fishing stories would you like them to be telling? What is the level of your holy discontent these days? Or are you still struggling with being a frustrated malcontent with everyone and everything else?

116 Around the Charcoal Fires of Healing

JOHN 21:12–17 ESV | Jesus said to them, "Come and have breakfast." Now none of the disciples dared ask him, "Who are you?" They knew it was the Lord. Jesus came and took the bread and gave it to them, and so with the fish. This was now the third time that Jesus was revealed to the disciples after he was raised from the dead.

When they had finished breakfast, Jesus said to Simon Peter, "Simon, son of John, do you love me more than these?" He said to him, "Yes, Lord; you know that I love you." He said to him, "Feed my lambs." He said to him a second time, "Simon, son of John, do you love me?" He said to him, "Yes, Lord; you know that I love you." He said to him, "Tend my sheep." He said to him the third time, "Simon, son of John,

do you love me?" Peter was grieved because he said to him the third time, "Do you love me?" and he said to him, "Lord, you know everything; you know that I love you." Jesus said to him, "Feed my sheep."

Consider This

A few unrelated-related observations heading in the same direction for today.

"Come and have breakfast."

Did you catch the full weight of that? After fishing all night and catching nothing, Jesus puts them on the fish (and not just a little bit). Next, he builds a fire on the shoreline as the sun rises and starts cooking some fish and biscuits. And something tells me there was coffee. Then the second person of the Trinity says this:

"Come and have breakfast."

This is what God is like. Let that sink in.

When they had finished breakfast, Jesus said to Simon Peter, "Simon, son of John, do you love me more than these?"

John was careful to set the sunrise scene with this little detail: "When they got out on land, they saw a charcoal fire in place, with fish laid out on it, and bread" (v. 9).

So what? He was also careful to set the scene of the darkest night with this little detail from the night of Jesus' arrest: "Now the servants and officers had made a charcoal fire, because it was cold, and they were standing and warming themselves. Peter also was with them, standing and warming himself" (John 18:18).

Three times Jesus asked Peter the question, saying, "Simon, son of John, do you love me?"

Same question three times—one for each of Peter's three disavowals of even knowing him.

This is penetrating restoration, deep healing of the breach . . . a total reset of the relationship. It's not about failure or guilt or shame or regret. It is 100 percent about love. Love absolves guilt. Love covers shame. Love buries regret. No matter what lives or lies in our past, Jesus only needs to know one thing from us. He asks, "(insert your name here), do you love me?"

This is what God is like. Let that sink in.

Peter was grieved because he said to him the third time, "Do you love me?" and he said to him, "Lord, you know everything; you know that I love you."

Finally, Jesus had reached the wound. How do we know? Because Peter was hurt. Jesus picked the scab in order to apply the salve of grace. He re-broke the bone in order that it might be reset in the form of mercy.

How desperately do we all need the gentle wounding of Jesus? We have been through so much in our lives. Many of us live almost constantly on the brink of tears, while so many others capped the well on them long ago. We have all been hurt, and yet we are in need of the wounding, healing wounds of Jesus, which would hurt us again for healing's sake. Too many times we allow our hurts to slowly calcify into the hardness of a broken heart. The hardened heart must become broken again in order to heal back into soft and pliable wholeness. I can't explain that sufficiently here. I only know it's true and that I need more of it in my life. And I know you do too. This is what Jesus does.

This is what God is like. Let that sink in.

The Prayer

Abba Father, we thank you for your Son, Jesus, who is, as the hymn says, "risen with healing in his wings."* Thank you for the gifts of his wounds, for by his wounds we are healed. Come, Holy Spirit, and open our minds and hearts to the healing we need, and give us the courage and the opportunity to receive it. Jesus, you know more than anyone else just how handicapped we are by our unhealed hurts. You know we love you, and yet we need this dialogue of healing with you to deepen like never before. We pray in Jesus' name, amen.

The Questions

- What is sinking in the most with you from today's text, reflection, and prayer? Try telling Jesus you love him today—three times in a row. Try putting your name in the place of Peter's and rehearse the conversation with Jesus. Where might the edge of healing be in your life from past hurts? Where have you been hurt in past relationships where the lack of healing has become calcified and hardened? How might the hurt in present relationships be tended to in a truly mending and healing way rather than allowed to become hardened?

---

* Charles Wesley, "Hark! the Herald Angels Sing," 1739. Public domain.

117 For Those Who Need to Be in Control

JOHN 21:18–23 ESV | "Truly, truly, I say to you, when you were young, you used to dress yourself and walk wherever you wanted, but when you are old, you will stretch out your hands, and another will dress you and carry you where you do not want to go." (This he said to show by what kind of death he was to glorify God.) And after saying this he said to him, "Follow me."

Peter turned and saw the disciple whom Jesus loved following them, the one who also had leaned back against him during the supper and had said, "Lord, who is it that is going to betray you?" When Peter saw him, he said to Jesus, "Lord, what about this man?" Jesus said to him, "If it is my will that he remain until I come, what is that to you? You follow me!" So the saying spread abroad among the brothers that this disciple was not to die; yet Jesus did not say to him that he was not to die, but, "If it is my will that he remain until I come, what is that to you?"

Consider This

A reader and dear friend, Brother Bill, texted me with a question about today's text:

> I have wondered if the love of Jesus was available to Judas as it was to Peter. If so, what of Jesus did Judas miss that Peter survived long enough to appropriate?

It generated a bevy of text responses, including these:

> I think in the end Judas was a zealot. Peter was only zealous. Judas was fanatically committed to the mission. Peter was in love with Jesus.

> I believe Judas did what he did, not in order to betray Jesus, but to take control of the situation in order to incite a revolution. He took matters into his own hands—as control-bound people are bound to do. Judas needed to be in control.
>
> Judas did not want the love of Jesus. Like so many others, he wanted the power.

The bigger question is: Why was Judas that way? What was underneath his need to be in control?

This, I believe, is the quandary of so many of us.

I think if Judas hadn't killed himself, he would have been sitting around that charcoal fire with Jesus too.

With the deep, deep love of Jesus comes the loss of control. That's where the text goes, right? Jesus told Peter about his future:

"Truly, truly, I say to you, when you were young, you used to dress yourself and walk wherever you wanted, but when you are old, you will stretch out your hands, and another will dress you and carry you where you do not want to go."

Jesus let Peter know that, henceforth, he would not be in control of his life or his death. It's interesting how Peter wanted to get into the other disciple's business—making the classic triangulating move of a controller:

When Peter saw him, he said to Jesus, "Lord, what about this man?"

Look at Jesus' "mind your own business" response:

"If it is my will that he remain until I come, what is that to you? You follow me!"

I suspect the conversation would have gone similarly with Judas—rigorously restorative—had he not been the controller even of his own death.

Lordship means control. It means an undivided heart, unflappable trust, and uncompromising obedience. It means me being out of control. Those of us who struggle with a controlling nature tend to be the first to excuse ourselves. We make wry references to our ethic of "trust but verify" while pointing to our apparently successful track record of wins and achievements in Jesus' name. When will we finally have the courage to name it? From the garden of Eden to the present day, control is the original sin. Control crucified Jesus. It made his prayer in the garden of Gethsemane all the more stunning, as he took himself out of control: "*Abba*, Father," he said, "everything is possible for you. Take this cup from me. Yet not what I will, but what you will" (Mark 14:36).

Controllers may win a thousand battles, but they always lose the war. The opposite is also true. Those who give up control may lose a thousand battles, but they always win the war.

"You follow me!"

"Feed my sheep."

The Prayer

Abba Father, we thank you for your Son, Jesus, who is Lord precisely because he surrendered his lordship, taking on the nature of a slave, humbling himself, making himself nothing, becoming obedient to death—even death on a cross. Therefore, you highly exalted him and gave him the name that is above every name; that at the name of Jesus, every knee shall bow, in heaven and on earth and under the earth, and every tongue confess that Jesus Christ is Lord, to the glory of God the Father. Come, Holy Spirit, forge and form this same mind of Christ in us (see Philippians 2:5–11). We confess our need to control as sin, and surrender all control to Jesus as we pray in his name, amen.

The Questions

- What do you make of this discussion of Peter and Judas and the matter of control? Are you or do you tend to be a controlling person? Are you willing to see it as sin? If not, why not? If so, will you reckon with it? What do you think is underneath that need to be in control of people and situations? What is it about your story that makes it that way?

118 The Gospel of John in a Sentence

JOHN 21:24–25 ESV | This is the disciple who is bearing witness about these things, and who has written these things, and we know that his testimony is true.

Now there are also many other things that Jesus did. Were every one of them to be written, I suppose that the world itself could not contain the books that would be written.

Consider This

"It is shallow enough for a child not to drown, yet deep enough for an elephant to swim in it." This statement by Augustine is where we began in our contemplation of the words that comprise the fourth gospel.

"In the beginning was the Word, and the Word was with God, and the Word was God" (John 1:1).

Today we come to the end, and we are still talking about words.

Now there are also many other things that Jesus did. Were every one of them to be written, I suppose that the world itself could not contain the books that would be written.

Don't hear me wrong. I do not mean to diminish John's magisterial twenty-one chapters, 879 verses, and 15,635 words by suggesting they are mere words. And yet, if we are honest, that is what they are—words.

Then there are my words about John's words: just shy of 86,000 words through 118 entries, over seventeen weeks, spanning nearly four months. And, of course, my words bear no comparison to John's words, and apart from John's words they have no meaning or even intrinsic worth. The point is to say that all these days, weeks, and months later, we are still where we started—words.

The greatest peril of the whole project is that we somehow allow the Word to remain at the level of words. If you ask me to land on one verse in the whole gospel—indeed, the whole Bible—that held the greatest importance, I think I could do it. I'll take it a step further and narrow it down to one sentence. You are probably thinking I'm going to land on John 3:16. Nope. Here's my choice: "The Word became flesh and made his dwelling among us" (John 1:14a).

This is the great point of God's whole project. When the Bible says this:

> "As the rain and the snow
>   come down from heaven,
> and do not return to it
>   without watering the earth
> and making it bud and flourish,
>   so that it yields seed for the sower and bread for the eater,
> so is my word that goes out from my mouth:
>   It will not return to me empty,
> but will accomplish what I desire
>   and achieve the purpose for which I sent it." (Isa. 55:10–11)

It means this: “The Word became flesh and made his dwelling among us” (John 1:14a).

And I think you see where this is heading. As Jesus was and is, so we are and shall become—words becoming flesh. That’s why we are doing this every single day, not to learn more words, but so that the Word might become flesh in us—in me and in you. All that said, which is still just more words, the most challenging word from today’s text for me is this one:

Now there are also many other things that Jesus did.

We get the feeling John has only given us a sample. My kids were talking among themselves the other day about how they respond to people when asked about what their dad does for a living. One of them said, “I say, my dad writes devotions.” I found it mildly hilarious, and yet it kind of haunts me, if I’m honest.

I want to do the stuff Jesus did and does. I want the Word to be made flesh in my hours and days and weeks and life. And that’s why I write devotions, because I know you want to do the stuff too.

So, here’s to the Word becoming flesh in our lives—to doing the Jesus stuff together.

The Prayer

Abba Father, we thank you for your Son, Jesus, who is forever and always the Word made flesh. Thank you, that he makes his dwelling not only among us, but within us. Thank you for John and his faithfulness to receive these revealed words and to write them down. Thank you especially for

Jesus. Come, Holy Spirit, and cause the Word to become flesh in my life and in our lives together. We want to do the stuff Jesus did and does. Let it be said of us, "They did it!" We pray in Jesus' name, amen.

The Questions

- So, how is the Word becoming flesh in your life? Where are the developing edges of his work in and through your hours, days, and weeks in this season? How has this journey through John helped you to know Jesus better? How has it helped you to know yourself better? What are your top takeaways from these past 118 days together in the gospel?

THE SOWER'S CREED

Today,
I sow for a great awakening.

Today,
I stake everything on the promise of the Word of God.
I depend entirely on the power of the Holy Spirit.
I have the same mind in me that was in Christ Jesus.
Because Jesus is good news and Jesus is in me,
I am good news.

Today,
I will sow the extravagance of the gospel
everywhere I go and into everyone I meet.

Today,
I will love others as Jesus has loved me.

Today,
I will remember that the tiniest seeds become the
tallest trees; that the seeds of today become the shade
of tomorrow; that the faith of right now becomes
the future of the everlasting kingdom.

Today,
I sow for a great awakening.

CPSIA information can be obtained
at www.ICGtesting.com
Printed in the USA
LVHW021223300421
686014LV00003B/3